Founded in 1807, John Wiley & Sons is the oldest independent publishing company in the United States. With offices in North America, Europe, Australia, and Asia, Wiley is globally committed to developing and marketing print and electronic products and services for our customers' professional and personal knowledge and understanding.

The Wiley Finance series contains books written specifically for finance and investment professionals as well as sophisticated individual investors and their financial advisors. Book topics range from portfolio management to e-commerce, risk management, financial engineering, valuation and financial instrument analysis, as well as much more.

For a list of available titles, visit our website at www.WileyFinance.com.

Goals-Based Wealth Management

An Integrated and Practical
Approach to Changing the Structure
of Wealth Advisory Practices

JEAN L.P. BRUNEL, C.F.A.

WILEY

For general information on our other products and services or for technical support, please contact our Customer Care Department within the United States at (800) 762-2974, outside the United States at (317) 572-3993 or fax (317) 572-4002.

Wiley publishes in a variety of print and electronic formats and by print-on-demand. Some material included with standard print versions of this book may not be included in e-books or in print-on-demand. If this book refers to media such as a CD or DVD that is not included in the version you purchased, you may download this material at http://booksupport.wiley.com. For more information about Wiley products, visit www.wiley.com.

Library of Congress Cataloging-in-Publication Data:

Brunel, Jean L.P.
    Goals-based wealth management : an integrated and practical approach to changing the structure of wealth advisory practices / Jean L.P. Brunel.
        pages cm. – (Wiley finance series)
    Includes index.
        ISBN 978-1-118-99590-7 (cloth/website) 1. Portfolio management.
2. Wealth–Management. 3. Investment advisors. I. Title.
    HG4529.5.B777 2015
    332.6–dc23
                                                                                        2014040792

Printed in the United States of America

10 9 8 7 6 5 4 3 2 1

To Léandre Eloise, Charlie, and Mason, and hopefully a few more still to be born!

Contents

Acknowledgments

I would first like to express my deepest gratitude to our clients, current and past. In the end, it is their kind pressure on me to help them find solutions to perfectly reasonable needs that has driven me to push the limits of whatever the envelope was. Without client pressures, I doubt that I would have done much with respect to goals-based wealth management. Admittedly, it was not clients—who would then have been clients of my employer—who pushed me to think of the need for wealth managers to think of tax-efficiency. There, I was compelled to move by academic literature and the obvious questions it raised. But the observation that traditional strategic asset allocation had serious limitations was directly suggested to me by clients who could not make sense of what their advisors were recommending. So, thank you, dear clients; you have indeed made me much better, and your pressure eventually led to the text within this book. What's next?

It also behooves me to thank you, our readers. Purchasing and reading this book is proof that the topic is important in your eyes, and that is already a great result. More importantly to me, I sincerely hope that you will allow me to achieve a crucial goal: making a difference and getting our clients—and yours if you are advisors—better served by an industry that is there to help them manage their wealth. Do not think that you have to copy the model I use to make my point. But please learn the principles behind it and then feel free to develop solutions that respect these principles and work even better in your own circumstances, whether you are a wealthy individual or family, or a professional wealth advisor.

I should also extend my thanks to the many authors who submitted articles to the *Journal of Wealth Management* and express my gratitude to Institutional Investor Journals. Authors, you have provided me with a unique opportunity to sit at the crossroads of many intellectual flows, and it has been a privilege. These many thoughts—quite a few of them ended up published as wonderful articles—inspired me to keep trying to innovate. Institutional Investor Journals also played a crucial role in the development of our industry by providing a forum where these thoughts could be shared: the *Journal of Wealth Management*. I want, therefore, to thank Gauri Goyal, who asked me to be the founding editor, and Allison Adams, who succeeded her, and with whom I have worked for the last ten years at least.

The many members of our Advisory Board also deserve special thanks, as they have helped me discern those ideas that were worth exploring from those that were not. I should add the CFA Institute to those I thank in this section, particularly people like Stephen Horan, Charles Henneman, and too many others to name them all, but they know who they are, for their willingness to invite me to speak at too many CFA Society meetings for me to remember. Interactions with the attendance at these sessions also kept me driven to get better. Annie Wee, Cynthia Teong Boey Choo, and Joyce Lee, of the Wealth Management Institute in Singapore, also deserve special mention as they supported me in my endeavors to develop and share these thoughts, with a huge degree of faithfulness. Last but not least, Jos van Bommel and the Luxembourg School of Finance should also be noted, as they invited me to teach a class at the capstone event of the Executive Program in Wealth Management and thus fostered further research that resulted in quite a few of the insights that make up this book.

A number of people were kind enough to agree to review the manuscript and to offer comments. They were chosen among friends who neatly fell in two categories: several of them believed in the concept of goals-based wealth management, but others were openly skeptical. They all, however, provided very insightful and useful comments without which the text would be less interesting, quite a bit poorer, and much harder to read and follow. So thank you, in alphabetical order, to Thierry Brunel, Mark Cirilli, Vera Cvijetic-Petrovic Boissier, Kevin Irwin, Jean Karoubi, Mel Lagomasino, Jack Parham, Todd Pines, Kevin Prinsen, Vincent Worms, and Michael Zeuner.

I should obviously thank Wiley for their willingness to support and publish this text. Laura Gachko, senior editor, Digital Business Development, Professional Development, stands as the first person I should thank, as she was the one who negotiated the contract that led to this book. Judy Howarth, senior development editor, helped me manage the writing schedule, gave crucial feedback along the way, and captained the team as the book went from manuscript to published book. Finally, Tula Batanchiev, associate editor, Professional Development, was always there to make sure that everything ran smoothly, from designing and selecting a cover to setting up the website. I could not imagine working with a more professional and helpful team.

Last but not least, I must thank my wife of forty years and business partner of almost fifteen, Debbie. She went through numerous iterations of the manuscript with an eagle eye for typographical or grammatical errors, but, more importantly, for flow and even contents as well. She tolerated my "mental absence" while we were entertaining friends in our home in the south of France last summer, as I would only appear at meal time and spend the rest of the day holed up in my office working at the keyboard. Without her patience and understanding, I surely would not have met the deadline we had agreed to meet with Wiley & Sons.

Preface

I have spent the last thirty-eight years in the world of investment management and the last twenty-three dealing with the people we all call "the affluent." Although I do not want to cast aspersions on anyone, I feel that we—as an industry—have not done the best job serving them, in part because we have not sufficiently adapted our processes to their specific needs and in part because the affluent have not always taken the time to discern what they really needed. My point in this Preface is to take our readers through the evolution of our industry and its market over the last forty odd years, to describe the way our industry is currently structured and operating, and to identify the mission I feel it needs to fulfill. I also want to discuss the three areas of focus that should help me achieve my goal of contributing to the further growth of the industry: (1) recognize the need for humility, (2) promote a sharper focus on the definition of the goals of our clients, and (3) discuss the potential for a restructuration of the typical advisory firm so that it can better serve its target market. But, first, we must define what we mean by "the affluent."

There are about as many definitions of that group of people as there are people trying to serve them. They can be described by the financial assets they possess, but this can be misleading, as assets can be income-producing or not; they can be owned or in some form of generational wealth transfer structure; they can be liquid or illiquid; they can even cost more to maintain than they produce in terms of income! Think of the aristocratic European families, for instance, who conduct guided tours of what is left of their castles or estates because that is the only income they have to live on and maintain these massive structures!

I define the affluent as a group of people who have liquid assets of at least $5 million and who could maintain their lifestyles drawing income and principal from these assets, even if they do not earn material outside revenue. Thus, a family with $5 million, where both husband and wife are in their early sixties and semi-retired and spend $250,000 a year would qualify. By contrast, a single individual—a young man, for instance—with $10 million who spends the same $250,000 a year and is in his thirties would not be affluent, by my definition. Our semi-retired couple does not have to change their lifestyle to enjoy a high likelihood of not running out of money in the next twenty-five or thirty years, which corresponds to their

current life expectancy, if they have taken the precaution to buy appropriate catastrophic insurance.[1] By contrast, the young man in his thirties has
a sixty-odd-year life expectancy; unless he is an excellent investor, he could
well run out of money spending about 2.5 percent of his assets each year,
particularly if inflation was to play dirty tricks on him. He could run out of
money in two different ways. First, he could run out of money by taking too
much risk that does not pan out into higher returns if he simultaneously tries
to grow the assets while being unwilling to cut his spending. Conversely, he
might run out of money by being too conservative in his investments, which
would then not earn enough of a return to carry him through the balance of
his life, let alone the possibility that his spending might change as and when
he decides to marry, start a family, and raise children! In short, you have to
look at assets, running spending rates, and required horizons before labeling
someone—a family or an individual—affluent in my definition.

Over the last twenty plus years, I have had the luxury to follow the evolution of this industry with a serious dose of fascination coupled with cynicism.
When I first started to work with the affluent, as the chief investment officer
of J.P. Morgan's (JPM) Global Private Bank, the vast bulk of the industry's
assets, at least in the United States, were comprised of inherited money. JPM
at the time had to be one of the largest players in the industry globally, and
probably the largest in the United States; we used to figure that 80 percent
of the financial assets entrusted to us were either in trust or inherited. Our
clients trusted their portfolio managers and trust officers, and these people
truly tried to do what was best for their clients, rather than for themselves
or their employer. In fact, I vividly remember our "big boss" reminding us at
every opportunity that "clients pay your salaries, not the bank!"[2] Fiduciary
responsibility—putting client interests ahead of our own, duty of care and
loyalty, avoiding conflicts of interest, and managing costs and expenses for
the benefit of the client—was our sole guiding light. In truth, the processes
we used were, with the benefit of hindsight, somewhat simplistic, but some
of that was driven by the law. Would you believe that we were told then that
hedging currency risk in foreign equities, for instance—which required us
to buy foreign exchange contracts—was a speculative activity?

Back in the late 1960s, the industry experienced a first important change,
which affected both private and institutional wealth management, although

---

[1]This is needed because some catastrophic event, such as a major health crisis, can
quickly and irreversibly eat up their savings and make it impossible for them to sus-
tain their lifestyle to the end of their lives.
[2]Note that he was only echoing the famous quote by Henry Ford: "It's not the
employer who pays the wages. Employers only handle the money. It's the customer
who pays the wages."

it is fair to suspect that private clients might not have totally accepted or even understood it. The advent of modern portfolio theory that resulted from the work of Nobel Economics Prize laureates Harry Markowitz and Bill Sharpe led us and many others to begin to view the investment "space" as a two-dimensional affair that comprised both return and risk. Hitherto, the principal focus had been on return.

Then two other changes impacted directly the private wealth management industry. First, the make-up of the clientele began to change. With the substantial equity market rally that followed the success experienced by Fed Chairman Paul Volker fighting inflation and with investment bankers much more diligent looking for mergers and acquisitions or initial public offerings, self-made money was becoming a much more important source of clientele for investment managers. These clients were different from inheritors in several ways. The two main differences were that they were less educated in the behavior of financial markets—their experiences were with creating and running businesses—and much more demanding of their financial advisors—they had achieved their status of financial wealth through and with the help of advisors and were not afraid of being tough with them. They quickly found trust officers too sleepy—little did they know that those officers were by and large simply doing their jobs and following the rules that were laid down for them. In addition, having dealt with investment bankers and brokers when selling their businesses, they were more inclined to hire them rather than those bank trust departments when it came to choosing a wealth advisor!

The second change was the growing recognition, which JPM pioneered in the United States, that individuals were very different from institutions in that they had to pay taxes. The phrase was coined: "It's not what you get, but what you get to keep that counts!" This moved us from our two-dimensional space to one that had a third dimension, tax-efficiency. It would prove to be an important source of innovation starting in the second half of the 1990s. Although that focus has not been universally accepted, in part because absolute levels of returns in the 2000s were often low enough to allow tax-efficiency to appear unneeded, it is one of the two innovations I fully expect will define our industry in the years ahead.

This was but the first step in a process of deepening our understanding of the needs of the wealthy, which has now expanded into many directions. We now recognize that wealth management is about much more than managing assets: the mission of the wealth management industry has thus been more broadly defined. We indeed "discovered" that capital can be financial, but also includes human, social, artistic, philanthropic, and emotional dimensions. We "discovered" that individuals do not typically have single goals and single risk profiles: they have multiple goals, each goal usually has a different time horizon, and they have different required probabilities—or levels of certainty—that each goal will be reached. We "discovered" that there are important—and quite complex—interactions between the various dimensions of the wealth management challenge. We explicitly set out tax-efficiency as a crucial interaction between investment and tax planning; but there are similar interactions between investment and financial planning: Who should own what and how liquid do I need my investments to be? Similarly, philanthropy interacts with investment, estate, and tax planning. Estate planning is another obvious dimension that cannot be taken up outside of a serious discussion with investment managers and other advisors.

Charlotte Beyer, who founded the Institute for Private Investors, used to compare each affluent individual or family to a company, which she called "My Wealth, Inc." Taking her point a bit further, you can observe that there has hardly ever been a successful chief executive officer of a successful large company who was not aware first that the company comprised many divisions—each focused on some different aspect of the business, such as research, engineering, production, marketing, client service, legal and regulatory, human resources, and the like—and second that these divisions had to be efficiently coordinated so that the whole was more than the sum of the parts. The same construct can be imagined for a wealthy family, even if wealth is modest, in that individuals need to be aware of the several issues on which the family, the head of which could be called the "CEO of My Wealth Inc.," should focus.

Today, the industry neatly divides into three general categories of providers. First, you have the manufacturers; their function is to create the products and services the affluent and their advisors need to use. Second, you have advisors who have elected to focus on only one or two of the many dimensions of the problem faced by their clients; they may be tax lawyers, estate lawyers, certified public accountants, investment advisors, philanthropic consultants or managers, family education or governance specialists, and many others. Finally, you have a wide variety of advisors and consultants who try to take a holistic view of the overall problem, effectively seeking to make money sitting next to the client, on the same side of the table as the family. That they are not all equally successful should not surprise; what may, however, be surprising is that quite a few of them naturally believe that they are exactly what the doctor ordered, when in fact the problem is quite a bit more complex than their current understanding of it.

In this book, my desire is to contribute to the further growth of the industry in at least three areas. First, I continue to think that the affluent need to know more about the questions they should ask and the issues they ought to feel are important. The initial insight must be a recognition that our industry—with respect to both advisors and clients—suffers from an imperfect ability to predict and thus deal with the future. We will go into this in more depth in the book, but I am still flabbergasted by the fact that so many people do not appreciate that God created weather forecasters to make investment managers look good! The late Sir John Templeton, an icon in the industry who died well into his nineties, once said that he had never seen an investment manager who is right more often than 65 percent of the time. Now, think what this means: the best managers are wrong at least 35 percent of the time! Most investment managers do not (or should not) have more than a modest confidence in their expectations: diversification matters, hubris should be out! Yet, how many individuals are still mesmerized by pronouncements of talking heads and expect their advisors to know when to be 100 percent in cash and 100 percent in equities? A corollary of this is that individuals should know that what is hard for trained advisors to do must, almost by definition, also be very hard if not harder for them. In short, a healthy dose of humility should permeate the thinking and dealings of industry participants and of their clients.

Second, I continue to think that a lot more progress is needed in the discernment of individual goals and in the formulation of the appropriate investment policy. Sure, this may not be an exercise that individuals enjoy—advisors do not often enjoy it any more than their clients. Yet, as Yogi Berra is quoted as saying: "If you don't know where you're going, you might not get there!" If you do not have a target asset or strategy allocation that is designed to meet your goals over time, what are the odds you will, in fact, meet them? Thus, individuals must recognize the importance of serious introspection to formulate their goals with some degree of granularity; correspondingly, advisors need to feel responsible for helping individuals in that endeavor that is not natural to many of them. In short, I feel it is important to recognize that the current tendency is fraught with danger: one misses the point when considering some form of "average" goal, rather than a list of actual goals, and constructing an "average risk profile" from the top down, rather than a bottom-up formulation of risk based on the risk associated with each goal and each time horizon. It exposes the industry to the real risk of not satisfying its clients. A corollary is that clients, too, must require their advisors to recognize that they, the affluent, are different; that they are no single-purpose institution; and that they need a tailored approach. It would really be too bad if individuals and families were to keep missing their goals and failing to "connect" with their wealth, simply because their advisors prefer to remain in the comfortable preserve of institutional asset management rather than adopt a framework explicitly designed around the specific nature of individual wealth management needs.

Third, I feel that the industry needs to consider restructuring. This may be the most controversial part of this book. Consider the difference you observe when comparing a lawyer's office, a medical practice, and the office of an investment advisor. The former two appear quite leveraged, with very few people at the top of the pyramid and a number of associates help-ing with the tasks that can be delegated. The latter typically comprises a number of senior people, the advisors, and very few other people. Not sur-prisingly, advisory practices tend to suffer from very low margins. As such, this gives rise to the obvious temptation to add to revenues by receiving var-ious forms of supplementary fees, for instance. Steve Lockshin, in his book *Get Wise to Your Advisor*,[3] offered the thought that these could easily be called kickbacks! Now, how can an advisor claim to be fully objective and solely dedicated to the client—each client—if he or she is receiving some compensation from people he will recommend to be hired? How willing will they be to recommend that someone who has paid them in some way be fired? Others try to raise profitability by degrading the client experience or by starting to accept certain forms of conflicts of interest; both should be viewed as highly unsatisfactory, as profitability is increased at the expense of the client, rather than by active internal management efforts. Consider an alternative that is equally potent and much more intellectually satisfying: How about an approach to raising margins that would rely on creating more internal operational efficiencies within the firm?

In conclusion, let me make two quick points and offer a disclaimer. This is an industry in transformation. In fact, you could even argue that this has been an industry being created before our eyes; in that frame of reference, creation continues. Thus, I certainly do not want to impugn the motives of certain actors and set them up as contrary examples vis-à-vis others who would be viewed as the pious alternatives. Second, industries that suffer from relatively poor profitability will naturally find it harder to change: change costs money and they have little excess money to spare to finance change and to live through the initially adverse consequences that might result. In short, I offer opinions and thoughts here that I have had a chance to test in the field. Yet, because of the very limited nature of the list of clients that we have served over the last fifteen years or so, and because of my strong belief that Templeton's comment extends way beyond investment management, I want to offer these thoughts with a great deal of humility. I am convinced that they are taking us in the "right" direction, but if I am wrong, I must honestly admit that it will not be the first time I was wrong!

---

[3]Lockshin, Stephen D. *Get Wise to Your Advisor: How to Reach Your Investment Goals without Getting Ripped Off*. Hoboken, NJ: John Wiley & Sons, 2014.

I wanted to write this book because I feel that a lot more is needed to help individuals manage their wealth. I think that a crucial first step is to help individuals understand the relationship between their wealth and what it does for them, and this may well be the most important failing I noticed in our industry over the last twenty-five years or so. The next step relates to creating a process that allows that relationship to prosper and develop, with all the necessary feedback loops so that individuals can avoid the pitfalls that await them at each turn in the road. Finally, I strongly believe that this will likely lead to changes in the way the industry structures itself so that clients can be effectively served while other stakeholders can earn the rewards they deserve.

I therefore invite you, each reader, to make up your own mind. A lot of considerably more academic literature has been written on a number of these issues. Not all of it is unilaterally in agreement with my views. It takes more than one to make a market. Thus, read the book, ponder the insights, consider how they apply to your own circumstances, and then decide whether and, if so, how much of them make sense and should be integrated into whatever part of the integrated wealth management process most directly concerns you.

Jean L.P. Brunel, CFA
November 2014

Introduction

The first book I wrote on the topic of Integrated Wealth Management was published in 2002, with a revised edition in 2006.[1] In truth, it was a textbook whose audience turned out to be chiefly comprised of students of the industry. One day, I actually told a friend who had asked me to sign a copy he had just bought that the best use I could think of for the book was as a means of propping up a table that had one leg shorter than the other three. Another joke I probably overused was that it should be prescribed to people who had trouble sleeping!

Clearly, I only half meant those jokes, as it had taken me quite a bit more than a year to write the book and I had poured everything I knew—or knew of—into the effort. I was quite pleased (and proud) of the end product. I saw it at the time as a bit of a reference book to which one could go to see not only what one person (me) thought about a particular issue, but, probably more importantly, what the current leading thinkers in the industry thought. I received some praise for it, and it was mentioned as a reason behind an award I received from the CFA Institute in 2011, which is quite close to my heart. Therefore, I still look back on the effort as both useful and quite worthwhile. With the second edition nearly nine years old, I could simply have endeavored to bring the text up-to-date, called it a third edition, and left it at that.

Yet, I decided to take a completely different route. I decided that the experience—quite a bit of it practical—gained over the last fifteen years or so required me to take a different tack. In truth, the theory behind our industry and its day-to-day activities has evolved somewhat, but the change has not been radical. Even something as "big" as goals-based wealth management, which was pioneered in 2002, has really not caused massive change in the last few years; we have seen slow evolution, at best. Goals-based policy formulation itself has only seen modest refinements, arguably in large measure because it has yet to be broadly adopted. We first need to see what really causes practical implementation challenges and what works well as is

---

[1]Brunel, Jean L.P. *Integrated Wealth Management: The New Direction for Portfolio Managers*. Institutional Investor Books, a Division of Euromoney Institutional Investors PLC, 2002. (2nd ed., 2006.)

before we can finalize the full specification of the approach. In short, you could argue that the baby has been born, but that it still needs to go through many of its normal growth phases.

This book is, therefore, about sharing that experience, with the main focus being on what I see as the cornerstone: goals-based wealth management. The vast majority of people who know something about managing assets or wealth agree with the simple statement that the key to long-term success resides in having the right strategy. This truth has often been phrased in ways that obscure rather than clarify the point: "Asset allocation is the main contributor to long-term returns." In fact, the statement is only partially true and, more importantly, is missing a key word. The correct formulation[2] is that one's "asset allocation is the main contributor to long-term *risk*." In fact, I take this one step further; I add the word "strategic" so that the phrase becomes: "Strategic asset allocation is the main contributor to long-term risk." This allows one to distinguish between the long-term investment policy and tactical portfolio rebalancing or tilting. The former is what drives the long-term performance expectations for the portfolio in terms of both return and risk. The latter involves the activities associated with shorter-term portfolio moves either to bring a portfolio that has drifted away from policy—as a result of market performance—back to it or to take advantage of occasional, perceived market opportunities. These rarely generate more than a minute portion of total return and, if properly managed and executed, return volatility; in fact, rebalancing or tactical tilting often fails to generate extra returns when it is executed in a tax-oblivious manner and taxes are taken into consideration. So, in short, the fundamental element of our thinking should be that strategic asset allocation drives long-term expected risk and, thus, returns.

Experience has taught me that goals-based wealth management is the best way to deal with the formulation of that strategic asset allocation, at least when it comes to individuals with more financial than human capital. Clearly, the experience I want to share does not exist in a vacuum. I will have to recall certain facets of theory from time to time; if only to stay grounded. Yet, I will refrain from detailed exposition of theory and will rather strive to keep linking it to what it means to the affluent and their advisors alike, in a very practical way. In fact, the conceptual framework used in each of the four parts of the book will involve setting out the issue with a sufficient recall of theory to provide the base on which and the principles with which we

---

[2] Brinson, Gary P., L. Randolf Hood, and Gilbert L. Beebower. "Determinants of Portfolio Performance." *Financial Analysts Journal*, 42(4), July/August 1986 or, Brinson, Gary P., Brian D. Singer, and Gilbert L. Beebower. "Determinants of Portfolio Performance II: An Update." *Financial Analysts Journal*, 47(3), May/June 1991, pp. 40–48.

can build. I will then translate this base and these principles into day-to-day language, illustrating one of the most important lessons I have learned in the last fifteen years: clients do not ask advisors how to make a watch; they ask them what time it is! To wit, they ask us to translate for them the stuff we learn in our jargon, which I have come to dub "financialese." Being a client certainly does not absolve any affluent individual from his or her share of responsibility in the joint enterprise in which we cooperate: the management of their wealth. However, these responsibilities do not extend to the need to learn a foreign language. Clients should feel able to rely on advisors to translate their needs into the realities of capital markets and to explain to them what is possible and what is not, how one can proceed and what to expect.

The goal here is to focus on the most important issue affecting the affluent: how their various goals, constraints, and preferences should drive the strategic—or policy—allocation of their financial assets and how the process has to take into account the very natural fact that we are all subject to a variety of emotions. Will these always help us? The effort must, therefore, reflect all of the client's personal circumstances to allow the advisor to feel safe that he or she does understand what he or she needs to do before actually doing anything. It should also allows the client to feel equally safe so that he or she can accept that there are emotional elements at play and that he or she has to learn how to deal with and control them. Last century, at J.P. Morgan, one of our standard lines was that we would not touch a penny of our clients' assets until we knew exactly what the client needed. This was not a principle limited to the Trust and Investment Division; the classic JPM advertisement, which displayed a blank mirror and stated that "Some time, the best thing to do is to do nothing," illustrates that it applied to the institution as a whole. The main message there and in what we told clients is that we would not start work and charge a fee if we did not think that the client's goals were feasible. And before we could tell whether these goals were feasible, we had to understand them. In the Preface, I mentioned the case of a young man with $10 million in assets who spent $250,000 a year. I stated that I would not consider him affluent because he could not maintain that level of spending unless he quickly got a job to add wages to investment income. I am sure that more than one family patriarch or matriarch will immediately think of this or that descendant who needs to adjust their lifestyle to be sure that some of the capital that the individual inherited is left for his or her own descendants; similarly, I am sure that a few of our readers within the wealth management industry will recognize real-life circumstances when they had clients who were trying to achieve the impossible. Just as no medical doctor would try to "sell" some expensive treatment or surgery to a terminal patient he or she knows will not benefit from it, advisors owe it to their clients to be honest. That one will almost inevitably lose prospects over that honesty is unfortunate; but one must believe that what goes around comes around: there is not a much better reputation than that of being honest!

I also said that we would discuss four issues. Ostensibly, one could write a tome that covered many more than these. It could be so long that few people would be prepared to labor through it. Alternatively, it could stay at such a level of generality as to be of limited use to practitioners and their clients, both of whom constitute our intended audience. I hope that students and members of academia will find a few snippets or insights in this book. Most often, I believe that it might stimulate further research, rather than provide the proverbial light bulb. Yet, I am ready to accept that many of them will find the lack of academic references—such as the massive bibliography found in the earlier book—and the much plainer language to be a bit disappointing. I sincerely apologize to them; the earlier book addressed the problem and many of its challenges from their perspective. We now must focus on the places where the proverbial rubber meets the road: the affluent and their advisors.

The first part of this book returns to the complexities of the many challenges experienced by the affluent and the wealthy. I feel that this is an absolutely crucial piece of the puzzle, as it is needed to remind all of us—practitioners and clients alike—that managing wealth involves more than managing financial assets. Being able to put the asset management piece—what the book eventually addresses—into the proper perspective is essential. In fact, were we not required to deal with this issue, we could simply take institutional asset management processes and tweak them for taxes. I suspect that this first part will be more interesting for service providers than for the affluent themselves. Indeed, many of the latter do know the multiple dimensions of their problem and understand them very well. They may at times—we have seen many instances of this in the last fifteen years—be frustrated that they cannot have these needs served effectively, but it is usually not for a lack of awareness. They are often frustrated because of their advisors. First, the industry—and its many participants—still suffers from a silo mentality. While there are many exceptionally knowledgeable and well-intentioned providers, they often reside in sub-segments of the industry. There are fabulous estate lawyers; but how many of them truly understand the investment business sufficiently? There are many great investors; but how many of them understand the implications of their actions on tax and estate issues, and vice versa? There are many financial or philanthropy planners; but how many of them understand the crucial interactions between what they do and what other service providers do? Second, almost perversely, it often appears that the better advisors are at their specialty, the less concerned or aware they are about the way they should cooperate with other advisors in different disciplines to ensure that their clients receive the best overall advice. Often, the market seems to reward the brilliant specialist more generously than the exceptional generalist!

The second part of the book delves more specifically into the issue of strategic asset allocation or investment policy formulation; although we are still conscious of the complexity of wealth management, we narrow our focus on asset management, understood within a wealth management framework. We start with a description of how that very process actually takes place in the institutional world. At some level, it may look anachronistic to discuss institutions in a book focused on individuals. I believe this to be very important because the bulk of the theory of asset management was developed and written with respect to institutional investors. This should not surprise as, at least until relatively recently, there was little dedicated research to the individual field, most probably in response to the simple fact that the individual space was not "where the dollars were" and the complexities created by trust law made study of the field rebarbative.

The key here is, thus, to bring out the assumptions that underpin the institutional investment management process and to show how these must be changed when dealing with individuals. Once we complete that step, the need for different solutions becomes both clearer and inescapable. This second part would not be complete without an honest exposition of the complexity that comes with having to deal with individuals. Although intellectual laziness at times explains why certain change has not yet been implemented, the more realistic and objective explanation simply is that advisors can feel lost in the face of the complexity that true customization would bring to their practice. We will come back to this point in the fourth part of the book.

The third part of the book is specifically dedicated to a model that allows one to deal with the individual strategic asset allocation process, despite the complexities described at the end of the second part. The model is not described here in a bid to find buyers for some related software. In truth, that software has yet to be written; the model currently operates within our firm in an Excel format—those readers who know Excel will recognize its features in the figures or charts presented. One hopes that readers will not cynically be asking the usual: "What's in it for him?" Although I certainly would love for some software package to be developed one day, your humble servant is neither a software developer, nor in the business of selling and maintaining software. Further, extrapolating a thought by Steve Lockshin in his book, there must be many ways to develop and sell software that are simpler and less time-consuming than writing a book!!! My goal here is simply to present one solution, showing the nature and sequence of the interrelated pieces and processes with the hope that this will encourage others to develop their own solutions, preferably well-adapted to their specific client circumstances.

The fourth part of the book deals with the structure of the typical advisory firm and the need to change it; it should be of the most direct interest to advisors, but clients will find interesting insights that should help them seek and reward those advisors who can serve them best and in a sustainable manner. It starts with a short diagnosis of what has challenged the industry: although most often well-intentioned, the industry as a whole has failed to create sufficient operating leverage within the typical firm to earn a decent return on equity. The wealth management industry—more specifically, fee-only advisors or multi-family family offices—often maintain a structure, as they have grown, which suits a single practitioner practice. They have not evolved from that to a more comprehensive advisory structure that is dedicated to outlive the founders. We will be showing that they should understand that, in reality, as they move from a simple individual practice to a business, they should rethink the way in which they are organized. Hitherto, by and large—with a few welcome and notable exceptions—firms grew from one to several advisors seemingly by replicating with two or three or four people the same processes the individual advisors had when they operated independently; the process repeats itself even as firms grow to ten, twenty, or even thirty advisors. This is not conducive to profitability and is made even more challenging as the straightjacket of regulatory compliance and information technology requirements become more demanding. Thus, many end up succumbing to the siren's song of product creation, where fees are no longer solely earned on advice, but also generated by selling products, which can destroy the integrity of the client experience.

There is a better way. We develop and describe simple solutions that might allow those advisors who want to do the best for their clients, all the while not losing their shirts meeting their clients' goals. In short, it revolves around the notion that, as they grow, they should think of mass customization as their goal, rather than Saville Row–like absolute customization to each client. In a mass customization model, each client feels that the service is truly custom-designed to his or her own needs, when, in fact, it is custom-designed, but comprises certain parts that are common to all. Think of a high-end, "custom-made" racing bicycle. The frame may be truly designed to your exact measurements. Yet, the tubes from which your own frame is cut are mass produced and the various mechanical parts, from the pedals to the brakes, to the gears and ball-bearings, are the same for all generically similar bikes. We will come back to that example later. The ultra, ultra-affluent may require the services of the equivalent of a

Saville Row tailor; but there are very few such clients and, in fact, they most often operate their own single-family offices.

When you finish reading this book, my most sincere hope is that you will realize that this remains a work in progress. With the change still needed in our industry, it is inevitable that certain ideas will prove either impractical or at least too difficult to implement until either they have been simplified or some form of change has occurred in the landscape. Being involved in a consulting role, my focus has always been to think of what the world could and should be. I am sure that there are quite a few operational aspects of this revised set-up I do not fully understand in their true detail or complexity. I also know that I am not the one who might have to accept lower profitability in the short term in a bid to raise profitability in the long term.

Yet, I also hope that you will realize that each of us needs to broaden our horizons. Most of us have approached this mission of ours from the perspective of a small fraction of the universe. I started life as a security analyst, became a portfolio manager, and then a strategist and member of senior management. Whatever I had to learn about taxes, behavioral finance, non-traditional investment strategies, transaction flows, client communication, and the simple discovery of multiple goals, multiple risk profiles, and multiple time horizons occurred through chance and experience. I would love to say that progress was always linear and in the right direction! That would be the biggest lie. I learned through trial and error—as we all do—always putting the best interest of the client first. I hope this book will allow readers to sidestep a few of the traps into which I fell. Perhaps it will confirm a few intuitions as well as relegate others to the "doomed" bin, thus speeding up the learning process. Most importantly, I hope it will convey the notion that this is not a job, but a profession, and that success will not come without passion. That passion must be geared toward our clients, who, as I was told many times when I was younger, do pay our salaries!

One

The Integrated Wealth Management Challenge

Part 1 of this book is dedicated to setting the stage pointing to the multiple challenges that wealth managers should expect to encounter and which are different from the institutional asset management norm. We look at the fact that managing wealth requires the applications of multiple disciplines and a solid evaluation of how they interact with one another; we illustrate one such interaction focusing on the issue of tax awareness and suggest that wealth management advisors should view being interpreters as a large part of their roles.

CHAPTER 1

Many Interrelated Disciplines

Crucial among these many challenges must be the notion that helping a family manage its wealth is much more than helping manage its financial assets. This misguided conception of the classical wealth management relationship is illustrated in Figure 1.1.

This first chapter discusses the fundamental truth that family wealth management is broader than simple asset management and the difficulties this injects into the management process. Our point here is not to be comprehensive about these difficulties, as they alone could be the topic of another book. Rather, we mean first to take inventory and second to introduce a few of the alternative approaches which we have seen at work over the last twenty years or so. The serious student of these challenges should dig further.

MULTIPLE SOURCES OF CAPITAL

At some elementary level, it is not hard to understand intuitively that there is more to any family than its bank or brokerage account. After all, if this is so obviously true for the average family, why would it be any different when the only change one makes from the average is to assume that the family is financially wealthy? No family can be simply reduced to its financial assets; if that were the case, why would it have occurred to anyone to create the phrase "from shirtsleeves to shirtsleeves in three generations?"[1] Money certainly is

---

[1] According to Richard M. Segal, "shirtsleeves to shirtsleeves in three generations" is an American translation of a Lancashire proverb, "there's nobbut three generations atween a clog and clog." Some say that Andrew Carnegie, the famed 1800s industrialist from Scotland, brought the proverb's message to the New World. Further investigation proves that the adage is not unique to any one country or culture. In Italian, it is "dalle stalle alle stelle alle stalle" ("from stalls to stars to stalls"). The Spanish say, "quien no lo tiene, lo hance; y quien lo tiene, lo deshance" ("who doesn't

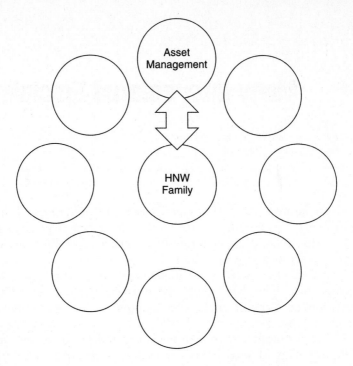

FIGURE 1.1   A Misguided Depiction of Family Wealth Management

a part of what a wealthy family is, but it is only a part, and hopefully not the most important.[2]

---

have it, does it, and who has it, misuses it"). Even non-Western cultures, including the Chinese, have a similar proverb. This quote was authored in 2008; Mr. Segal is the chair of the Family Business Council, a membership organization of family-owned businesses. The Chinese version of this proverb mentioned above, but not quoted is: "wealth never survives three generations," while the Japanese say "rice paddies to rice paddies in three generations."

[2]This is the point at which readers who are interested in detail might want to brush up on the differences between the concepts of total and marginal utility in economics. The simple insight is that marginal utility decreases as more and more of a good or service is consumed, while total utility is the sum of all marginal utilities for a given good or service. Thus, one can have a good that has a high marginal utility but a low total utility, as only small quantities of that good are purchased and vice versa. Ostensibly, the concept is applicable to financial wealth.

Lisa Gray coined the phrase "authentic assets"[3] to refer to the many different sources of wealth that exist within a family; her crucial point is to warn us that financial assets are only a part of the management challenge faced by the wealthy and their families. At a minimum, let's consider just a few: clearly, the wealthy do have financial assets. But human, intellectual, social, emotional, philanthropic, and artistic dimensions cannot be ignored; and there are others. Each has its own definition, which can be generally accepted or hotly debated and many have been studied in the halls of academe for quite a while. Whether a family is indeed financially wealthy or not, it is still a grouping of related individuals who exist within a broader social context. Maximizing their financial wealth is rarely enough for all members of the family to feel duly fulfilled. In many ways, certain families have even adopted a mental framework that is well worth considering: financial wealth is an enabler in that it facilitates family members to seek overall, complete fulfillment, while less wealthy individuals often cannot focus on much more than making financial ends meet.

EXPANDING ON THE CORPORATE ANALOGY

There is even more to the wealth management challenge than the fact that there are various sources or definitions of capital. Families must deal with a variety of issues that are common across the whole wealth spectrum, although financial wealth or social prominence tend to magnify them somewhat. They must pay taxes on their income and need to meet their ongoing expenses. They must pay transfer taxes when some of the wealth passes from one generation to the next or simply from one individual to another. They must comply with rules and regulations, whether in the management of financial assets or otherwise. They often have important philanthropic intensions that require planning and executing. Last, but not least, they must manage a wide range of risks for which insurance exists in certain cases and not in others, and which wealth can exacerbate, for instance with respect to reputation risk!

Figures 1.2 and 1.3 help put this notion in the proper perspective by drawing on the comparison once suggested by Charlotte Beyer, whom we already met in the Preface. The first step in our logic is to illustrate the broad

---

[3] Gray, Lisa. *Generational Wealth Management: A Guide for Fostering Global Family Wealth*. Euromoney Books, 2010, pp. 11–13. Lisa Gray acknowledges that the term "Authentic Capital" was coined by James E. Hughes, Jr., and inspired her in the differentiations of the various forms of assets on which a family can draw.

FIGURE 1.2 The Multiple Dimensions of Corporate Management

management problem facing the chief executive officer (CEO) of any corporation. Figure 1.2 provides a graphical depiction of the issue. It is mighty
hard to think of the successful CEO of a successful company who only
focused on a single dimension of his or her job: the business world is littered
with failed companies where the CEO only had time for research, engineering, finance, or marketing—to pick four areas at random. While not a totally
inescapable proof, as there must be an exception to any rule, this helps set
the simple proposition that a corporation is a complex assemblage of multiple functions and that the person at the top of the ladder must understand
both how each of these functions operates individually and how they all
work and come together to create the business of the whole firm for which
he or she is responsible.

Now, let's apply the same analytical framework to a family, assuming
that a family is no different than a corporation. Making this assumption
requires us to leave aside a number of important considerations, but the case
can simply be made that these are not crucial to our point here. Let's imagine

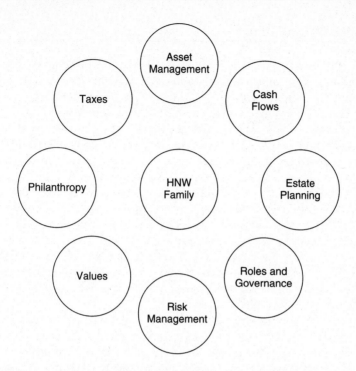

FIGURE 1.3 The Multiple Dimensions of Family Wealth Management

the head of the family as the CEO of his or her family's wealth, a company Charlotte Beyer calls My Wealth, Inc. Just as was the case for a corporation, there are multiple dimensions and the successful high net worth individual must first realize the multiplicity of these dimensions, and, second, be able to deal with all of them. Figure 1.3 illustrates this point and recalls a number of the dimensions we mentioned in the introduction for this chapter.

Just as it would be silly for a corporate CEO to focus on a single aspect of the business, it is equally misguided for an individual to consider just one aspect of the wealth management challenge. And yet, the traditional approach would be exactly that. For years, the industry had us and many of our clients believe that their focus should be solely on managing their financial wealth, their financial assets. This may have made sense when financial wealth was primarily inherited and in the form of stand-alone trust structures; but it certainly no longer applies when these financial assets were created by the current senior or immediately preceding generation.

MULTIPLE INTERACTIONS[4]

Now, if the challenge was simply to recognize that the problem is more complex and has more dimensions than initially thought, there would be little need to make dramatic change. Yet, just as is the case in a corporation, all these various "divisions" within the family structure do not exist in isolation. They have both their own issues that have to be addressed directly and a variety of tentacles that extend toward and into other dimensions. This is what makes it impractical for any service provider to the wealthy to argue that he or she can serve the family by simply focusing on a single aspect. I vividly remember the time when we first introduced the concept of tax-aware investment management to J.P. Morgan's clients: I could be my own wealthy client if I had a penny for each time I heard people tell me that "the tax tail should not wag the return dog." Most individuals who were raised in a world where taxes did not matter simply could not understand that there was a need to change the traditional investment process if one was going to focus on maximizing after-tax returns or terminal after-tax wealth at some future point in time.

Similarly, I was recently involved in a panel focused on asset allocation issues; it was sobering to observe highly gifted and successful people who principally operated in the world of institutional investors seemingly become "frazzled" when individual investor-related "complexities" were brought into the picture. Years ago, this was understandable to the extent that the bulk of the financial assets to be managed were owned by defined benefit pension funds. Now, with individuals owning more than 50 percent of all financial assets and with several institutional markets sharing "individual complexities" (Australian pension funds are taxable, for instance), what could uncharitably be viewed as a myopic inability to look beyond the theoretical and into the practical is rather surprising.... Yet, their hearts

---

[4]The term "interaction" here and in subsequent occurrences within this book is meant to convey the idea that the various disciplines do not exist in a vacuum. Although a few of these interactions may be unwitting, most reflect the fact that what is done within one sphere has a direct—and often predictable—impact in another, in somewhat of an inevitable manner. A well-known Georgia family suffered from on such interaction, which did not have to be: the family hired two private jets to fly to a holiday event, and one of the two planes crashed. A wealthy family does not have to, but certainly may fly private. Yet, sticking to the example, the plane that crashed was said to have all trustees of all family trusts onboard; a different choice as to who sat in which plane might have helped avoid the catastrophe. This could, in the words of the Family Office Exchange founded by Sara Hamilton, have come under the "risk management" header.

are definitely in the right place; it is just hard for them to accept that some cherished framework might need to be amended.

There are many other interactions beyond the simple integration of taxes into the investment process.[5] Consider philanthropy, a very important activity for both wealthy and less wealthy families, particularly in the United States.[6] Let's limit this discussion to the idea of giving away financial assets, be they money or securities, although the rarest and most precious asset that families often have is the time of their members. Clearly, giving away cash will achieve the purpose of benefiting the philanthropic activity chosen by the family and may well provide the donor with some tax benefit. How much more powerful, from the overall wealth management standpoint of the family, might some different form of giving be? Giving away appreciated securities might provide the same ultimate philanthropic impact at a lower real cost to the family, as it might avoid their having to pay taxes on the unrealized gain. Assuming that the family has both some cash available for giving and appreciated securities within an equity portfolio, for instance, a smarter strategy emerges: the family may give the appreciated stock, thus satisfying its charitable intent. It can also use the cash that it has available to top up the equity portfolio (some part of which has just been given away). This could provide an interesting additional benefit: it might lower the ratio of the market value of the portfolio to its tax basis (the stock that was given away had the most imbedded unrealized gains, while the new stocks purchased with the cash have no unrealized gain). This increases the flexibility of the manager to be tax-efficient in his or her handling of that portfolio. Although beyond the scope of this book, one might also mention other routes, such as charitable lead or charitable remainder trusts as a means to achieve either tax or transfer benefits.

So far, we have discussed interactions between investment management and income taxes, between philanthropic and tax planning, and between these last two and generational planning. We have also discussed interactions between philanthropy and investment management. The list does not stop here. Consider interactions between investment management and social capital; this occurs when a family wants to reflect certain social concerns in its investment management activities, which might lead it to consider so-called "socially responsible investing," or, more recently "impact investing." Consider interactions between strategic asset allocation and the development of the business skills of future generations. This occurs

---

[5]A family we serve has a particularly complex set-up, including inter-generational loans to combine investment management with income and estate tax efficiency.
[6]Brooks, Arthur C. *Who Really Cares, America's Charity Divide: Who Gives, Who Doesn't, and Why It Matters.* Basic Books, 2006.

when some portion of the family's assets is dedicated to financing some or all of the entrepreneurial activities of younger generations. Consider the interaction between the management of a family's philanthropic activities and the education of future generations, either in terms of the values the family wants to steward from one generation to the next or with respect to promoting family unity across different branches. In truth, the list of these interactions, if not endless, is only limited by the imagination of the family and of its advisors and its willingness to countenance what can become somewhat daunting complexities.

EDUCATING FUTURE GENERATIONS AND WEALTH TRANSFERS

Although we looked into these two issues a couple of paragraphs ago, the topic deserves more attention. Educating future generations is always important, whether a family is or is not financially wealthy. Yet, wealthy families often feel that they must dedicate a disproportionate amount of time and attention to it. The logic is simple and is best illustrated by an example. More than ten years ago, I found myself in the office of a multi-billionaire who had just stepped down from the chief executive position in the company he founded, which was the source of the family's financial wealth. After having spent some time focusing on the family's goals and fears, I asked him the same two important questions I had been asking all clients, in a bid to create a sort of a feedback loop. The first was: "We are now five years from now and you want to say that the program we have designed and implemented has been successful. How will you justify that?" The second was the obvious reciprocal: "We are now five years from now and you want to say that the program we have designed and implemented has been a failure. How will you justify that?" At that point, this hard-nosed executive simply broke down in tears. He answered the second question saying: "I have ruined my grandchildren!" The point was made, and nothing more needed to be said.

Ensuring that financial wealth transferred to future generations does not "ruin" them is one of the highest priorities of most financially wealthy parents and grandparents. Yet, there are many schools of thought as to how the process can be structured. Certain families choose to hide the money from future generations, at least until they are required by law to disclose its existence. A family once told me that the wealth had been almost totally dissipated one generation ago, because they had not been aware of the wealth or prepared to deal with it; the younger generation squandered it when it received it. Others choose to disclose the wealth very early, but place a great deal of emphasis on values, as opposed to the wealth. Family meetings are opportunities to discuss achievements and the family "history" as a means of reinforcing the traits that the currently controlling generation feels should be emphasized. Others finally choose a trickle approach to make future generations aware of the responsibilities they will one day have and to teach the skills required with small amounts, one at a time. In short, there is no such thing as a one-size-fits-all solution, but there is a one-size-fits-all requirement: the issue deserves to be thought through carefully and in depth, and whatever decision is made must be carefully implemented.

I remember a meeting with a family with two of the three current generations in the room. One of the members of the second generation was defending his spouse's decision not to attend the meeting and the fact that their two boys did not want to be involved with the management of the family's wealth. I felt it was my job to make a simple point: whether the boys and their mother were comfortable or not was not the issue. They did not object to the treats the wealth made possible, did they? They would one day have to take responsibility for the management of the wealth, would they not? With that, I suggested that there were really only two options. First, they could decide to add the wealth to what was already in the family's substantial private foundation. The members of the family who were reluctant to participate would then truly be "normal," in that they could not draw any income from the financial wealth and would have to live "like their friends." If they were not prepared to dispense with the wealth, then they had no option but to take responsibility for it and thus be adequately trained in its future management! The patriarch and his wife were beaming!

Related to the issue of education is the truism that wealth transfers should not be driven solely by tax issues, but really reflect what the family expects future generations to do. Thus, sheltering the family against all taxes could work wonderfully well, if younger generations were simultaneously prepared for the advantages that wealth might bring to them and for the responsibilities that went with them. In other circumstances, sheltering the family against transfer taxes might play directly against crucial family goals and would not be the preferred approach. Helping families deal with this issue is one of the most important tasks a good advisor can perform and, back to the topic of this book, is one of the great benefits of a goals-based wealth management approach. As it indeed demands that future goals be made quite specific, both in terms of dollar amounts and time horizons, it requires one to have thought through all these issues. Simply postulating some equity/bond mix as the risk profile that best characterizes the family misses out on an important opportunity to raise issues early that can otherwise be irrevocably set in stone once wealth transfer strategies have been implemented.

A final concern relating to intergenerational transfers cannot be ignored. Whose money is it anyway, and when? Although many families do carefully prepare wealth transfer plans, I have seen several cases where future generations were not or did not want to be aware of the way in which the passing of the ownership baton was orchestrated and of its timing. There were conflicts in that the generation owning the assets ostensibly had different goals than the one to which the assets would pass; one could see either open bickering or at least muted resentment at times. This may be less frequent when the "older" generation happens to have created the wealth: then, subsequent generations often tend to respect the fundamental role of the wealth creator and accept that his or her will should prevail, whatever documents may say. It can become a bit harder when the current owner of the wealth did not directly create it: he or she might have inherited it or received it in some form of legal settlement. Then, following generations do not always have the same natural willingness to stand aside; they can openly worry that spending patterns or clinging to some property—real or financial—may deprive them of what they see as ultimately and eventually theirs.[7] To me, the heart of the solution must be in appropriate communication and education, with some measure of mutual understanding and respect promoted to foster family continuity. It is indeed part and parcel of dealing with the risk of creating an entitled mentality, which can pollute virtually any generation, including the non-wealth-creating senior family members, at any point in time.

THE MAKE OR BUY DECISION

Although selected very large families, in terms of number of members, with substantial financial assets continue to prefer to "make" most of what they need in the management of their wealth, it has become much more frequent for families to delegate certain functions to outsiders while retaining others with the family. The single-family family office has often morphed into multi-family family offices. Indeed, the cost and regulatory burden associated with running a single-family office have increased substantially over the last twenty years, to the point that a fully staffed family office that carries out all the required activities has become the exception rather than the rule. Another contributor to that trend has been the gradual realization, on the part of families as well as within the wealth management industry loosely

---

[7] I actually saw one such conflict between the management committee of a trust and its beneficiaries. There, a member of the management committee—who was not a trustee—seemed to object to the fact that the beneficiaries were living too well. Was he reacting that way because he knew the grantor of the trust or because he himself did not feel it was right to live ostentatiously?

defined, that the number of disciplines is just too large. How can anyone be an expert or have an in-house expert in so many fields?

Yet, families at times find themselves making the decision about what activity they will conduct by default, rather than consciously. They tend to keep inside the office those functions that have typically been there, rather than asking themselves what they should and should not delegate.

The decision to delegate or not to delegate can be influenced by many factors, all of which can be analyzed in terms of some cost. One can think of four generic forms of cost. The first, the most obvious, because it adheres to the most traditional definition of what a cost is, looks at dollars and cents. Paradoxically, this may well be by far the easiest one to handle, if only because these accounting costs can be somewhat precisely determined. The second is a variant on the same theme, but is harder to assess. It relates to sustainability rather than current circumstances. Families might be able, for instance, to attract a top flight chief investment officer, who could be someone who has decided to step down from the world of the rough and tumble and to focus more sharply on a single client. However, will he or she be able to attract and retain the talent that might be needed if the assets are not growing sufficiently to provide for growing revenues from which to draw the compensation increases that this younger talent might expect?

This naturally leads to the third decision, which relates to confidentiality of family information. Any staff turnover means that someone outside of the family and of the office is aware of family circumstances. Despite the many "legal" precautions that can be taken through "non-disclosure" agreements in various forms, it is only a small step before one worries that the information will eventually leak! The final such cost is driven by the ability of staff to grow: certain disciplines are in a state of flux and the ability of individuals to be exposed to more than one set of circumstances or to more competing ideas can be an essential element of professional growth.

THE CREATION OF A WISDOM COUNCIL

One of the families we have been serving ever since our company was formed came up with a brilliant idea years ago. They created a Wisdom Council, which they defined as a group of specialists, all of whom had to have an interest in discussing and the ability to understand the various interactions that had to take place across the disciplines that were crucial to the family and its sustained well-being through time. We have since had the opportunity to see this put in place by a few other families and feel that it is a smart way to create an advisory and supervisory process within a family. These councils, as we have grown to appreciate them, tend not to meet more often than once a year, as theirs are strategic rather than tactical roles. The best analog would be to view them as a corporate board of directors stripped of its governance role. It takes a fairly insightful patriarchal generation to recognize its own limits and seek "counsel," but the rewards can be high. Yet, it is fair to say that the importance of the council should be expected to fade over time as the patriarchal generation gains the experience it lacked at the outset.

A Wisdom Council can be incredibly helpful to the family's development as long as its members recognize that they are not involved in day-to-day matters and that they should never become advocates, least of all for their own specialty areas. Members would typically be "experienced" enough that they are at ease within their specialties and have seen a large enough number of different circumstances to be able to react to them. They should also be "young" enough mentally that they are not set in their ways and are always prepared to speculate on or consider new angles and perspectives. Wisdom Council members also can "mentor" various individuals within the family or the office. Such a Wisdom Council may well be a requirement for families who decide to "make" most of what they need in-house. It should indeed serve as a useful sounding board for the family to make sure that they are fully exposed to all that is happening outside of their office. Though not the same as a Wisdom Council, which comprises skilled external professionals, the Family Council is also an important dimension of family governance, as it serves as the forum where important family decisions can be made, relying on more decision makers than the sole patriarch or matriarch.[8]

SUMMARY AND CONCLUSIONS

The point of this first chapter was simply to set the broad stage for the challenges that wealthy families face. Managing their wealth cannot be subsumed into the simple action of managing their assets; it must be set in the proper framework. That certain families will choose to focus on asset management primarily is not an indication of misguided decision making; it is fine provided that decision has been made actively, rather than by default, after having considered all the other dimensions of the challenge. Yet, most families will want to consider and work across several of these dimensions and actively manage the numerous interactions that exist. Whether they do this all internally or through the use of external service providers is very much the result of an internal cost/benefit analysis.

---

[8]As discussed in Dickstein, Sidney. "The Family Council: A Useful Adjunct to the Functions of the Wealth Management Professional." The *Journal of Wealth Management*, Spring 2003, pp. 12–14."

CHAPTER 2

An Example of a Crucial Interaction: Tax-Efficiency

The first professional article I ever wrote was entitled "The Upside-Down World of Tax-Awareness" and was published by *Trusts and Estates,* in 1997.[1] At that time, the classic article by Robert Arnott and Robert Jeffrey had already been published (it came out in 1993) and the fundamental question had been asked: "Is your alpha big enough to cover its taxes?"[2] Yet, I can vouch for the fact that practitioners, although intellectually interested in the question the article raised, seemed singularly unwilling to change their ways. In fact, when J.P. Morgan introduced the first active tax-aware equity investment process a little more than eighteen months after the Arnott and Jeffrey article was published, it really seemed to us that we were blazing a trail and yet only got minimal press coverage for it!

In this second chapter, we will be looking more deeply at the issue of tax-efficiency and the ways in which it forces us to change the way we think. A book could be written on this topic—and in fact a few of them have been—but our point is not to take our readers to the full depth of the issue, but rather to use it as a proxy for the way in which considering the interactions identified in Chapter 1 require practitioners and families alike to revisit the way they have been working. We'll start with a simple exposition of the effect of the tax bite on compound returns, and then focus on three ways in which our thinking must change: (1) the definition of active management may need to be expanded; (2) portfolio architecture may need to be altered; and (3) for families who can handle the complexity and minimum asset requirement, there may be a place for a greater reliance on derivative securities. I should note that quite a material part of this chapter is inspired

---

[1]Brunel, Jean L.P. "The Upside-Down World of Tax-Aware Investing." *Trust and Estates,* February 1997, pp. 34–42.
[2]Arnott, Robert D. and Robert H. Jeffrey. "Is Your Alpha Big Enough to Cover Its Taxes?" *Journal of Portfolio Management,* Spring 1993, pp. 15–25.

by Chapters 3, 4, 6, and 9 of my prior book,[3] readers are invited to go back to these for more detail and a more complete list of the other articles cited.

THE TAX BITE AND ITS IMPACT ON COMPOUND RETURNS

One of the first implications of the need to be tax-aware—which we define as appreciating that taxes should not be ignored[4]—is that the cherished focus on total return may need to go by the wayside. Institutional investors who are most often—but not always—tax-exempt have very much led the asset management industry away from the traditional observation that there are several components to return, preferring to focus on total return. At the very least, there are three components: interest and dividend income, realized capital gains or losses,[5] and unrealized capital gains or losses. Absent taxes, it is perfectly sensible not to draw much of a distinction among them, other than to the extent that one can argue that interest and dividend income is probably more predictable, in the short term at least, than capital gains. With taxes a relevant dimension, distinctions are inevitable, to the extent that tax codes[6] frequently distinguish among them by applying different tax rates to each. Many tax codes add another requirement: one must distinguish between "short-term" and "long-term" realized capital gains, as well!

With tax rates often in excess of 25 to 40 percent for income and realized capital gains, the difference between pre- and after-tax returns is quite significant, and this difference is magnified through time by the normal compounding. It takes about ten years to double your money with a 7 percent pretax return; apply a 35 percent tax to that return and your assets will only have grown 55 percent after ten years!

The only piece of good news in this otherwise sad state of affairs is that returns involve risk, which statisticians often measure in terms of the

---

[3]Brunel, Jean L.P. *Integrated Wealth Management: The New Direction for Portfolio Managers.* Institutional Investor Books, a division of Euromoney Institutional Investors PLC, 2002 (2nd ed., 2006).

[4]A fuller definition I used in quite a number of presentations expands on the idea. I define tax-awareness as the process by which one avoids unnecessary and defers unavoidable taxes.

[5]Certain jurisdictions differentiate between realized gains and losses on securities that were held for short- or long-term periods and apply different taxes to each.

[6]They certainly do in the United States and many OECD countries, for instance, but do not in countries such as Taiwan, where transaction taxes are used.

standard deviation of these returns. Investors who do not worry about taxes are left bearing that risk alone. Taxable investors are lucky, as they have a partner with whom to share that risk: the government (as most jurisdictions allow one to use realized capital losses to offset realized capital gains)!

A NEW ANALYSIS OF CAPITAL LOSSES

I used the phrase "upside down" in the title of that original article of mine, because of the fact that the government becomes a partner of the investor when taxes enter into the equation: this is a bit of an upside-down world indeed! Let me state the conclusion up-front and work to explain it. Although one should never wish for capital losses, the taxable investor has some positive use for them, while tax-exempt investors do not. More to the point, an unrealized capital loss can be viewed as a free option! It is a free option to realize a capital gain elsewhere in the same taxable pocket tax-free (as the investor can choose to realize that loss, use it to offset some unrealized capital gain in the portfolio and thus, having no net realized capital gain, manage to avoid taxation on a realized capital gain)! Similarly, for jurisdictions in which it matters, one can arbitrage between short- and long-term gains and losses, for instance, by waiting until a gain is long-term before taking it.

Consider capital markets over the long term. Returns are positive, although they oscillate more or less violently and regularly around that upward-sloping trend line. This has two important implications. First, we expect to make money over time. Second, random market fluctuations over the short term will make it inevitable that individual positions may be in an unrealized capital loss position from time to time. Post the advent of Modern Portfolio Theory, capital market theorists will tell us that the return pattern of any security, or asset class for that matter, comprises a risk that is specific to the security or asset class and another that is systematic. They have demonstrated that specific risk can be diversified, while systematic risk cannot.

Diversified specific risk means that the various securities in the single-asset class portfolio—or asset classes in a multi-asset class portfolio—will experience diverging return patterns from time to time, but that these individual fluctuations will be offset by other securities or asset classes. It should, therefore, follow that I might be able to take any one of these random losses and use them to offset some gain! Not using a random loss means two things. First, it may well disappear as the security's price pattern reverses. Second, the gain I had in that other security may easily disappear as well for the same reason.[7] Thus, not taking the loss when it occurs prevents me from taking advantage of a gain when it is available and can be taken with no adverse tax consequence; this is an important insight when that gain is in a security whose weight in the portfolio has, for instance, risen to a point where it should be trimmed, were it not for the adverse tax consequences: taxes can indeed at times prevent appropriate risk management when that would involve trimming substantially appreciated positions; tax-awareness can help restore the balance when it is focused on systematic unrealized loss harvesting.

AN EXPANDED DEFINITION OF ACTIVE MANAGEMENT

Although several authors have focused on this issue, no one has written more on the topic than David Stein, who was a pioneer in the space.[8] David Stein postulated that there are two ways in which a portfolio can be actively managed. The first, the most traditional definition, is illustrated in Figure 2.1 and involves being active with respect to security or asset class selection. Simply, a manager will incur higher risk—in absolute terms or relative to some index—to earn higher returns—in absolute terms or still relative to some index. Many authors are now arguing that such a form of portfolio

FIGURE 2.1   A Traditional View
of Active Management

---

[7]In fact, we might fear that such a gain might disappear, but be loath to "take" it because of the adverse tax circumstances. Thus, being able to take advantage of some unrealized loss can reduce—if not eliminate—the pain associated with taking a gain we fear may not remain.
[8]Stein, David M. "Diversification in the Presence of Taxes." *The Journal of Portfolio Management*, Fall 2000, pp. 61–71.

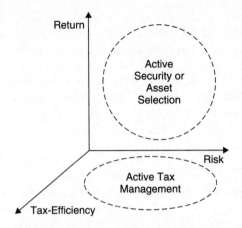

FIGURE 2.2 An Alternative View of
Active Management

activity might be self-deluding, suggesting that markets are too efficient for such value added to be sustainably captured.

Figure 2.2 presents a different definition of active management. There, the manager still accepts that he or she will incur some more risk—again in absolute terms or relative to some index—but the goal is not to earn higher returns, but to increase the portfolio's tax efficiency.

This new definition is crucial, as it suggests that one can raise after-tax returns in one of two ways. One can raise them by earning higher pretax returns and hoping that the incremental return is not wiped out by taxes. Alternatively, one can raise them by working to reduce the tax rate that is applied to the entire portfolio,[9] and as discussed further below, this principle can be applied both within an individual asset class or sub-asset class and to the portfolio as a whole.

APPLICABILITY TO BOTH ASSET AND SECURITY DECISIONS

Although the large bulk of the literature dedicated to active tax-management has focused on security selection decisions, the process it describes is

---

[9]Note that this discussion puts a new light on the traditional—and in my opinion too narrow—active versus passive management debate. While there may be good reasons to argue that active security selection is becoming increasingly hard to justify (elusive value added and the impact of fees), the notion that one should eschew active tax management does not follow.

practically almost as relevant to asset class decisions. In fact, Clifford Quisenberry[10] demonstrated that it might be more tax-efficient to dispense with size and style capitalization distinctions when managing a U.S. equity portfolio. As the composition of the each index representing small and large capitalization stocks, as well as value and growth stocks, changes over time, each sub-portfolio needs to be rebalanced. As it is rebalanced, gains may be realized that would not need to be if one stuck to the broadest definition of U.S. equities.[11] These gains lead to the unnecessary incurring of taxes![12]

This principle can be extended in two dimensions. First, it suggests that one should use as broad a definition of asset classes and strategies (or risk factors) as possible, so that it comprises as many independent sources of volatility as possible. These independent sources of volatility maximize the chances that individual losses may occur while the overall allocation is still in the black. Consider this: while large capitalization stocks might be appreciating, small capitalization equities might be under pressure. Within an all-capitalization stock portfolio, potential small capitalization random losses can be used to take large capitalization gains tax-free.[13] In short, whether limited to an equity portfolio or more broadly applied, multiple sources of independent—or semi-independent—volatility allow managers to realize a few of these unrealized gains without incurring capital gains tax liability. Second, it suggests that the relative volatility of different asset classes can also be used to enhance the tax-efficiency of the portfolio. Consider high yield bonds and emerging market equities, for instance. A sudden increase in interest rate levels or widening in credit spreads can provide a random capital loss in a high-yield bond portfolio. This might provide an opportunity to take "tax-free" gains in emerging market equities, for

---

[10]Stein, David M. "Equity Portfolio Structure and Design in the Presence of Taxes." *The Journal of Wealth Management,* Fall 2001, pp. 37–42. Quisenberry, Clifford H. Jr. "Optimal Allocation of a Taxable Core and Satellite Portfolio Structure." *The Journal of Wealth Management,* Summer 2003, pp. 18–26.

[11]We will see an echo of this point in our next chapter when we discuss the concept of the "market portfolio."

[12]We will discuss in a few paragraphs the potential use of derivative securities in a bid to manage or control that challenge.

[13]This statement is true when the portfolio as a whole is either actively managed or indexed using a sampling rather than replication approach. In a replication index approach, one would not want to take profit, as any stock that appreciates in the portfolio would appreciate in the index as well, thus obviating any need for rebalancing.

instance. Although it may be harder in this context to avoid straddle rules in the United States, or their equivalent in other jurisdictions, there are ways to take losses in an asset class that is falling in price and to use them to take profits tax-free in another.

ABANDONING THE MURKY MIDDLE: THE BARBELL PORTFOLIO[14]

Traditionally, people select investment policies that reflect some balance between too much and too little portfolio activity, which has some direct impact on expected portfolio risk and return. In this context, risk and return have two dimensions each. The first relates to the traditional capital market line: return rises alongside risk, although not in a straight line. Thus, a portfolio will typically comprise a mix of risky and less risky assets. The second dimension may be more subtle, but it is equally important. Certain strategies used on the portfolio will involve low manager risk, in part because this typically means lower fees and in part because investors have learned that high portfolio activity usually means lower tax-efficiency. Others will accept a higher degree of manager risk, as people have also learned that managers must take risk relative to their benchmarks to generate alpha—or excess return.

It should, therefore, not surprise that portfolios often represent some mix, aiming to strike a balance between low and high activity levels. Figure 2.3 represents this graphically. It describes this typical portfolio design as the "murky middle," which is defined as a portfolio that maintains a balance between little or no activity (we can call this passive within the context of Figure 2.1) and high activity (which would reflect concentrated and very actively managed portfolios). Portfolio activity is represented on the sole axis in the graph: it is assessed using the degree to which managers deviate from their benchmarks, whether this relates to policy asset allocation or to individual asset classes or strategies. As portfolio activity increases, the expected value added, or alpha captured by the manager or managers should also increase: expected alpha should be a linear function of portfolio activity, as no portfolio manager would incur portfolio activity if its marginal efficiency was negative![15] This is depicted

---

[14]Brunel, Jean L.P. "A Tax-Efficient Portfolio Construction Model." *The Journal of Wealth Management,* Fall 2001, pp. 43–50.
[15]Note that this may not be true in terms of actual alpha in that higher activity does not guarantee that the activity will be successful.

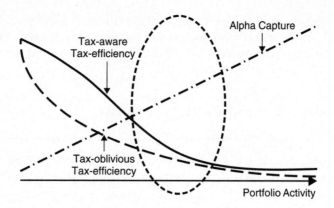

FIGURE 2.3 The "Murky Middle" and Its Challenge

in the graph as the upward sloping alpha capture line. The graph also shows two tax-efficiency lines; they are meant to show that tax-efficiency falls quite rapidly as tax-oblivious portfolio activity increases; this is the Arnott and Jeffrey argument. The tax-aware tax-efficiency line allows some deferral of the onset of tax-inefficiency, but there are limits to how much taxes can be deferred. The murky middle portfolio is hurt by the fact that the alpha capture increase is linear, while the loss of tax efficiency is not: it falls off quite rapidly. Thus, that "murky middle" portfolio only captures some of the available alpha, and yet is virtually as tax-inefficient as possible.

Figure 2.4 transforms the picture shown in Figure 2.3 and illustrates how the right portfolio structure can contribute to better overall portfolio

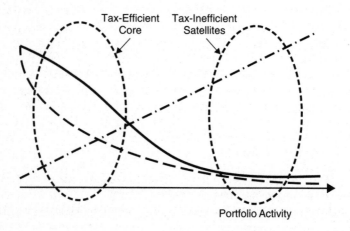

FIGURE 2.4 The Barbell Portfolio

tax-efficiency. A portion of the portfolio is invested in a tax-efficient core, which may even be "hyper tax-efficient," a name we give to strategies such as the one pioneered by David Stein that seeks to enhance tax-efficiency. Using a systematic tax loss capture, they are able to produce net realized losses than can be used elsewhere in the portfolio. Another part of the portfolio is invested in high-activity, low tax-efficiency strategies whose purpose is to find some way for the investor to benefit from some measure of active value added. Note that the losses generated within the "hyper tax-efficient" portion of the portfolio can then be used in these tax-inefficient satellites. While both "portions" will experience materially different levels of activity, it is quite conceivable that the "average activity" for the portfolio as a whole can be similar to what might have been found in a typical "murky middle" portfolio.

THE POTENTIAL ROLE AND LIMITS OF DERIVATIVE STRATEGIES

Whether they deal with portfolio rebalancing or security selection, investment managers must suffer from a curse: they are wrong a fair portion of the time. I've already quoted the late Sir John Templeton's observation that he had never seen a manager right more often than 65 percent of the time. Take this statement and observe that portfolio activity must involve some net capital gain realization in a world where the long-term return line is upward sloping. Being right at most 65 percent of the time must mean that one is wrong at least 35 percent of the time, too. Since activity involves some gain realization, it also involves paying capital gains taxes. Note the irony: at least 35 percent of the time, investment managers will pay taxes for the privilege of making a poor decision. This is the fundamental reason why generating after-tax excess return is so hard.[16] This after-tax return must not only bear the taxes it should bear when it is positive, but it must also cover for the taxes that were still paid even when excess return was negative!!![17]

This is where derivative securities can come into play in tax jurisdictions where they can be used effectively. In the United States, for instance, the buying or selling of a derivative security is considered an "opening trade,"

---

[16]Brunel, Jean L.P. "Revisiting the Fallacy of Market-Timing in an After-Tax Context." *The Journal of Private Portfolio Management*, Fall 1999, pp. 16–26.
[17]As you can have a positive absolute return, which will thus create a realized capital gain, and yet have a negative relative return.

even if the portfolio has exposure to a similar general risk factor, provided a number of arcane rules are respected. They include but are not limited to so-called "constructive sale" or straddle rules! Anyone considering such a strategy should first consult with his or her tax advisors, as this is quite complex a topic. Yet, in broad principles, an opening transaction does not attract tax. Thus, hedging some Japanese equity exposure, for instance, and creating an equivalent dollar amount of, say, European equity exposure could be done via derivative contracts, rather than through the sale of physical securities. Rather than selling specific Japanese equities, one could simply be selling the appropriate notional amount of Japanese equity index futures; on the other side of the trade, one could be buying an equivalent amount of European equity index futures. More simply, but with different counterparty risks and "minimal bite size" considerations, one could consider swapping Japanese equity index returns for European equity index returns for a notional amount of exposure equal to the desired geographical allocation shift. This is the practical equivalent of reducing the portfolio's Japanese equity exposure and adding to its European equity exposure, in this example in equal amounts. If this had been done in the physical security markets, one would have to assume that there would have been some capital gain realized on the Japanese equity sale.

Thus, in a physical portfolio, the manager pays taxes first and then observes whether the transaction produced value added. In a derivative overlay, the manager first changes the portfolio exposures and then observes whether the transaction produced value added. If it did, then taxes must be paid. But if it did not, not only were taxes not incurred at the outset, but the loss realized on this overlay trade can now be used to offset some gain elsewhere in the portfolio. One should however note that certain arcane rules governing how these positions are accounted for at year-end may or may not affect the advisability or the timing of the decision to consider them. This latter example is intentionally simple and one could complicate it easily. Yet, the point here is not to argue that derivative transactions always make sense, but to suggest that families might discuss them with all their advisors and make up their own minds as to whether they do or do not make sense in their own circumstances. Beside the need to comply with rules that can be quite complex, there are two principal additional issues to consider. The first relates to counter party risk. Certain derivative transactions may involve individual counter parties rather than broad market clearing houses; the cautious investor will want to make sure that these risks are both well-understood and appropriately managed. The second relates to bite sizes. Derivative strategies usually involve dollar amounts that can appear quite high for certain families. This simply reflects the expenses associated with the creation of the position on the part of a family and the maintenance of the position on the part of the counter party. The practicality of considering such a transaction within the context of each family should therefore be very carefully evaluated.

SUMMARY AND CONCLUSIONS

The interactions between investment and tax management activities are among the most numerous and the most complex. This chapter serves as an illustration of the changes one must consider making to the traditional, tax-oblivious investment process once taxes enter into the picture. In short, a tax-aware investment process looks and feels quite different from its traditional tax-oblivious alternative. This will be true along many dimensions: the need to accept that an unrealized loss represents a valuable free option; the recognition that the traditional portfolio balance between active and passive strategies should be reconsidered; or even the realization that there may be room for the use of derivative securities. The same could be said when considering many of the other interactions we discussed in Chapter 1. Our strong suggestion is thus for families to recognize the challenge and seize the opportunity!

CHAPTER 3

The Need for a Financial Interpreter

(Given the Complexity of the Investment Process)

Although in fairness this trait is not the sole province of wealth managers, I have heard many families complain that their advisors do not speak the same language as they do. Whether this refers to advisors using jargon or simply to families not knowing enough about the environment in which they must operate in the end is a moot point. The role of any advisor is to help the family, and his or her first focus should be a diagnosis of what the family needs in order to be able to participate in the management of its wealth. This chapter, which is dedicated to asset management issues, focuses on the principal environmental variables that a family must understand, as well as on the activities the family must be prepared to carry out. Note that we do not mean to absolve advisors by saying that there are things a family has the responsibility to learn. Far from it. Our main point is indeed that financial advisors should see themselves as interpreters. That role comprises both the classic interpreter function and that of the teacher who should help the family learn what it needs to learn, but not more than it has to! The old adage that families are asking us the time and not how to make a watch applies in spades! Although it is tempting to think that many advisors already know this, I really feel that both clients and advisors need to recognize that they must communicate and thus have some common language and knowledge base: this is where it is important to suggest to advisors that they should be financial interpreters and to families that they should reward them when they fulfill that role well. We start with a discussion of capital markets and the development of rational expectations and move onto three important family asset management responsibilities: performance analysis and reporting, manager selection, and financial governance.

WHAT MAKES MARKETS WORK?

My main concern here is to develop a mutually agreed on view of a thought framework that describes how and why markets work. One of the most challenging statements often made by investment managers is the idea that "fundamentals move markets!" Families often do not really know what we mean by fundamentals and, when they do, are not sure how these fundamentals actually work. Further, it can be counterintuitive that one might see substantial price volatility from one day to the next because fundamentals tend to develop and change through time rather than instantaneously. Such a thought framework postulates that markets are driven by real macro- and micro-economic developments: strong corporate earnings growth leads to higher equity prices and vice versa; strong economic growth eventually begets higher interest rates and vice versa; or strong economic growth should lead to higher commodity and energy prices, and vice versa. While this makes a great deal of intuitive sense, it may well miss an important point and thus mislead families into the wrong expectations or sheer befuddlement at certain points in time.

I have always preferred to lead with the simple proposition that buyers and sellers drive markets. It first has the benefit of being the plain truth and, second, it is considerably more intuitive from the point of view of a family. Thus, prices will tend to go up when buyers are keener than sellers and vice versa. The discussion, however, does not stop here; far from it! If it did, one would simply have to accept that no serious forecast can be made over any time horizon longer than a few days. Indeed, if traders are only driven by mood swings, how could one have any hope of determining how their moods will swing weeks or months from now? Yet, the key here, if the activities of buyers and sellers are the main market drivers, is for us to see how we can anticipate how they might behave in the near future or the middle-term horizon.

The insight that brings fundamentals back into the picture is that they can be said to be an indicator that will help us anticipate how buyers and sellers may act in the future. One would first assume that markets will fluctuate somewhat randomly for as long as actual fundamental—that is, economic or corporate—developments turn out to be more or less in line with expectations. Although considerably simpler an exposition than the original efficient market hypothesis,[1] the idea is just that markets should reflect all currently available information that should have been discounted

---

[1]Fama, Eugene, "Efficient Capital Markets: A Review of Theory and Empirical Work." *The Journal of Finance*, May 1970, pp. 383–417.

into current prices. From this it follows that material price moves—upward or downward—should be expected to be the result of some form of surprise. Thus, it would be reasonable to argue that buyers will flock to the market when they are favorably surprised, and vice versa. Interestingly, this also brings to the fore a very important notion: what matters is not how good or bad a development is; what matters is how it compares to prior expectations.

Where efficient market supporters and detractors part ways is in the likelihood that anyone can have access to that "premonition that a surprise is imminent;" efficient market supporters tend to believe that no one can reasonably expect to have access to these kinds of insights frequently and reliably enough. Efficient market detractors argue that careful analysis can point to opportunities, whether related to macro- or micro-economic factors. It is not our point to argue one side or the other here, but simply to show that the debate exists and illustrate what one would need to believe to take one side or the other.

It is not hard to point to the beliefs of the investor who argues that nobody knows the future: he or she simply postulates that the future depends on way too many variables, none of which can be known with any certainty. What might be interesting, but beyond the scope of this book, would be to point to a few circumstances when history tells us both that there was an extreme of emotions and that some structural change was taking place. This indeed would tend to be one of the few instances when arguing that no forecast is possible might be the hardest. The rest of the time, it does indeed appear to many observers that randomness prevails, providing plenty of fodder to the supporters of the efficient market theory.

The careful investor who believes that markets are not always perfectly efficient simply postulates that general trends, cycles, and fundamental relationships can be identified that have tended historically to be reliable enough indicators. He or she will, therefore, feel the need to develop a framework within which the behavior of fundamentals is described in "normal" or "equilibrium" circumstances and to assess the relationship that may exist between market prices—whether these markets comprise equities, fixed income securities, or real assets—and relevant macro-economic or corporate variables. One must consider "normal" circumstances because this should be the environment in which the greatest degree of reasonableness and lack of emotion might prevail. That "normal" conditions rarely exist in the short term is what makes the exercise more interesting. Once that framework is formulated, it becomes easier for anyone to evaluate the extent to which one or several variables differ from their so-called equilibrium state and thus the extent to which markets should be expected to experience "valuation" swings.

ASSET CLASSES, SUB-ASSET CLASSES, AND STRATEGIES

Before setting out the formulation of rational return and risk expectations, it is necessary to agree on the definition of asset classes; once that is done, we can then define sub-asset classes and even expand this to strategies that are defined as active investment processes around either asset or sub-asset classes.

I still have not found a better framework to define asset classes than the one I outlined in Chapter 7 of my earlier quoted book. There, I argued that the three most important differentiating financial asset class attributes were the relative importance of income in total returns, the relative predictability of income, and the term of the instrument. Thus, we found ourselves with three primary financial asset classes. Cash has a return that comes entirely from income, with a set coupon and a short time horizon. Equities derive the bulk of their total return from capital appreciation, have a less predictable income flow because dividends can be raised or cut, and do not have a formal maturity date. Fixed income securities, bonds, are in between these two, as income accounts for the bulk of their returns and is predictable, as they have fixed coupons[2]; however, because they have a maturity date and because that date can be several years out, changing interest rate levels in the broader environment can cause price fluctuations that can have a material impact on total return at least in the short to medium term. The only change I would make in this original framework would be to specify real assets as a fourth category, whose returns and risks are driven by the size and the volatility of the premium they should earn above inflation.

Sub-asset classes[3] are defined as segments within an asset class that differ from it as a result of some structural premium that reflect some additional dimension of risk. High-yield bonds involve more credit risk than

---

[2] Aside from events of default, where the risk applies potentially both to the coupon that stopped being paid and to the eventual repayment of the bond when it matures.
[3] Note that the list of possible such sub-asset classes is almost limitless. In fact, a few of these may even be viewed to straddle asset classes: convertible bonds are a good example. The accounting profession has created specific measures determining whether a convertible is an equity-equivalent or not, but this does not really help one resolve the problem. My own solution is to accept to place such "hybrid" instruments into one spot, knowing full well that my definition is somewhat biased or subject to debate. The most material such issue relates to instruments that do not have linear pay-off patterns, such as options and variants on the theme. I address this by postulating that they are not individually a part of a strategic asset allocation, although a strategy trading option might be.

investment grade bonds. Small capitalization equities involve some additional risk relative to the broader equity market in that the underlying companies are less mature in one or several dimensions. There are many other similar illustrations.

The leading edge of the investment management industry is gradually moving away from the concept of asset class, preferring the idea of "risk factor." Risk factors are defined as those broad macro-economic or environmental variables that drive changes in asset prices. The advantage of sticking to asset classes is that it is a well-understood and very familiar concept; the main disadvantage is that asset class prices can and do vary in response to a variety of different factors (few of which may be specific to an asset class while most straddle the full universe); they can actually affect different asset classes in different ways. What are these factors? The list can be as long as one might wish, but the following few should illustrate the concept sufficiently: inflation, economic growth, interest rate sensitivity, corporate profitability, credit worthiness, geopolitical circumstances, global capital flows, liquidity, and so on. At this point, there is no readily available and affordable software that maps a normally diversified global portfolio across individual risk factors, but the time is coming when investors will need to become more familiar with an approach that can provide more textured and granular insights into portfolio risk exposures.[4] Looking ahead, one can hope that asset allocation based on risk factors rather than asset classes or strategies will become the norm, as it allows a more differentiated and finer analysis and management of the risks involved in a portfolio.

Anticipating somewhat on future chapters, I am comfortable postulating that the process that will be described based on asset classes and strategy can easily and readily be transposed to replace them with whatever list of risk factors the industry eventually settles on.

DEVELOPING REASONABLE EXPECTATIONS[5]

Capital market forecasting is not for the faint of heart. Yet, without some reasonable framework for determining longer-term expectations, any desire

---

[4]One can assume that a variant on the software originally developed following Bill Sharpe's work on style analysis can provide a possible solution to this quandary. See Sharpe, William F. "Determining a Fund's Effective Asset Mix." *Investment Management Review*, December 1988, pp. 59–69.

[5]This clearly begs the question of whether one can escape the need to forecast capital market expectations altogether. I personally do not believe this is possible simply because of our need—as we shall discuss it in Part 3—of being able to compute the size of a sub-portfolio needed to fund any and all client goals.

to create some policy allocation, whether guided by Modern Portfolio Theory or a result of goals-based analyses, will be frustrated. A total reliance on history is fraught with danger, as the past is not always the appropriate prelude. A total rejection of the past is equally problematic, as it is hard to see how such expectations would relate to reality, to the extent that it would be a very unusual situation indeed when no historical relationship would be said to hold any value.

Note, however, that more recent thinking in the asset management industry is leading a number of well-known and respected authors to promote the concept of "the market portfolio" and to argue that each individual's portfolio is simply a mix of that portfolio and cash—or leverage for those seeking additional risk. While the concept is interesting, it is, in my view, one of those instances in which an excessive reliance on theory and a lack of understanding of what taxable investors need might create distinctions without differences and, more problematically, less efficient portfolios. A simple example illustrates why I hold this view, until someone convinces me that I am wrong. In 1988, Australia elected to change pension fund—they call them superannuation funds—taxation. Further, the Australian tax system incorporated and still incorporates certain features to avoid the double taxation of dividends. This feature combined with the newly taxable status of superannuation funds to change the traditional fixed income/equity mix in the typical fund, raising the equity exposure. The higher equity risk was more than offset by the potential for using the equity dividend "franking credits" to shelter some of the tax on interest income from bonds. The "market portfolio" had not changed and neither had the risk profile of the average fund, yet the optimal portfolio for the "average fund" had changed, because of new tax realities.

The forecasting model—framework might be a better word than model—I developed and that is described in my first book referenced earlier remains my best hope, although a number of variants exist, many of which are not without value. The model I prefer to use starts with a simple premise, illustrated in Figure 3.1. It simply postulates that four main macro-economic variables (we call them building blocks) drive both the return and the volatility of the major asset classes. They are all evaluated in "equilibrium" conditions, a hypothesis that refers to an environment in which an economy is midway between the top and the bottom of a business cycle and the various asset classes are fairly valued relative to one another.

Return and volatility estimates for sub-asset classes can then be computed as a derivative of each of these asset classes by applying a structural premium—also evaluated in equilibrium conditions—to both return and volatility expectations for each of the main asset classes. In this context, real assets can be viewed as a sub-asset class to cash, except that the premium

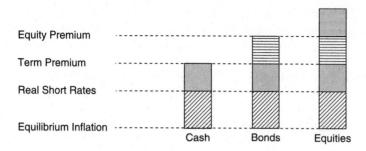

FIGURE 3.1 A Building Block Approach to Capital Market Forecasting

that they command is measured relative to inflation rather than vis-à-vis cash returns. Strategy return and volatility can similarly be estimated based on the returns and volatility of the asset or sub-asset class in which they are applied combined with reasonable manager value added and tracking error assumptions. Correlations across these various estimates are best based on historical data for reasons that relate to matrix mathematics and are not crucial to our point here.

It should by now be clear that this framework is only as good as the assumptions that are made with respect to the building blocks as well as the various premiums. Yet, an important feature of this process is that it benefits from three different dimensions of clarity. It is clear with respect to the structure of capital markets; the definition of each asset class, sub-asset class, or strategy is explicit and can thus be challenged and verified through time. It is clear with respect to its assumptions, which can also be challenged and modified through time; yet, any modification in any single assumption will apply equally to each of the forecasts that rely on it. Finally, it is clear with respect to expectations: one is not looking so much for absolute accuracy as for some relative hierarchy across all forecasts. Orders of magnitude matter more than precision to the second or third digit after the decimal point.

In short, this framework respects the lessons from history, as any assumption must be calibrated based on some historical pattern, with any deviation from historical norm being actively explained rather than ignored or simply postulated. At the same time, by allowing the investor to reflect his or her best guesses of how economic and market developments might unfold in the years ahead, it ensures that the policies that are designed are internally consistent and represent at least somewhat educated assumptions and structural relationships. I should add that experience has demonstrated, to me at least, that the intellectual discipline and rigor that underpin the model did allow us to avoid a few of the most serious errors that befell several investors in the alternative investment space. Had these investors taken the time to understand what the managers were purporting to do, how their value added could be reasonably calibrated, and what risk they were taking relative to what had to be a logical benchmark, they would not have fallen victim to the mistaken belief that many hedge funds provided "equity returns with bond risk," as the saying went until 2008!!!

PERFORMANCE ANALYSIS AND REPORTING

The same intellectual honesty and rigor ought to drive performance analysis and reporting. Whether focused on pre- or after-tax data, performance reporting is actually not terribly complex. It can be cumbersome. It may require access to pricing data that can at times be deferred or simply hard to find. But it is relatively trivial, as the return of a portfolio is the weighted average return of all its individual positions! Volatility—or risk—measurement is somewhat more complicated, but it is again not terribly arduous, as long as one respects the generic domain within which all the various statistics one wishes to use remain valid! A standard deviation of monthly returns over three months is about as useless as bringing ice cubes to the North Pole!

Performance analysis, on the other hand, is always a bit more challenging, as it relates to comparing certain actual return or volatility numbers to standards, be they market- or peer-benchmarks. It is also made no easier by the ever-present challenge of distinguishing—or trying to distinguish—between skill and luck. It is indeed a truism that, after the fact, one can only make a single observation: Were the results good or not? Objectively, whatever result we observe is a function of a variety of interactions between decisions that were actively made and how markets actually behaved; between various biases or prejudices and whether these were rewarded or not; between circumstances that were within someone's control and others that were not.

Detailed—and at times complex—performance analysis is the discipline that allows one to make educated guesses—and these become more and more so with time—as to how a portfolio did and which decision worked or did not work. Ostensibly, in this brief overview, we do not have the time or space to go into any detail, but three simple comments may help make the broader point. First, performance should always be analyzed over a time period that makes sense. The more detailed—and complex—the process, the shorter the period over which some insight can be derived; the complexity of the process can indeed serve to eliminate several of the random dimensions of performance. Yet, any result assessed over anything less than at least three years is probably not worth the effort. Second, performance should always be analyzed relative to "naïve" expectations. In this instance, naïve expectations relate to what should have been expected, rather than what we might have wished. Comparing the performance of a small capitalization stock manager to a high yield bond index is senseless—and virtually anybody would agree with this; yet, it is not a lot more so than comparing the performance of a relative value hedge manager focused on arbitrage strategies to the returns of the S&P 500 Index—and there, one can point to many people who actually regularly fall into the trap! Finally, performance analysis should always be multi-dimensional. This simply means to make the argument that multiple points of view often help gain a better picture: while a single point of view can present a distorted picture in that it does not allow one to see an important feature, looking at that same edifice from different perspectives helps create a much better and more accurate image.

Performance analysis plays directly into one of the most difficult tasks families and individuals must perform: selecting the managers who will be charged with certain portions of the family's or the individuals' financial assets. Chapter 19 in my earlier book goes into a lot more detail than I can here, but the points are still essentially valid. Manager selection should incorporate an analysis of performance, but the latter should only serve to illustrate and confirm that the processes a manager claims he or she employs both worked as they should have been expected to and experienced success. Fundamentally, the sad truth is that selecting managers is often—somewhat analogous to what the Hippocratic Oath requires of physicians to do—about avoiding errors rather than displaying flashes of genius. Thus, one should first be concerned that the philosophy on which a manager bases his or her processes is reasonable and has some chance of being successful.

One should then make sure that the processes that are thus employed are designed in a way that is consistent with the professed philosophy and that the resources brought to bear are in line with what one should expect. A manager who proclaims that the crucial element of his philosophy is security selection based on detailed research should, for instance, have sufficient research resources to cover the relevant universe. Once one can feel convinced that philosophy, processes, and resources are internally consistent, then an analysis of past performance,[6] calibrated to show whether the expected performance drivers did, in fact, do the trick can go a long way to justify taking the manager to the next and final step.

---

[6] One should not take this too far, though. I remember a well-known multi-family family office where manager selection analysts did not seem to conduct much performance analysis, focusing on the first three dimensions instead. That was a mistake, as the careful analysis of past data will tell us what the key drivers of that performance might have been. Having done that work and knowing the results it produced can help drive manager interviews much deeper than generic conversations or the misguided—and arrogant in my view—idea that a young analyst can realistically have an opinion on whether a successful hedge fund manager really is "smart" or not!!!

The notion that different managers will follow different processes because they believe that price variations can be explained and captured differently is at the very basis of manager diversification. Let's face it; we would only have one manager—at least one manager in any given strategy—if it was clear that the same principles apply universally and through time. Would it not be nice if that were the case? Unfortunately, experience demonstrates that, although a few basic principles may still apply through time, markets have a way of rewarding different twists at different times. Thus, one's manager stable should be constructed so as to preserve enough diversity to have a chance to avoid being carried out on a stretcher when an approach is temporarily out of fashion, all the while eschewing so much diversity that one is simply creating an expensive replication of a market index. Tax-efficiency issues, such as the barbell principle discussed in Chapter 2, militate into building manager stable diversity along several dimensions: highly focused universes versus some measure of "freedom-to-roam"; active risk taking versus a more passive "beta capture" strategy; solid expected value added with correspondingly higher management fees versus "beta replication" and lower fees; tax-oblivious alpha capture versus systematic tax loss harvesting portfolio indexing; and many others.

In the end, each family or individual will need first to question the nature of the decisions he or she wants to retain control over and those he or she is willing to delegate. This should be preceded by an in-depth reflection as to where he or she believes value can and should be generated, what active—or management—risk or fee budget should be applied, and the extent to which he or she is able and willing to contribute to the process.

Combining the results of this reflection with the principles enunciated earlier naturally leads the family or the individual on the path to creating a financial governance structure that is appropriate to him or her. Investment policy statements often are the embodiment of this overall governance, although they also extend into topics we will cover in much greater detail in the next two parts of this book. It might help readers to think in terms of that policy being a letter that they write to themselves related to how their assets ought to be managed. Stating ahead of time the key beliefs that underpin their investment philosophy, the way in which various decisions should be made and by whom, the circumstances that might cause them to change their minds, and a few other general principles such as these have a way of lowering the stress that naturally comes with bad surprises or disappointments. Having taken the opportunity to think these through before they occur removes a lot of the emotionality that can crowd out logic and common sense in the heat of the moment.

SUMMARY AND CONCLUSIONS

Although this chapter was all about the need for a financial interpreter, we spent most of our time discussing and illustrating the complexities associated with the management of one's financial assets. While this may appear contradictory at first blush, there is reason behind the madness. The point was to show to both the wealthy and the managers that the issues at hand were complex and at times highly technical. When you think about this, the process is not all that different from instant total immersion in the world of language education: total immersion prevents one from looking for the safety of known territory; it forces one to accept the challenge and move on. Here, the idea is similar. Which client advisor realizing how complex and specialized his or her world is cannot appreciate that clients should not be forced to learn the new language if they do not wish to? Having realized this, the advisor is left with the clear understanding that being a faithful interpreter is a crucial element of the job. Correspondingly, which individual or family realizing how much new material there is to learn will not be ready to work with a professional advisor who truly seeks to understand their needs expressed in plain English (or their native tongue) and translate them into "financialese"? Given the many shortcuts I chose to take to avoid the myriad of details each sub-topic would deserve to have discussed, I am left hoping that the argument for taking the role of interpreter seriously is even more powerful.

More broadly, the first part of this book was meant to illustrate the nature of the wealth management challenge. Again, space constraints and the desire to focus on an element of the problem—goals-based wealth management—made this review cursory; at times, it was even probably frustratingly so. Yet, my goal was to convey three key messages:

1. Managing one's wealth is a highly complex enterprise that should not be reduced to its simplest dimension: investment management.
2. Using tax-awareness as an illustration, it becomes obvious that there is a lot more to wealth management than asset management, and one ignores these additional dimensions and their multiple interactions at one's own peril.
3. The wealthy need advisors who are willing to serve their needs and to work with them to meet these needs, understanding that they need interpreters rather than pundits.

Investment Policy Formulation: Goals-Based Allocation

In this second part of the book, we begin to discuss the crucial issue of investment policy formulation, with a particular focus on the need for a strategic allocation of the assets of the individual or the family. We first consider the theory of strategic asset allocation via a detour in the institutional investment world, in large measure because it is there that the bulk of the theoretical analysis has been conducted. We then map the key features of institutions and individuals to draw out the major relevant differences, and thus articulate the need for some different approach. Finally, we outline how that different approach might work, introducing the fundamental principles behind and the structure of a goals-based allocation process.

CHAPTER 4

A Brief Journey through Institutional Theory

You might reasonably ask why we need to worry about institutional investment management theory in a book focused on the affluent. Yet the logic is deceptively simple. The large bulk of academic literature and of what is learned by many students today relates to the classical tax-exempt money management world. The Chartered Financial Analyst (CFA) Institute has made major strides incorporating private wealth management issues in the CFA curriculum, but you will still today find people—advisors, that is—who will argue that other certifications, although admittedly less arduous to earn, are at least as relevant. Often the logic is based on the fact that other certifications provide a deeper understanding of non-asset management dimensions. I do not want to inject myself into the debate as I find it a bit sterile. But the fact is that the moment you start thinking of individuals, you need to be ready to take an almost iconoclastic stance; you simply cannot take what you have learned in one space—the institutional world—and replicate it in the individual world with the hope that this will be sufficient. It is not a total coincidence that the first peer-reviewed article I submitted and had accepted by *Trusts and Estates* was entitled "The Upside-Down World of Tax-Aware Investing," as I have already mentioned. You must see the upside-down nature of the new world before you could begin to think of a possible solution; that takes an iconoclast!

Again, if this is correct, why focus on something that is irrelevant? The answer must be that the learning process we need to see financial advisors follow will inevitably require them to "unlearn" certain things. Starting the conversation—or the educational process—with postulates that makes people uncomfortable, because they are so radically at variance with what they have learned, is dangerous unless they have been suitably prepared. Without that proper preparation, the risk is serious that they will recoil and thus fail to learn what they should. By contrast, setting them back into a universe with which they are familiar and in which they are comfortable may actually serve as the necessary step that allows them to progress. Our goal in this chapter is, thus, to review the main aspects that generally characterize both the institutional asset management problem and the way it is most often solved. In Chapter 5, we will work to map that structure to the affluent universe, showing those elements that remain unchanged and those that must be revised. Hopefully, being able to understand how we moved from here to there will make it much easier to accept what the "there" is and that we do need to change our perspective.

FIVE IMPORTANT FEATURES OF THE TYPICAL INSTITUTIONAL INVESTMENT ORGANIZATION

In my opinion, the single most important feature of the institutional world is that assets are there for a single purpose. Consider an insurance company. Is there any other reason for them to have an investment portfolio than to be able to provide their customers with the money they need when the event against which they were insured occurs? Consider a pension fund. Is there any reason for a pension fund to hold assets other than to provide pensions to retired members? Consider an endowment fund. Again, is there any reason for there to be money set aside other than to provide the funds the institution needs to defray certain expenses? Finally, consider the most obvious case of all, foundations. Why do foundations hold assets other than to be able to finance their philanthropic purposes? In fact, as we know it in the United States, tax authorities set minimum distributions that a private foundation must make annually to preserve its tax-exempt status.

Note that this single-purpose existence is not always absolutely perfect. I have had foundation managements tell me that the larger their endowment the more readily new donors might feel inclined to support them. It is equally clear that a corporate pension fund could "top up" its assets from the company's income statement if needed, or vice versa (reduce their current contributions if the fund is in substantial surplus). Yet, while I may be drawing the contrast in overly bright lines, the fact is that institutions have assets for the primary purpose of achieving a mission, which is usually defined in terms of a simple, single goal.

The second and third important features are that the liabilities of most institutions are numerous and individually relatively small. While this generalization may be a bit broader and thus still less reliable than the first, you can easily imagine the case of a pension fund. It typically covers thousands of employees—in certain cases hundreds of thousands or more. Why is that important? It is important because it allows the fate of any single employee, or two or ten, to have very little impact on the actual life of the fund. In short, liabilities can be determined using actuarial processes, and what probability theorists call the law of large numbers applies. This provides two crucial sets of inputs that can be used to deal with the formulation of an investment policy, which is the issue we are tackling here.

The first such set of inputs is that it makes the liability stream easier to forecast and that forecast considerably more reliable. Imagine here the contrast between a family of twenty and a pension plan covering 20,000 people. The death of one member of the family can have crucial implications on the management of the family assets in many ways. It can trigger the maturity of one or several trusts. It can lead to a significant change in the family's living expenses. It can trigger an estate event with significant tax implications, leading to the possible material diminution of the size of the family's assets. It certainly can cause a material change in the ratio of the market value of the assets to their tax basis, as the deceased individual's assets might benefit from a step up in tax basis. There are many more, and quite a few of them may actually have non-financial and emotional ramifications, but they are beyond our current scope. Now turn to the pension fund and assume that a bus traveling with 100 retirees runs off the road and into a ditch, killing everyone on board. What will that change? Probably next to nothing of a material nature! Any potential adjustment will be at the margin, and were it not for the affection members of the board might have for any and all retirees, the topic would probably not even make the agenda of the next meeting.

We have already dealt with another difference in prior chapters, but it might be worth mentioning it again in passing, as our fourth feature: most institutional assets benefit from a tax-free or at least tax-deferred status, while most private assets are taxable. Ostensibly, the distinction must be blurred a bit, as this is another case where shades of gray are more accurate than the dramatic contrast between black and white; insurance company funds are typically taxable, for instance. It is instructive here to remind ourselves that a predecessor of tax-awareness for individuals was found in U.S. nuclear decommissioning trusts that were taxable. Yet, it is fair to say that the bulk of the assets entrusted to the institutional management industry are tax-exempt—or at least managed as such.

A final dimension (and fifth feature) is inescapable. Although there are exceptions—which confirm the rule, as the French would say—institutional assets tend to come in larger sizes than those of the affluent. Clearly, one can easily come up with these exceptions, focusing on the pension funds of small organizations or on small family foundations and then drawing a contrast with the assets of a handful of multi-billionaire families. Although these must be recognized and taken into consideration, the comment on relative asset size stands. Note that this should not affect investment policy formulation,

other than in terms of taking certain strategies that require large individual
bite sizes (minimum investments) out of the feasible realm of possible investment for smaller families or investors. Thus, even for families that are large
enough to invest in so-called alternative strategies—such as arbitrage, relative value, long/short equities and the like—it may well be that many of them
will need to consider funds of funds rather than individual managers; this
would be because of the need to diversify individual manager risk despite
the fact that funds of funds impose an additional layer of fees.

Figure 4.1 illustrates these five major features, which we will recall in
Chapter 5 when we look at how individual investors fit relative to these same
features.

	Institutional Investor
Major Purpose	Single
Liabilities—Number	Large
Liabilities—Individual Size	Small
Tax Status	Mostly Tax-Exempt
Asset Size	Mostly Very Large

FIGURE 4.1   The Five Features of
Institutional Investors

Although these five features are important, fairness requires me to mention one element that can inject non-institutional emotions or realities in
the process. While one must always remember the concept behind Robert
Swanson's agency risk concept, most of the overseers of institutional assets
are professional managers and typically do not have any direct ownership
relationship. The concept of agency risk is worth revisiting for a second, as
it suggests that people whose careers are dependent on the performance of
a pension fund, for instance, may well tend to inject some of their own risk
preferences into the definition of the investment risk that the pension fund
can take. However influential such a consideration might be, it is still not
unreasonable to think that the overall risk/return trade-off point selected for
the pension fund will likely be driven more by the needs of the funds than
by the personal job insecurity felt by its manager.

How do these five features affect the way in which investment policy
formulation has evolved in the institutional space? Very prosaically, the large
size of the pools of money created a very profitable business niche that was

able in its early history to sponsor significant academic research. The fact that these funds were managed by people who were professional financiers rather than "normal" individuals made the sponsors ready to look for the "theoretical" solution to their management problem. Remember that, in a business, the role of senior management often is to design business processes that are proven sound, auditable, and repeatable and that are implemented appropriately by lower management layers. Thus, whether it does or does not really make sense in practice, intuition only plays a modest role, and a solution is more likely to be adopted because it appears sensible and is justified by solid research or consultant reports than because it is truly the one that will yield the best results.

Thus, with the advent of Modern Portfolio Theory, it stands to reason that the institutional environment was ripe for experimenting with the new ideas, particularly if one could argue that one would produce similar results with less risk. What senior or middle manager would not succumb to that siren's song? Actually, it turns out that Modern Portfolio Theory added a material amount of value to the process, although many old-timers will easily argue and point to circumstances under which certain assumptions did not work out. Returns are normally or log-normally distributed, people will say; old-timers will reply that this is totally true except when it is not! Correlations help us combine assets in ways that allow us to generate similar returns with lower risk; yes, except when correlations all rise in periods of crisis! However, it would be grossly unfair to both Modern Portfolio Theory and the industry not to recognize that the general thrust of Modern Portfolio Theory has worked to produce better results, even if one saw the occasional excesses. Did it make sense to diversify a pension fund portfolio by appointing more than 100 managers? Probably not! Should one have been more reasonable in understanding the time horizon differences between policy goals and performance assessment periods? Probably! But on the whole, these shortcomings are small in relation to the benefits that accompanied them.

The classical proposition of Modern Portfolio Theory is that there exists a series of points that describe the risk/return characteristics of portfolios that are such that you cannot earn a higher expected return without taking more risk, or incur a lower amount of risk without accepting a penalty in the form of lower expected returns. Risk, here, is defined in terms of the volatility of the expected return stream. This set of portfolios is said to form "the efficient frontier," an example of which is depicted in Figure 4.2. Note that the frontier can be unconstrained, that is, you allow any combination of the assets or strategies you are prepared to consider, or constrained, in which case, minima or maxima are set that restrict any and all asset classes or strategies.

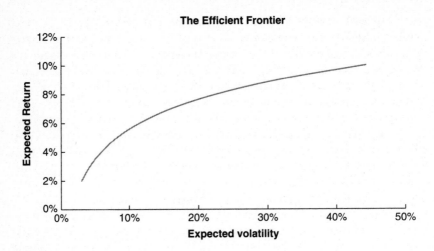

FIGURE 4.2   The Efficient Frontier

The next step is for the fund to find the one portfolio that is "best" or "ideal" for it. The process is illustrated in Figure 4.3. The fact that institutions typically have single purposes and a liability stream that can be estimated with a high degree of confidence first led to the proposition that one could describe each institution's ideal risk return trade-off; that trade-off would reflect the institution's preferences as to how much risk

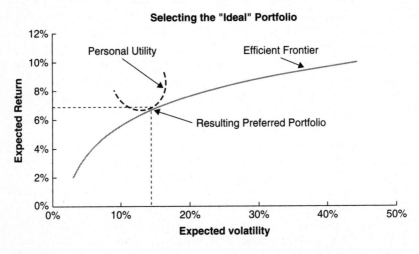

FIGURE 4.3   The Efficient Frontier and the Utility-Determined Preferred Portfolio

was acceptable for any given return, or vice versa. Macro-economists and game theorists call this preference a "utility" and define it as the amount of risk one is prepared to accept to earn a certain return or the return one is prepared to require in order to accept a certain level of risk. Figure 4.3 starts with the same efficient frontier as shown in Figure 4.2 and adds the personal utility.[1] The point at which the utility touches the frontier without crossing it is called by mathematicians the *tangency point* and the portfolio mix represented by that point is said to be the "best" or "ideal" or "optimal" portfolio for that institution.

A QUICK DETOUR VIA ASSET LIABILITY MANAGEMENT

Another way of conceptualizing the process is to perform what traditional finance calls an *asset liability analysis*. We have already seen that you can view and estimate the future cash outflows likely to be required from the fund. We postulate that these are the liabilities of the fund and then argue that the fund's assets should have a structure such that they are as well matched as possible. Saying that they are matched effectively is arguing that changes in the external capital market environment should ideally affect both sides of the balance sheet equally. One of the most readily "controllable" elements would be the level of interest rates. Indeed, it stands to reason that the fund's future cash flow must be discounted to some present value. That discount rate must be based on current or prospective prevailing interest rate levels; these also, coincidentally, affect both the value of all fixed income assets in the portfolio and, by extension, of its equities as well—the asset side of the fund's balance sheet. Indeed, although we regularly talk of the price to earnings (P/E) ratio of equities as a measure of their valuations, we often fail to recognize that this ratio is the inverse of any equity's earnings yield, which we would naturally represent as E/P. There should logically be a relationship between the earnings yield of the equity market and the yield of the bond universe.[2]

---

[1] Recall that this "personal utility" is defined as the preferred risk/return trade-off of the investor.

[2] This concept arguably led to bond immunization, which will find an echo in the declining balance portfolios we discuss in Chapter 6 for the individual world. For more detail on bond immunization, see Granito, Michael R. *Bond Portfolio Immunization*. Lexington Books/D.C. Heath and Company, 1984.

SUMMARY AND CONCLUSIONS

In short, the nature of institutional assets lends itself to a systematic—or quantitative—analysis. This process naturally leads to the determination of some "ideal" long-term portfolio, which is called the *policy portfolio*. It should be viewed as the fund's flight plan, which would only change if general conditions change; these might include changes in the prospective cash flow patterns, for instance because of a change in the average age of the prospective retirees served by a given pension fund or different expectations with respect to the occurrence of the events covered by an insurance company or changes in long-term capital market risk and return expectations. They could also reflect a change in utility or the fund's risk/return preferences or be due to the emergence of new strategies or vehicles that should henceforth be included in the investment universe and were not until then. Note that the policy would *not* be expected to change in response to shorter-term market conditions, unless one could make the case that the change one is seeing is structural rather than cyclical.

In the next chapter, we will draw a series of contrasts between the assumptions we can make with respect to an institution and those we cannot make when we look at individuals or families. We already alluded to the fact that there are many fewer data points when we look at a family, as compared to the vast universe that characterizes pension plans or insurance companies, for instance. But there are many other such differences that naturally force individuals to adopt a different approach. However, our point will be that the framework remains exactly the same and that we are adapting theory to the need for different assumptions, not reinventing the wheel.

Mapping Institutional and Individual Issues

The first contrast we should draw is in the way in which the factors we identified as important for institutional investors affect individuals. Figure 5.1 recalls Figure 4.1 and adds a column to the right, in order to describe individual investors. Ostensibly, there is bound to be quite a bit of oversimplification in any such analysis. Yet, although I do not view it as conclusive, Figure 5.2 tells me that I need to dig further into the factors differentiating the needs of individual investors: just assuming that they are like institutional investors does not cut it. Later on, we shall look not at these factors per se, but at how they affect the way institutional and individual investors should approach setting their goals. Figure 5.3, at the end of this chapter, will summarize that work. It will show a strong parallel to Figure 5.1, but will be more practical, as it focuses on goals rather than the broader question of the nature of the two universes.

So individuals are different. There is not much that is truly surprising here for anyone who has worked to serve individuals for an extended period of time. However, this statement can initially be destabilizing to many an institutional investor. Institutional investors have been quite comfortable with their theories and processes for many years; managers who focus on private assets were not, at the outset, necessarily the most progressive or innovative of the industry. Rather than digging a bit more into whether there were real differences, the institutional investment management industry preferred to stay with the simple conclusion that it knew what it was doing and that private wealth managers did not. That convenient—but ultimately proven dramatically incorrect—stance led a number of money management firms that served both sets of clients to think of the "private bank" as a distribution channel! The role of private advisors was simply to convince

	Institutional Investor	Individual Investor
Major Purpose	Single	Multiple
Liabilities—Number	Large	Small
Liabilities—Individual Size	Small	Variable
Tax Status	Mostly Tax-Exempt	Mostly Taxable
Asset Size	Mostly Very Large	Variable

FIGURE 5.1 The Five Features of Institutional Investors and Individuals

individuals that they ought to invest in the same products and strategies as their institutional brethren. Changes to product specifications could only be considered if they were mere tinkering rather than fundamental rethinking!

The first crack in the proverbial clay feet of the statue appeared when tax-efficiency—or tax-awareness as we called it then at J.P. Morgan—emerged. There, we had an undeniable difference, and it quickly became obvious that it required a different investment process. We discussed this in more detail in Chapter 2, but the notion that "tax day is every day" or that an unrealized loss is a free option to take an unrealized gain tax-free made it plain that something different had to be done. It took at least another six to eight years for people to identify the second major crack.

This came about with the gradual recognition that individuals did not necessarily react the same way as institutions did to general market circumstances, and that the differences were not due to stupidity or a lack of sophistication. Advances in the behavioral finance field started to make a crucial point: our brains are not wired to be absolutely rational; we experience emotions and we cannot ignore what that does to the way we make decisions. It certainly helped, in my view, that we could almost immediately demonstrate that certain of the actions of our industry's paradigm of genius—institutional investors—actually were not immune to these emotions. How else could we explain that a high share of cash in the portfolios of equity mutual funds was a good indication that equity markets were about to tear up, and vice versa? The Nobel Economics Prize won by Daniel Kahneman[1] for his work on prospect theory in 2002 arguably must have

---

[1]Most of which he conducted with Amos Tversky, who unfortunately died in 1996 and was thus not eligible to be a Nobel Prize Laureate.

played a role in giving respectability to those who had been studying individual behavior and developing the field of behavioral finance.

Behavioral finance simply argues that traditional finance is prescriptive, while it is best to be descriptive. Traditional finance tells us how we should react. Behavioral finance shows to us how we behave. Demonstrating, as it did, that we all have a variety of preferences and biases, it tells us to be careful when setting forward-looking rules. The classical example involves pointing out the apparent stupidity of simultaneously owning insurance policies and lottery tickets.[2] Insurance policies suggest that we are trying to protect the value of our assets, another way of saying that we are averse to losses. Lottery tickets, with their incredibly low probability of paying out, suggest that we are prepared to lose it all in the almost self-deluding hope that we can win a big jackpot. Traditional finance argues that both attitudes cannot be in the same person, who should have a single "utility" describing his or her risk/return preferences. Behavioral finance takes a completely different tack. In essence, it says: "Suppose that I do not have one, but two goals! Suppose that each goal is associated with a different risk profile. Then would it not make sense that I should have two utilities?" Translating this into plain English, it postulates that one of my goals would go very well with a bumper sticker that would say: "I'd rather not lose what I've got!" It also postulates that I have another goal, the bumper sticker for which would say: "I'm sure I could find a way to use a sudden windfall!"

THE FIRST CRUCIAL DIFFERENCE

Meir Statman and Hersh Shefrin[3] developed the concept of the behavioral portfolio, which reflected Abraham Maslow's hierarchy of needs,[4] published in 1943. Statman and Shefrin's behavioral portfolio is based on two deceptively simple assumptions. The first is that individuals have multiple goals, echoing Maslow's concept that individual needs range from physiological, safety, love/belonging, esteem, and self-actualization. The second, which I personally find the most insightful and powerful, is that individuals have different risk profiles for each goal, as we just saw in the apparent contradiction of having insurance and a lottery ticket. Armed with these assumptions, it

---

[2]Friedman, M., and Savage, L.J. (1948). "The Utility Analysis of Choices Involving Risk." *Journal of Political Economy*, 56, 279–304.

[3]Shefrin, Hersh, and Meir Statman. "Behavioral Portfolio Theory." *The Journal of Financial and Quantitative Analysis*, 35(2), June 2000, pp. 127–151.

[4]Maslow, A.H. (1943). "A Theory of Human Motivation." *Psychological Review*, 50(4), 370–396.

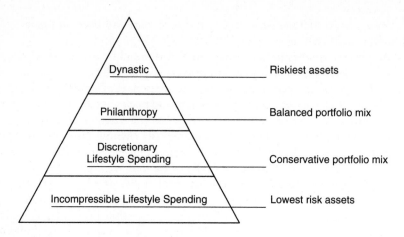

FIGURE 5.2 Behavioral Portfolio

is almost inevitable that one should have not one, but as many portfolios as one has goals and risk profiles.

Figure 5.2 shows my own representation of their behavioral portfolio; it makes the case that one could, in the example shown, have four sub-portfolios, rather than one overall one. My four portfolios in this case would thus be:

1. A very low risk sub-portfolio to ensure that my incompressible lifestyle expenditures[5] are met for the material forward looking period;
2. A modestly higher risk portfolio to allow me to continue to spend money on things or services that are not absolutely essential, but I would still like to keep acquiring;
3. A higher risk portfolio designed to fund my philanthropic activities; I am prepared to take some more risk there as I would love to give more, but I am not willing to take that extra giving out of my lifestyle spending and

---

[5]There are two important aspects of what I call here incompressible lifestyle expenses. The first is that experience suggests that the worst nightmare of most wealthy families is to have to cut their lifestyle. We will come back to this later. Thus, any risk—perceived or real—that some need is imminent that expenses may have to be cut will take on horrendous proportions for many families and thus expose them to the most extreme emotional reactions. The second is that some of these expenses are literally out of the family's control, at least as far as factors such as inflation or taxation go, to mention the two most important. This sense that the family is thus not fully in control exacerbates the potential risk of an uninspired emotional reaction at the worst possible time.

I recognize that if the extra risk I am taking actually hurts that spending, I will accept it; and

4. My riskiest sub-portfolio is there to allow me to build capital I would love to leave to my children or grandchildren, recognizing that what I can give today is not big enough, but also recognizing that it cannot be larger without hoping that markets will make it grow for me.

This is very similar to the hierarchy of needs described by Abraham Maslow.

A SECOND IMPORTANT DIFFERENCE

Although we have so far accepted that we have multiple goals and multiple risk profiles, we have not explicitly noted that my goals do not all live over the same time horizon. But they do, and this should have an impact of how I see them.

My incompressible lifestyle spending is something that I need covered immediately and for some time. I expect to begin to draw from the portfolio tomorrow! One way to think of how long the time horizon would be here is to consider two important variables. One is inflation and the other is the cyclicality of capital markets. Ostensibly, in the short term, I need to be able to minimize risk, in order for my steady withdrawals not to create the risk that the portfolio is depleted too early. When the value of a portfolio fluctuates somewhat materially, the regular withdrawal of a fixed amount can indeed deplete the portfolio faster than expected. Mathematicians would explain this by noting that there is an asymmetry in the return compounding process. In plain English, this simply means that I need my portfolio to go up 25 percent to get back to the value it had before it fell 20 percent. Consider this: my $100 drops to $80 when they experience a 20 percent decline. Yet, the $20 I now need to earn to get back to $100 represent 25 percent of $80! Thus, a portfolio from which I will need to draw a regular amount should have an expected return stream that has as low volatility as possible. With any asset or strategy that can protect somewhat against inflation being at the riskier end of the volatility spectrum, I tend to define the short term as whatever period during which I can safely assume that inflation will not spike up. Note that this does not mean that there is no inflation; current inflation expectations are reflected in current market prices, as we saw in Chapter 3. What we cannot hedge, without significant short-term fluctuation risks, is unexpected inflation.

The other dimension is to consider capital market cyclicality. Although Japan is the most notable exception to this rule, it is extremely rare for any developed equity market to have produced negative compounded returns over any period longer than twenty years. I can generally assume that I should cover my lifestyle expenditures for the next twenty to twenty-five years and assume that capital markets will allow me to replenish my reserves as and when needed, with or without a safety cushion.

In short, my lifestyle sub-portfolio will probably be divided into a couple of further sub-pieces. One will take care of the next five years or so, if I can assume that inflation is unlikely to spike in the next five years; the other will cover me for the ten to twenty years after that, depending upon my willingness to deal with the vagaries of capital market cyclicality.

The non-lifestyle part of my portfolio here represents two totally different needs, with two different time horizons. The example as presented does not specify whether my "philanthropy" sub-portfolio is supposed to start paying out right away or at some future point in time. By contrast, it is probably safe to assume that my "dynastic" portfolio is expected to take time to build. Thus, depending on whether the "philanthropic" portfolio starts to pay out early or not, it may or may not have to be divided further into short-term and longer-term components, following the thought process we used for lifestyle. The "dynastic" portfolio, however, can safely be assumed to have a single, long-term time horizon.

A DIFFERENT WAY OF DEFINING RISK

So far, as institutions do, we have accepted the traditional proposition that risk is best measured as the volatility of expected returns. However, is that really the way individuals think? I do not think so. Most of the people I meet would love to experience upside return volatility—Who hates a raging bull market? Most of them, at the same time, hate downward volatility. In fact, behavioral finance predicts this, arguing that a given gain is less pleasurable to individuals than the pain associated with a loss of similar magnitude![6]

Four authors produced a seminal paper in 2010 that helped deal with this quandary. Sanjiv Ranjan Das, Harry Markowitz, Jonathan Scheid, and Meir Statman bridged the theoretical gap between traditional and behavioral finance by suggesting that they could be viewed as equivalent if one were prepared to change the definition of risk[7]: rather than the volatility of

---

[6]Theory would say that the disutility generated by a loss is greater than the utility produced by a commensurate gain. This is mentioned in Zamir, Eyal. Chapter 8, *Law, Psychology and Morality: The Role of Loss Aversion*. OUP, 2014, publication forthcoming.

[7]I must apologize to these authors for grossly oversimplifying their work. Yet, I hope that in so doing I make their insights more broadly available without destroying their insights.

returns, one should define risk as the probability of not achieving a goal. Note how intuitively appealing this suggestion actually is. While volatility is indeed inconclusive—as I like some version of it and not others—not achieving a goal is exactly the way I would view risk! This leads to another major change in the way we can argue that an individual should define his or her goals. Each goal should be associated with a minimum required probability of being achieved over the time horizon that applies to it!

THE LAW OF LARGE NUMBERS

It is worth going back to the point that we made earlier, as it will close the list of the major differences that force us to look at setting a strategic asset allocation in a different way for individuals.

Many of the computations that are made in the spaces of probability or statistics rely on what specialists call the *law of large numbers*. In simple terms, the law of large numbers says that the average result from a large number of experiments should come close to the expected result, even if individual results from each of these experiments can appear to occur in a random manner. The easiest example one can use to illustrate this law is a coin flip. We all know that the result of a single coin flip is totally unpredictable; we cannot say whether we will get heads or tails. Yet, we know that we should get each about 50 percent of the time if we repeat the coin flip a sufficiently large number of times. Whether the original probability is 50/50, as in the case of the coin flip, or somewhat imbalanced, as might be the case with a roulette wheel, the generic expectations are the same. We have no real idea as to where the ball will settle the next time the wheel is set in motion, but we know that, over time, we should get heads or tail 50 percent of the time or get a specific number 1/37th of the time on a European wheel, which has only one zero. This law allows institutional investors to disregard the fluctuations that might be due to one or several unusual occurrences, based on the view that any given time period will involve such a large number of occurrences that the few unusual ones will be lost in the greater mass.

Individuals, as we have already seen, cannot hide behind this law. They live in a world of relatively small numbers. Thus, although they can state that the expected return of this or that part of the portfolio or even of the whole portfolio should be X percent over time, they really do not know what that return could or should be in any given time period. This gives rise to yet another difference between institutions and individuals. While institutions can be—and often are—concerned with average returns, individuals should look for the minimum return they can expect when evaluating their goals. Thus, if I want to have a 95 percent chance of being able to meet a certain lifestyle spending level in the next five years and want to determine how much money should be set aside for that goal, I cannot discount the projected cash flow using an average expected return for the part of the portfolio that is set aside for that goal. The 95 percent probability of success I require means that I must discount my cash flow with a return that my portfolio will meet or exceed 95 percent of the time. Note that this does mean that I could well often find myself with money left over at the end of five years. But, just as I do not mind upside volatility and hate downside risk, I should not mind having money left over. My goal was to be able to meet my goal in at least 95 percent of all instances!!! Figure 9.1 (Chapter 9) and the discussion surrounding it expand on this point.

IMPLICATIONS

It is first worth noting that the concept of an investment policy, which we aim to develop here, is considerably less natural to individuals than it might be for institutions. So it is important to find a way to frame the idea for individuals, in plain language, so that they may find it acceptable because more understandable. Once we have done this, it will be the time to summarize the key differences between individuals and institutions and to see how these differences force us to react differently with individuals.

In its simplest form, one I used in my first book, one can liken the investment policy of any investor to the flight plan of an airplane. Assume for a minute that two people board an airplane at the same time. One turns right and takes a seat in the passenger cabin. The other turns left and heads for the cockpit. Is there any real doubt that they both have the same ultimate goal? I would argue they have exactly the same goal: they want to reach their destination safely, on time, and with the least possible amount of disruption. Yet, how different their lives will be over the ensuing few hours. The passenger will eat, drink, watch a movie, sleep, surf the Internet, work on his or her computer, and only occasionally, if the service is available, glance at the moving map that shows where the airplane is relative to the origin and the destination of the flight. The other will fasten his or her seatbelt knowing that the skies are crisscrossed by a myriad of virtual highways that planes follow. He or she will know that the plane is supposed to fly at a certain speed and a certain altitude over a number of beacons, which you can think of as the towns that used to pop up at irregular intervals along our land-based roads. The pilot will be able to tell whether the plane is on schedule or not by simply looking at whether it passes the various beacons at the time projected in the flight plan.

Compare this to the investment policy. Nobody knows what markets, be they equities, bonds, currencies or commodities, will do tomorrow, next week, next month, next quarter, or even next year. We can surely guess,

	Institutions	Individuals
Goals	Single	Multiple
Time Horizon	Single	Multiple
Risk Measure	Return Volatility	Probability of Missing Goal
Return Determination	Average Expectations	Minimum Expectations
Risk Determination	Top-Down	Bottom-Up

FIGURE 5.3 Institutional and Individual Ways of Defining Their Goals

but our guesses are singularly imprecise. Yet, we can begin to have a bit more confidence in both the relationship among the various asset classes or strategies and their prospects over the intermediate to long term. Thus, by comparing how the portfolio is doing relative to its long-term target over the shorter time frame when our return predictions are notoriously fickle and inaccurate, we can deduce whether we are about in line, behind, or somewhat ahead of schedule.

These four simple changes that we have to make in the way we think lead us to a very material change in the way we must deal with our investment policy formulation, relative to what an institutional investor might do. Figure 5.3 illustrates this and can be summarized simply: while success for institutions is defined as meeting liabilities, it is defined for individuals as achieving their goals. I appreciate that a purist would argue that the two are not all that dissimilar; but while true from a pure linguistic standpoint, most families would agree that the two definitions are dramatically different. As a start, when was the last time one heard a wealthy individual describing the need to meet lifestyle expenditures as a liability?

SUMMARY AND CONCLUSIONS

It is probably worth summarizing our findings at this time before moving to the next chapter, which will describe the goals-based strategic asset allocation process in more detail:

1. We should not be surprised by the first two rows in the figure. We discussed the notion that institutional pools of assets typically have a single purpose, and thus a single time horizon. The behavioral portfolio

construct clearly tells us that individuals have multiple goals and that there is no logical reason that should compel all these goals to have the same time horizon.

2. We also covered in detail the idea that individuals are not interested in the volatility of returns, but in whether a goal is likely or unlikely to be met.

3. The law of large number also clearly suggests to us that individuals should form return expectations that fit both the time horizon selected for each goal and the minimum required probability they seek of achieving their goal.

4. The last line in the figure requires a bit more explaining. The idea is simple, but so many people miss it. There is a chance that I can describe a risk tolerance if I have a single goal. In fact, even if I find myself having trouble doing it, my advisor should be able to help me there. However, how could I arrive at an average risk tolerance if I have several goals, with different time horizons and different required probabilities of success? At best, I can compute a derived risk tolerance from the bottom up, by aggregating the various risk profiles associated with each goal and weighting them with the percent of my wealth that needs to be allocated to each of them. Note, however, that such a derived number does not necessarily mean very much. An old statistical professor of mine said it best: "If you put your head in the oven and your feet in the freezer, on average you might be comfortable, but I doubt you will feel that way!"

CHAPTER 6

Goals-Based Strategic Asset Allocation

This is where the rubber meets the road. The concept is simply to change the way the typical strategic asset allocation process is conducted by recognizing that the goal of formulating a simple return/risk trade-off for the typical individual or family is elusive and misguided at best. Again, it is worth remembering here that there are always at least two ways to proceed toward a goal. The top-down approach starts at the top and is the province of what I would generously call the easier process. It involves identifying the key assumptions and following them to the logical conclusion: given some return/risk preference and a few other assumptions in terms of specifics such as liquidity, taxation, and regulatory constraints, one can proceed to a long-term asset mix that makes sense and should, through time, achieve the investor's goal. The bottom-up approach observes that tackling the overall picture is too complex and unlikely to work; thus, one starts at the bottom, identifies the various goals, works to find a way to defease each of them, and then combines the various individual asset mixes into some overall policy formulation. Goals-based strategic allocation is unabashedly a bottom-up exercise.

THE BASIC PRINCIPLE

The fundamental idea, as we have seen in Chapter 5, is that individuals have multiple goals, multiple risk tolerances, and multiple time horizons. Attempting to aggregate all of these into a single, one-dimensional process takes us back to the quip that having our head in the oven and our feet in the fridge makes us comfortable, on average! While that may be true from a theoretical standpoint, it does not pass the simple common sense test. At some point, trying to combine things, either to simplify the process or to make it conform to a theoretical basis that is prevalent in some variant of the universe but not adequate to the circumstances, is plain silly. In fact, one could argue that it is arrogant and not correct from a fiduciary standpoint: the role of the advisor is to help the client meet his or her goal. Forcing a square peg into a round hole is either an indication that one does not understand the issue or a sign that business process simplicity—and thus prospects for higher profits—dominates. Both options are unacceptable; individuals and families deserve better.

The principle revolves around creating individual and tailored solutions for each of the client's goals. Part 3 and Chapters 7 through 10 will deal with this process in considerably more depth, but the basics are deceptively simple. You increase the probability of serving the needs of the client the moment you agree that you will look for each of his or her goals, understand the specifics that relate to each of these goals in terms of time horizon as well as implicit risk tolerance, and build portfolios that are specifically designed to them.

The goals-based strategic asset allocation process comprises seven principal steps at the level of a firm:[1]

1. Determination of generic asset or strategy preferences and constraints;
2. Creation of strategic goal modules to meet a series of representative goals;
3. Determination of the number and identity of each of the multiple goals, the cash flows associated with them, and the minimum required probabilities of success;
4. Specification of the module most likely to meet each goal or creation of new, custom modules if one or several goals cannot be met with a standard module;
5. Quantification of the assets required to meet each goal;
6. Aggregation of all modules into a combined portfolio; and
7. Specification of maximum deviation ranges for each of the asset or strategy allocations.

Each of these elements can and should be seen as parameters or process steps that the firm—and each of its advisors—fully understands and is perfectly capable of explaining. Part 4 of this book will delve in more depth into the way in which the current typical firm structure is ill-suited to perform these functions economically, but at this point let us simply postulate that

---

[1]Note that the client is really only concerned with four of these steps, with Steps 1, 2 and 7 being more the province of the advisor and his or her firm.

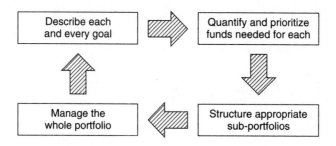

FIGURE 6.1 The Goals-Based Allocation Process

certain of these steps are internal to the firm—for instance, the first two and the seventh—while others are directly related to each client and specific to him or her. From the eyes of the client, you can therefore conceptualize the process as comprising four crucial steps, illustrated in Figure 6.1.

The first involves listing the goals individually, being careful to specify the time horizon over which they are expected to be met and the minimum probability of success that the client requires. See, as suggested earlier, how this is a better definition of "risk" than the traditional volatility of returns—actual or expected: it speaks directly to the question of how crucial the goal actually is and thus tells us how much risk can be taken trying to achieve it. Taking this further, one could easily imagine a "goal matrix" that reflects all the years in the possible time horizon on the vertical axis and various categories of goals on the horizontal axis. One could imagine these horizontal categories to reflect who the beneficiaries of the goal might be (recalling Figure 5.2, we could use incompressible lifestyle spending, discretionary lifestyle spending, philanthropy, and dynastic), but one could also consider categorizing the goals with respect to their degree of urgency (needs, wants, wishes, and dreams, for instance, as we will discuss in more detail in Chapter 7).

Second, one should list which asset classes or strategies are consistent with this implied risk profile. For instance, a goal that requires liquidity cannot be met with strategies that are partially or totally illiquid. Knowing which asset classes or strategies are eligible and which are not and understanding the time frame over which the goal must be met and the required probability of success tells us what discount rate should be applied to the cash flow requirements associated with the goal.

Third, one must size the assets needed to meet each goal. In certain instances, it will mean applying the appropriate discount rates to a set of cash flows; in others, it will mean selecting a lump sum that the client decides to allocate to goals for which there are no specific future cash flow forecasts.

Finally, one must create "optimal" sub-portfolios for each goal and combine them into an aggregate overall policy that can reasonably be claimed to be both goals-based and intimately client-specific.

INITIAL THEORETICAL OBJECTIONS

Initially, this approach—goals-based wealth management—was proposed[2] by a small group of practitioners, each of whom offered his own version of a solution to what had hitherto appeared a daunting challenge. All contained some measure of sub-portfolio level allocation, as opposed to the creation of an overall top-down policy asset mix. Others subsequently followed, arguably the most prominent and prolific of whom is Michael Pompian,[3] (who was a part of the initial list) who has since authored several books on the topic.

Yet, all were viewed to suffer from a significant degree of inefficiency. The main issue revolved around the argument that it is sub-optimal to break a portfolio down into several sub-portfolios. Doing so meant that one was giving up any diversification that could possibly occur between and across these various sub-portfolios. That criticism is certainly valid in theory. I initially attempted to answer the criticism by pointing out two potentially mitigating circumstances.[4] I first looked into the conceptual reasons why individuals require a different process and proposed a possible traditional finance interpretation of the approach they actually follow. I then attempted to quantify the level of possible sub-optimality, accepting that our optimization only addressed the risk/return trade-off at the level of each sub-portfolio. I concluded that the minor difference that arises between the goal-based portfolio and a theoretical traditional finance solution is such that a strong case cannot be made that goal-based allocation

---

[2]Brunel, Jean L.P. "Revisiting the Asset Allocation Challenge Through a Behavioral Finance Lens." *The Journal of Wealth Management*, Fall 2003, pp. 10–20. Nevins, Dan. "Goal-Based Investing: Integrating Traditional and Behavioral Finance." *The Journal of Wealth Management*, Spring 2004, pp. 8–23. Pompian, Michael M., and John B. Longo. "A New Paradigm for Practical Application of Behavioral Finance." *The Journal of Wealth Management*, Fall 2004, pp. 9–15. Chhabra, Ashvin B. "Beyond Markowitz: A Comprehensive Wealth Allocation Framework for Individuals." *The Journal of Wealth Management*, Spring 2005, pp. 8–34. Brunel, Jean L.P. "A Behavioral Finance Approach to Strategic Asset Allocation—A Case Study." *The Journal of Investment Consulting*, 7(3), Winter 2005–2006, pp. 61–69.

[3]Pompian, Michael M. *Behavioral Finance and Wealth Management: How to Build Optimal Portfolios That Account for Investor Biases*. Wiley Finance, 2011.

[4]Brunel, Jean L.P. "How Sub-Optimal—If at All—Is Goal-Based Allocation?" *The Journal of Wealth Management*, Fall 2006, pp. 19–34.

is sub-optimal. I should, however, observe that this article did not really change the opinions of those who saw sub-optimality.

With the benefit of hindsight, my analysis and demonstration did not focus on the appropriate topic. I was trying to argue that a small, but still visible, decrease in return per unit of risk was a small price to pay to promote greater policy sustainability; that was true, but it did not really play in the same register as the theoretical argument that there was a measure of sub-optimality. Similarly, I was trying to demonstrate that the margin of difference was well within the input forecasting error; in other words, there might be some theoretical sub-optimality, but it was something that we should not care about. Again, that might have been correct in practice, but it did not deal with the issue head on.

AN ACADEMIC IMPRIMATUR

The situation changed dramatically when an article was published by four very well-known authors. Das, Markowitz, Scheid, and Statman[5] took a totally different and much smarter tack. Using considerably more sophisticated mathematics, the authors integrated the key features of Markowitz's mean variance portfolio theory and a new framework, Shefrin and Statman's behavioral portfolio theory, which they dubbed "mental accounts" (this is the equivalent of what we call "goals-based allocation"). As stated in the abstract of the paper, they "demonstrate a mathematical equivalence between mean variance theory, mental accounts and risk management using value at risk. The aggregate allocation across mental accounts is mean-variance efficient with short selling. Short selling constraints impose very minor reductions in certainty equivalents, only if binding for the aggregate portfolio, offsetting utility losses from errors in specifying risk-aversion coefficient in mean-variance theory applications."

The last sentence of the abstract, which summarizes the key contribution of this article, is very telling: "These generalizations of mean-variance theory and behavioral portfolio theory via a unified mental account framework result in a fruitful connection between investor consumption goals and portfolio production." In short, it helps make the point that had eluded me in

---

[5]Das, Sanjiv, Harry Markowitz, Jonathan Scheid, and Meir Statman. "Portfolio Optimization with Mental Accounts." *The Journal of Financial and Quantitative Analysis*, 45(02), April 2010, pp. 311–334. Das, Sanjiv, Harry Markowitz, Jonathan Scheid, and Meir Statman. "Portfolios for Investors Who Want to Reach Their Goals While Staying in the Mean-Variance Efficient Frontier." *The Journal of Wealth Management*, Fall 2011, pp. 25–31.

the earlier article: creating comfortable and thus sustainable allocations that meet the specifics of individual circumstances is theoretically possible, even if it requires one to make a number of minor changes and substitutions to traditional finance. To me, the critical element is the notion that the definition of risk that matters to the individual, as noted in Chapter 5, is the probability that he or she may not meet the goals set for any sub-portfolio, rather than the more frequently used statistical constructs such as the standard deviation of returns, some form of semi-variance, or even Value at Risk.[6]

A FEW SIMPLE PRINCIPLES[7]

As we shall see in much greater detail in Part 3, the goals-based approach to strategic asset allocation—which I view as nothing but a subset of the broader issue of goals-based wealth management—requires adhering to a limited number of simple principles. In practice, four principles apply.

The first is that *the process must be centered on the client*. This requires a very careful effort, up front, to make sure that the advisor understands all of the client's goals and risks in as much detail as possible. For instance, although a client might initially state a single dollar amount as his or her annual spending requirements, there may be a need to look at the various elements of that spending and recognize that (a) they do not all persist for the same length of time (different time horizons) or (b) they do not all have the same priority or necessity (different required probabilities of success).

Second, *most goal-defeasing portfolios will tend to be of a "declining balance" variety*. Conceptually, they are analogous to immunized bond portfolios in the institutional world, in that the quarterly, or annual, expense needs are met by using income that has accrued during the period as well as the maturity—or liquidation—of certain positions. An "endowment" portfolio may be considered only in circumstances when expenses only require a minor portion of an individual's or family's capital and, most importantly, if issues of inter-generational transfers at the end of the life

---

[6]Note that the two categories of measures are indeed related. Yet, one stops at a statistical definition, while the other takes it to its direct consequence.

[7]Different authors have dealt with the issue in different ways, but they typically apply generally similar principles. Ashvin Chhabra, for instance, formulates three generic categories of goals he calls Personal, Market, and Aspirational. Although these are certainly different from the categories we use, we can see the same principles at work: individuals are concerned with the journey as much as with the destination and this is a client-specific variable, and various asset and strategies are differently suited to help meet different goals.

of current beneficiaries are not relevant.[8] Indeed, in this case, expenses are met solely from the income accruing into the portfolio. The most binding constraint here usually is not the percentage of the portfolio consumed each year, but the eventual transfer of the assets. It goes without saying that expenses must be paid out of income on assets that belong to those who are incurring the expenses. Thus, creating an endowment—rather than a declining balance—portfolio requires that the assets remain the property of the beneficiary. This creates an eventual need for these assets to be transferred when the estate matures.[9] Declining balance portfolios nicely side-step the issue, as they allow the current beneficiary generation to retain ownership of assets whose total value declines through time, all the while planning for and executing orderly and efficient transfers of the assets surplus to their requirements.

Third, *the process must include understanding up front how various asset classes and strategies interact with client goals.* Certain strategies are perfectly suited to meeting certain goals and totally unacceptable for others. Earlier, we showed how liquidity considerations can be one such dimension that transforms the eligibility of a strategy. Yet, there are others. Recently, a client asked why I would not use equities—or would place significant constraints on the size of any such exposure—in certain sub-portfolios designed for income replacement. His point was valid, as it was based on the truthful observation that equities currently often have a higher yield than many bonds. Yet, the issue was of a different nature: the declining balance expense defeasing portfolio needed to sell some set portion of its assets each year.[10]

---

[8] Another possible mitigating circumstance would be when the assets remaining in an endowment portfolio at the death of the current owners are in fact meant to be given away to charity (directly or in combination with some structure that can will the assets to some next generation, such as Charitable Lead Trusts). The initial nature of this quandary was suggested to me by a participant in a CFA Society conference in London and, although I do not recall his name, I hope that he will find the appropriate thanks here if he should happen to read this book.

[9] This is the wonderful euphemism that certain estate planners use to describe the death of the current owner or beneficiary!!!

[10] Clearly, one could object here that one would only use dividends. Yet, to me, this takes us back to a different debate: endowment versus declining balance portfolio. One could also consider using private equity distributions as a source of liquidity, but the objection here would be that these are considerably less predictable in terms of their timing than expenditures that are meant to be defeased. Although either of these would indeed be potentially more tax-efficient investments, one must go back to the question: What are we trying to achieve? When dealing with needs or wants, one is seeking a measure of probability of success that appears incompatible with the uncertainty associated with equity markets.

However, owning equities could hurt the sustainability—or eventual probability of success—of the portfolio, since they can experience volatile price swings through time. Some major equity market sell-off might indeed require that more equities than anticipated might be sold in any given year, meaning that the investor would have felt the full blow of the downdraft but could not experience any recovery in full.[11]

Finally, *the outcome of this process needs to be revisited at frequent intervals, usually yearly or at least bi-yearly*. This reflects two truisms. The first, which everybody intuitively knows, is that individual asset classes or strategies—indeed, markets as well—will rarely perform in a "normal" manner. While one may actually be correct forecasting some medium- to long-term compound return, the likelihood that returns will be exactly at that forecast level year after year is next to nil![12] Thus, it is important to look at how markets have treated portfolios and sub-portfolios and to determine whether the allocation remains appropriate or requires some measure of rebalancing. The second is less intuitive and yet is also totally reflective of human nature. It reflects the notion that a time horizon that was set one, two, or three years ago has often not declined in length one, two, or three years later. Often, I define the short term for our families as the next five years or so, viewing this as a time span for which certain forecast variables are less unknown—I often argue that economic growth and inflation are more knowable over that time period, as they rely on policies that take time changing. Yet, a few years into that five-year horizon, we are still likely to be looking at the next five years as the same definition of "short term." Thus, it may be necessary to rebalance the assets held in the various buckets with some degree of regularity.

IT CHANGES EVERYTHING

Although the process is only marginally different,[13] it is perceived totally differently by both client and advisor: it does change everything.

---

[11]However, one cannot totally discount the role of equities in certain well-controlled circumstances in view of issues of tax-efficiency, for instance when dividends are not taxed at the same rate as interest income.

[12]This insight is powerfully explained in Meyers, Darryl L. "Investment Considerations Under the Prudent Investor Act: Applicable Law." *The Journal of Wealth Management*, Fall 2005, pp. 25–35 and Meyers, Darryl L. "Investment Considerations Under the Prudent Investor Act: Part Two: Translation Analyses." *The Journal of Wealth Management*, Winter 2005, pp. 50–64.

[13]Rather than averaging the different goals into some aggregate return/risk trade-off or utility, one looks at and deals with each of them in turn. Note, however, that in

Clients have told me that the process has two important dimensions that make it vastly superior from their standpoint. The first is that it is totally centered on them. This may be trite, but it is true that many of those advisors who rely on "model portfolios" as a means of both meeting the risk/return trade-off of their clients and yet maintain enough simplicity to their business that they can execute profitably give clients the feeling that they are being pigeon-holed. The goals-based process cannot lead to that perception, as it starts and ends with the client discussing goals and risks in his or her own language, as we shall see in Chapter 7 in more detail. The very fact that these are explicitly brought out together with the reality that actual forward-looking expected cash outflows required to meet goals are formulated gives a strong impression that the effort is truly custom-made.

The second is more subtle, but it may be the one that has the most lasting impact: it creates a visible and real link between "My Wealth" and "My Life." Many families would indeed readily admit that they did not really know how much of their wealth had to be allocated to meeting their ongoing expenses. In fact, one family told me that they "needed to change their burn rate" when they discovered how much of their wealth was required to meet it. Note that the issue here was not that they could reasonably expect to run out of money before they ran out of breath: it was a case of feeling that it simply "was not right" to be spending that much!!! Simultaneously, by providing an opportunity to see how various portions of the wealth are doing through time, families begin to appreciate how markets interact with their own wealth and well-being. At a minimum, this feedback loop helps families live through nasty market conditions by experiencing at least some success. Families we serve experienced success in their "lifestyle defeasing" portfolios in the "crash of 2008." As equity prices fell, bond prices rose; thus, families were able to meet all expenses as planned and saw the value of the sub-portfolio decline (net of spending) by less than forecast. They did see their "growth" portfolios decline in value—as they contained significant equity exposure—but they naturally migrated to a relative return yardstick, which hitherto had appeared anathema to many of them.

It changes the life of advisors as well. First, it requires that advisors understand who does what to whom and thus who plays what role in the firm. Often, advisors have tended to reserve client advisory roles to the most senior people in the firm, whether they were truly gifted to be client advisors or were, in fact, first-class specialists in one of the several crucial disciplines—investment management being one, but certainly not the only

---

theory at least, the questions asked by the advisor should broadly be the same in both cases.

one. With the need to be able to be totally client-centered, advisors must have certain qualities that not all specialists have. The two crucial requirements, in my view, is that they be able to understand—and thus translate—client goals and general specialist requirements, and that they have sufficient client experience that they can help clients appreciate when they have truly unique requirements or when these are, in fact, pretty much "generic." Second, it certainly modifies the way they conduct business. It elevates the role of broad-based advisors and tends to relegate specialists to secondary or supporting roles, cosmetically at least. In fact, the dynamic is considerably less dramatic: it forces people to begin to think in terms of teamwork rather than "me" or "you." Although there may be certain instruments that can be argued to be "more important" in orchestras or certain positions that can be argued to be more critical in certain sports teams, the reality is that successful orchestras and teams do not see it that way. The proverbial quip that the weakest link is the one that causes one to win or lose still applies. Thus, firms are required to be able to manage their various team members in their respective roles, making sure that each member of the team—advisor or specialist—does the best he or she can do, but never pretends to play a role that is not his or hers.

AN INTERESTING IMPLICATION

Although we will devote Chapter 12 to the discussion of the issue of portfolio reporting, it is certainly worth it at this point to plant a seed. One of the observations many advisors have shared with me—and which I observed on my own in a number of instances—is that clients often do not seem satisfied. Institutional investors do not necessarily find the performance of their investment advisors any more exciting, but they have grown used to accepting the value of relative performance and more detailed forms of performance attribution. It has been a well-accepted truism in the private wealth management industry that "you cannot eat relative returns" and that performance reporting must, therefore, if not avoid relative return reporting altogether, surely at least deemphasize it.

To me, we are observing something incredibly simple, which is totally predictable. If we are correct in stating that individuals have multiple goals, why would we expect them to be satisfied with reporting focused on a single portfolio? Assume with me that markets have been "kind," by which I mean that equity markets produced superior returns; assume further that most individuals will need some lower risk asset exposure to take care of the goals associated with maintaining their current lifestyles. Then, is it not absolutely obvious that their portfolios will underperform a long-only equity portfolio? If this is the case, with the risk of losing money not the main worry—returns have been good—is it not natural that the individual "forgets" the goals associated with meeting expenditures—they have been met—and focuses instead on the loss of opportunity associated with a balanced rather than equity-only portfolio? In some way, our investor has effectively "converted" to a relative return frame of mind, because the absolute return constraint has been exceeded. Contrast this with the case in which the same individual has experienced negative equity market returns. Assume that his or her portfolio is down for the year. Rather than being satisfied that the portfolio has done better than the equity market, the individual shifts to the absolute return framework in which one typically considers the expenditure defeasing part of the portfolio. In short, there is a good—or at least rational—reason why our individual should be unhappy—or at least not fully satisfied—irrespective of market circumstances.

This takes us back to the quip at the end of Chapter 5: you would on average be comfortable in a statistical sense if your feet are in the oven and your head is in the freezer! The point is that there are cases when computing an average of incompatible events may make statistical sense, but does not make human sense. Thus, having established that individuals have multiple goals and also multiple risk profiles—not to mention multiple time horizons—it should not surprise that we cannot hope to satisfy them unless we use an approach geared to—and report on—multiple sub-portfolios. Thus, still focusing on the reporting part of the challenge, we need to be able to report on each of the various sub-portfolios as well as on the aggregate, to ensure that we have at least a fighting chance that investors will be satisfied with their results.

SUMMARY AND CONCLUSIONS

As we investigate the issue in greater depth, individuals require advisors to adopt a different approach to the management of their wealth. This should not surprise as, their needs being different, it would not be reasonable to pretend that the same set of solutions would apply equally to different sets of problems. The focus on the specific goals of an individual or a family forces us to look at different horizons, different required probabilities of success, and, in fact, different allocations of the wealth across the wide spectrum of possible goals. This creates a more tailored approach, which cannot ever be described as pigeon-holing. In fact, assuming that the percentage of the family's assets allocated to each goal is expressed down to the first decimal (12.1 percent allocated to short-term expense defeasance, 24.6 percent to medium-term expense defeasance, and so on), there will be 1,001 possible asset and strategy combinations, and thus 1,001 possible client-specific performance benchmarks. For all but the largest advisors, it is therefore likely that no two clients will have the same benchmark. This is the ultimate form of customization. Yet, as we shall see in Part 4, this will eventually require an even greater rethinking of management processes if firms need and want simultaneously to provide such a high degree of customization to their clients and yet retain sufficient profitability to satisfy legitimate shareholder requirements.

Three

Goals-Based Wealth Management Implementation

The third part of this book delves into the detail of the implementation of a goals-based wealth management process, leaving the issue of the implications this has in terms of the preferred structure of the advisory firm for the fourth and final part. We start with activities we briefly discussed in prior chapters: how goals-based asset allocation requires the management process to change and, more specifically, what it requires us to do to start. We will then, in Chapter 8, turn to the creation of the goals-based modules that will form the building blocks of our policy allocation. Our subsequent chapter, the ninth, has the rubber meeting the road as we begin to work with clients and to see how our process and our building blocks must be handled to make sure we can help them meet their goals. We then turn to the finalization of the investment policy before discussing how that strategic asset and strategy allocation can be managed from a tactical standpoint and how performance reporting needs to be modified to handle the specifics of our new process.

Before going further, let me restate an important point that was already made in the Introduction. This book, and this third part of the book in particular, is not a commercial for a specific model. Ostensibly, it is based on the model I use, but I certainly do not want to be seen to argue that it is the only valid alternative. Other models, based on the same general principles and having a similar—but not necessarily exactly the same—architecture can certainly do the trick. There may be a few debates among different authors, for instance in the way this model describes goals or portfolio modules, or in the approach taken by this or that other practitioner; but this is what makes markets. The real distinction I hope to create is between models such as ours, which look at individual client goals and their specific characteristics (time horizon and required probability of success) and others that work from some holistic aggregate return goal and risk tolerance. It would be fun to contrast the results of one such model and those of ours, but that is not practical, as I would of necessity be comparing apples and oranges somewhat.

An example will illustrate the impact which this approach can have. A family needed to spend about 7 percent of its financial capital—or 4 percent of its financial and real assets, the balance being comprised of exceptional, and thus concentrated, real estate and art. A goals-based asset allocation effort recommended that the strategic cash and fixed income risk exposure be raised from a current 15 percent to 61 percent, because of the focus on the need for short- to medium-term spending to be protected from potentially excessive equity market fluctuations. The cost of such a change was that the family had a virtual certainty that certain real assets would have to be sold in ten to fifteen years, simply reflecting the truism that a 7 percent "burn rate" in today's environment cannot last forever. Although this certainly would be a big change, it would be something that the family readily understood, and the ten- to fifteen-year time line gave it time to prepare and decide which of these prized real assets were truly part of their legacy and which were not. Contrast this with the more traditional approach which would lead the manager to raise the expected riskiness of the portfolio to earn a sufficient return, with the corresponding risk of a catastrophic loss in value and sudden requirement for the family to adjust its life style immediately if that added risk did not pay off. An alternative to that traditional approach might be to keep arguing that spending levels are excessive, but fail to provide guidelines as to how the assets would need to be redeployed to allow the family to keep on its current spending patterns if that is how it chose to lead its life, even if it meant that spending might have to be cut later.

CHAPTER 7

Dealing with the Implications of the Process

At this point, it will not surprise readers to see me postulate that the goals-based process changes things quite a bit. After all, the penultimate section of Chapter 6 was entitled "It changes everything!" As in most things, we need to be sure we have positioned ourselves so that we can start. In part, this means that we know we have looked at the most important issues, that we have made key decisions as to which assets or strategies belong where and why; and that we understand the limitations of our process, which, however good we might make it, will never neatly fit each and every situation imaginable. It has limitations and we are in danger of getting things very wrong unless we fully understand where we are standing on firm ice and where we are exposed to the risk of tumbling through it into very cold water indeed. Finally, we must have anticipated the various objections clients will inevitably throw at their advisors when the process appears to impose constraints with which they are, at least initially, uncomfortable.

COVERING A SET NUMBER OF BASES

Earlier, I mentioned that our focus was going to be primarily on the asset management dimension of the wealth management problem. Without presuming to take the analogy too far, let me state that we do need to maintain some form of peripheral vision. If it is true—and I think it is—that the asset management problem is only one dimension of a family's or individual's challenge, how could we claim to address it if we do it in some vacuum? I have come to believe that there are five essential bases that must be covered.

The first base we need to cover relates simply to the *interdisciplinary relationships* that are most likely to influence our effort. Ostensibly, our eventual objective is to describe the various goals our client will seek to achieve. We already know, from Figure 6.1, that these objectives will eventually be translated into some portion of the total assets being allocated in some way to maximize the chances that we will meet the goal these assets are meant to defease. Yet, upstream of that effort, we certainly need to have looked into the distinct pockets that already exist within our client's wealth structure. They will help us understand both who owns what—which represent the interaction between estate, financial, and investment planning—but they should also inform us as to the tax status of each of these individual pockets.[1] We will need to accommodate or even consider selected existing or prospectively created structures or instruments that the family needs for generational or philanthropic planning rather than for investment purposes.[2] We will have done this by working to understand what matters to the family and by doing so while speaking in the family's own language rather than what I have come to dub "financialese."

Avoiding financialese, our second base, can be hard, both because it is never easy to give up bad habits and, more importantly, because many of us have grown so used to financialese that our second language is close to becoming our mother tongue. We often do not even know we are speaking it! Discussing goals and risk issues in financialese can have both traumatic and complicating implications. Dealing with a family in the Middle East one day,

---

[1] William Reichenstein has contributed arguably more than most on the topic of "asset location." For more detail, see Reichenstein, William. "Savings Vehicles and the Taxation of Individual Investors." *The Journal of Private Portfolio Management,* Winter 1999, pp. 15–26. Reichenstein, William. "After-Tax Wealth and Returns Across Savings Vehicles." *The Journal of Private Portfolio Management,* Spring 2000, pp. 9–19. Reichenstein, William. "Frequently Asked Questions Related to Savings Vehicles." *The Journal of Private Portfolio Management,* Summer 2000, pp. 66–82. Reichenstein, William. "Calculating the Asset Allocation." *Journal of Wealth Management,* Fall 2000, pp. 20–25. Reichenstein, William. "Asset Allocation and Asset Location Decisions Revisited." *Journal of Wealth Management,* Summer 2001, pp. 16–26. Reichenstein, William. "Notes on "Applying After-Tax Asset Allocation." *Journal of Wealth Management,* Fall 2007, pp. 94–97. Also see Brunel, Jean L.P. "Asset Location—The Critical Variable: A Case Study." *Journal of Wealth Management,* Summer 2001, pp. 27–43.

[2] At this point, I would only mention one: inter-generational loans. In his first book, Jay Hughes describes one of the efforts a family should make to limit the size of the chair occupied by the government at the family meeting table. He thus pioneered the use of inter-generational loans, which can be seen as the fixed income exposure of the lending generation and the means to fund long-term growth portfolios for the borrowing generation. See Hughes, James E., Jr., *Family Wealth: Keeping It in the Family,* Princeton Junction, NJ: Netwrx, 1997, pp. 61–66.

I found myself asking the patriarch what his goals were. He mentioned a couple of "motherhood-and-apple-pie" truths, which, when processed down to numbers, only used up a minute portion of the family's newly liquid wealth, as it had floated one-third of its until then privately held business. That is when I came up with the idea of using a different word to discuss goals. I asked him about his *dreams*. Boy, did I open the floodgates!

The lesson I took away from this episode is that I needed better words to discuss goals and risks. After some measure of trial and error, I came up with a couple of word sequences. For goals, I invite clients to discuss *needs, wants, wishes, and dreams*. For risk issues, I suggest that they talk in terms of *nightmares, fears, worries, and concerns*. This is but a linguistic artifice, and I am sure other approaches might work as well. Yet, this one is a simple manner for us to develop the insights we need within our sophisticated financial infrastructure without having to drag the client along for the ride. A side benefit is that the artifice also helps us gauge the required probabilities of success discussed in Chapter 6, as the connotations of words such as nightmares and needs suggest a much higher degree of urgency than words like dreams and concerns; we know we will all die with a few unfulfilled dreams and remaining concerns. We cannot attach more than a 50 to 60 percent probability of success achieving or avoiding them.[3] By contrast, needs and nightmares must be at the top of any priority list!

The third base relates to the observation that *there may be other, more subtle issues that we will need to consider*. For instance, even within the narrow category of what a client might call lifestyle expenditures, it can be the case that not all such expenses are created equal. A family we know considers the taxes they pay on grantor trusts for the benefit of their descendants a part of their living expenses. Yet, while they expect to be paying taxes on generation skipping trusts "until further notice," they clearly have set a five-year time limit on paying the taxes associated with grantor trusts geared for the benefit of the next generation. We must be ready to deal with this, and our process must have a conceptual solution at the ready; in our own practice, we simply create different "goals" within the lifestyle component.

The fourth important base is to understand that *there are at least two "doors" into the process*. I have come to think of these as "cash flow" or "label" driven. There will be instances when a family or an individual is simply not willing or able to produce detailed cash flows with respect to each goal. On the surface, one could easily elect to force the issue and squeeze cash-flow projections out of the client or feel that one has enough data to create these projections ourselves; this would allow us to work around client

---

[3]Tables 9.1 and 9.1 in Chapter 9 illustrate this more fully.

reluctance or lack of information. Although this might be conceptually possible, that avenue is fraught with danger, as the truth is we must work with our client, as a team, throughout the process, if we are trying to achieve what I called the marriage between "My Wealth" and "My Life" in Chapter 6. In the end, the simplest alternative is to have a generic view of what we mean—or what is typically meant—by labels such as lifestyle, capital preservation, and growth. One could add other labels, for instance, using the very insightful "aspiration"[4] label postulated by Ashvin Chhabra and mentioned in Chapter 6. Although one could argue that it overlaps with "growth," it may, in fact, speak more eloquently to certain families than "growth." At the same time, it may be different from "growth," as it has a richer texture that might suggest a greater willingness to miss the goal.

The preferred alternative, whenever practical, would likely be to base the analysis on cash-flow planning. It offers many advantages in that it can more easily be tailored and can reflect uneven cash flow patterns, which often characterize the real world. We will discuss a bit later how one can make this detailed effort work in a practical sense, but suffice it to say here that, although quite a bit more complex, it is the approach with which I have encountered the greatest success with families. However, I am prepared to concede that it might be simpler and thus more practical to default to "label driven" processes for advisors whose clientele is both numerous and often less complex that the ultra-affluent who may need the greater detail. Just for the sake of completeness, I should add that these two "doors" are not mutually exclusive: I often find that certain "goals" can be described with cash flows while other really fit better with a label. It is therefore not unusual for me to use a combination of the two approaches in one single client situation.

A final important base relates to the *need to make sure that whatever thought model is developed is consistent with and can incorporate insights into the three basic dimensions of a family's or individual's goal structure: personal, dynastic, and philanthropic.* Ostensibly, perhaps in some form of contrast with Maslow's hierarchy that may be a bit more strict than ours, individuals generally think of their goals in one of these three dimensions and view the hierarchy among them differently. Unfortunate stereotyping can help visualize the problem. Certain individuals, usually among those who generate very high incomes for some possibly short period of time,[5] will view their personal goals as their primary concern, with little or no

---

[4]Chhabra, Ashvin B. "Beyond Markowitz: A Comprehensive Wealth Allocation Framework for Individuals." *Journal of Wealth Management*, Spring 2005, pp. 8–34.
[5]Leading figures in the world of sports or entertainment, for instance.

attention paid to dynastic or philanthropic issues. By contrast, immigrants in most cultures and countries are notorious for dedicating the bulk of their efforts to the goal that their descendants will never have to suffer the same fate as they. Their focus is dynastic rather than personal. Finally, a number of very wealthy individuals may be more conscious than others that some form of luck underpinned the creation of their fortune and will view philanthropy as the most important element of their wealth management effort.

As is so often the case when looking at hard-and-fast classifications, most families have some combination of these three dimensions when they formulate their goals. We need to remember that the goal that has the lowest priority will tend to be taking the bulk of the investment risk. Imagine that I have $100 and that I plan to divide it 50 percent for personal, 30 percent for dynastic, and 20 percent for philanthropic goals, prioritized in that order. Now imagine that the value of the portfolio falls by 20 percent before I have had the time to allocate the assets to the appropriate independent structures: philanthropy is out of luck! Ostensibly, a well-constructed goals-based portfolio will ensure that such an outcome does not materialize. This may well be the most powerful argument in favor of distinguishing among the various goals, their various required probabilities of success, and their various time horizons. The greater and better match between any goal and the sub-portfolio designed to defease it will be stronger and more explicit, thus making it less likely that the law of unintended consequences or simple bad luck will interfere with our intentions.

MAPPING ASSET CLASSES AND STRATEGIES TO GOALS

We do not need to spend a huge amount of ink on this, as we covered the topic when we discussed capital market expectations in Chapters 3 and 6 and will need to revisit it in more depth in Chapter 8, which is dedicated to the creation of goals-based modules. Yet, it is worth reminding ourselves here of the nature of the issue. As discussed in Chapter 3, the four main determinants of the nature of an asset class are the share of total return accounted for by income, the predictability of income, the process by which terminal value is determined, and the extent to which the value of the asset is liable or not to protect against inflation. Another important feature, although not one distinguishing one asset from another, relates to the liquidity of the strategy that is applied to the asset class.

From this, it follows that at least three questions should be asked when considering the suitability of an asset class or strategy for any goal. The first relates to the liquidity characteristics of a given strategy: Is it compatible with the time horizon associated with this goal? This is a topic we already reviewed in detail and the answer is almost intuitively obvious: one would not pick an investment in a strategy that is relatively illiquid for the next ten years or more if the goal has a time horizon that is less than ten years!

The second relates to the predictability of income—and by association the share of total return that it represents. Is it consistent with the characteristics of a goal? The classic example would be a goal that is associated with lifestyle expenditures or with expenditures that have highly predictable characteristics (these might include the grant share of the budget of a foundation that has significant pledges requiring annual grants). Thus, I must be able to have a good sense of the likely cash inflows into the sub-portfolio if I need to liquidate a material portion of its assets each year. A corollary to this is that, the more predictable and material the income component of total return, the more stable annual return patterns are likely to be; this is important, as it means that regular withdrawals will not be materially affected by underlying asset price fluctuations.

The third relates to the interaction between each asset class and strategy and inflation. How likely is it to protect the sub-portfolio against inflation? The longer the time horizon for a goal, the more likely it is to be exposed to the risk of unexpected inflation. Unless the nature of the cash outflows associated with the goal are specifically expressed in current—as opposed to constant—dollars, the risk of unexpected inflation is all the more relevant. A classic example here would be a goal expressed as the desire to pass a set, inflation-adjusted capital on to descendants at some future point in time. Particularly when that time horizon is in some distant future, the need to ensure that the capital that is accumulating is protected against the ravages of inflation is crucial. It may be useful here to signal an important distinction we will not develop at this point, but revisit in Chapter 8: there are two forms of inflation, cost-push and demand-pull. While demand-pull inflation can typically be at least partially hedged with equities, cost-push inflation cannot be explicitly hedged unless one owns the asset whose price increase is responsible for the increase in the overall price level. Just think of the inflation that resulted from the twin oil shocks of 1974 and 1979 and the length of time it took for equity prices to recover and the point will become obvious.

A few other dimensions can be argued to be derivatives of these three questions. For instance, one might want to argue that high-probability expenditures in some currency should principally be defeased with investments in that same currency. However, is that not simply a derivative of the second question above? Currency fluctuations can indeed be viewed as reducing the predictability of income. Similarly, although illiquid strategies can generally be viewed as unsuited to goals that require a high annual liquidation of a sub-portfolio, it is also true that certain illiquid fixed income strategies that generate and distribute material cash flows—interest income and loan amortization, for instance—may be acceptable when those illiquid strategies applied to equity or real asset markets would not be. In short, the foregoing three questions should be viewed as guides rather than strict branches in a decision tree.

UNDERSTANDING LIMITATIONS

One of the classic errors many people make when dealing with any form of model is that they fail to remember that any model is dependent upon its structure, the nature of the shortcuts taken to make it workable, and the inputs it requires. In short, one can suggest six important limitations.

The first is that *key assumptions must make sense*. At some level, this almost goes without saying: no one would purposely select senseless assumptions. Yet, one does need to ensure that all assumptions make sense in the context of the client environment in which one operates. This includes making sure one is dealing off the correct base currency and that the fundamental structure and outlook are appropriate and consistent with current circumstances. Some inconsistency can be acceptable, provided it can be explained in the broader framework. This is where cyclical versus secular elements may be reviewed, particularly to the extent that certain client goals may have to be viewed in a cyclical rather than secular sense.

The second is that *one must avoid determinism*, by which I mean coming to a single, non-negotiable view. It is clear that one does not adopt any forecasting framework with the idea that it is not well thought-through and useful, or that the outcome is just one out of many equally valid alternatives. But it is also clear that very few people would ever truly believe that they have the sole privilege of brains. Often, rather than getting stuck with the view that only one's own conclusion makes sense, it may well help to be open to other views. Thus, it is useful for one to consider not only what one thinks is correct, but also to ask what one would have to believe in order to justify other forecasts. The idea is not to be so "wishy-washy" that one has no real conviction on any view. The insight is that one could be wrong and that a good way of identifying possible errors is to ask oneself what makes others come to a different conclusion. I have found that trick quite valuable to the extent that being forced to place oneself in other people's shoes is a good way to make sure that one has as broad a perspective as possible, and that one has not jumped to a conclusion with respect to an assumption or to a process—by which I mean a series of logical linkages supporting the framework within which my decision is made.

The third is that *one must promote discussions of trade-offs*. While this is certainly more valuable when dealing directly with clients, this is also a useful extension of the last statement in the prior paragraph. It means ensuring that one understands not only the primary statements and expectations of others, but also that one extends this understanding to their assumptions. Any test of what I believe can only make my beliefs stronger if they survive that challenge.

The fourth relates to *the need to maintain multiple feedback loops*. Again, this is particularly important when dealing with clients; it is an equally important dimension of any forecasting, as discussed in Chapter 3, where we highlighted the need for clarity of assumptions and of structures. The feedback review of how our analyses are panning out is very relevant to the goal of ensuring that we understand limitations. When dealing with forecasts, challenges never arise when things come out as expected; the real opportunity is when things do not turn out as anticipated. The real question is: Is this a short-term blip or is it a true forecasting error? The best analogy to explain this is the prototypical radar screen; for a while, the dots tracking a plane seem to proceed in some more or less straight line. Then, the next dot is to the right or the left of that line. Does it mean that the plane changed direction or is it a case of inaccuracy of the system?

The fifth is a caveat: *beware of potential errors of interpretation*. Whatever hard work has gone into formulating what we need to have to start our process, we should always remain sensitive to the fact that we might here or there have misinterpreted the actual facts. This is also true when we turn to mapping client goals to the generic goals we establish in order to create some measure of standardization of our business, a topic on which we will spend more time in Part 4. The analog here would be the general sizes that tailors might use to create patterns, which are then customized to each individual client. Remember that we discussed mass customization rather than Saville Row in the Introduction.

Finally, but does this really need to be said: *remain humble and flexible*. At some level, this is a good summary for the foregoing five issues, rather than a distinct and separate one. Humility and flexibility are the two essential qualities that underpin any effort to remain close to market realities as well as client concerns. This does not mean that one should eschew any form of philosophical foundation or conviction; but it does mean that one should not think one is the only guardian of the "Total Truth."

DEALING WITH CLIENT OBJECTIONS

Paradoxically, the major challenge with a process that is more client-friendly is that it requires securing client buy-in all the way through the process. Using an institutional approach tends to obviate this need, as the client is never truly expected to participate in the process other than picking one of a few model risk profiles and being satisfied with the outcome.

Client objections come in a series of flavors, but one can generally focus on three, together with the ways to deal with them. The first relates to an *inability to understand the process*. This happens most often when advisors fail to connect with their clients. Obviously, an excessive use of "financialese" can be blamed, but it is not the only issue. I have found that not being able to connect is often a function of not being able to use examples and concepts with which the client is familiar. Remember that clients usually do not make their fortunes in the financial economy; they do it in the real economy, more precisely in a special sector of the economy. Thus, the advisor has to be familiar with a number of the generic dimensions of that sector of the economy and experiences that clients encountered in that sector, and then use examples that reference these experiences.

There can also be *modest or even serious disagreement with key assumptions*. This is not a first-degree challenge, but happens at a second stage. At this point, clients have asked advisors to go deeper into their model, either because of a personal interest or, more frequently, because they disagree with some outcome and look to the assumptions to find the culprit. Although I often suggest to advisors that they should avoid going too much behind the curtain because it is a very difficult discussion to have, they may at times be forced to do so. The challenge is to keep things as simple as possible, going as deep as the client desires, but doing it in stages and as invited to do so by the client, rather than immediately volunteering total transparency. Again, transparency is not a problem, but it can take the focus away from client goals toward markets, which clients often do not know as well as they should. While one should always go as far and as deep as required, one should avoid the temptation to abandon the translating role and to revert to an engineer-to-engineer dialog, recognizing that clients are not always prepared for the technicalities.

Finally, there can be client challenges because the *suggested outcome looks too different from past experience*. Although this does not typically happen early in the process, it can happen later when the client looks at the overall policy that comes out of the analysis and views the change as too significant. Dealing with this is challenging because it can have at least two radically different causes, and clients cannot always distinguish between causes and effects. I have seen times when a prior policy simply did not fit the client's actual circumstances. For instance, significant expense defeasance was not incorporated into the picture when an investor who needed more than 50 percent of his wealth to deal with expenses for the next twenty years had a portfolio that was more than 80 percent in equities! Taking the investor back to the actual evaluation of his or her goals can help, as can what I might call a "forensic process" that would suggest what kinds of goals might be met by the client's previous allocation. The alternative cause is more difficult to handle because dealing with it requires a level of granularity that can be a significant hindrance to communication: the expectations underpinning the prior policy in terms of capital market returns and the like were simply in a different country relative to ours.[6] Helping the client visualize these differences is necessary, but it is not always satisfactory, as explaining these differences is more important than pointing them out.

A THREE-PHASE PROCESS

Although this is the meat of Part 4 of this book, it is worth planting the seeds here. The process that an advisor should follow, if he or she adopts our philosophy and what we call the goals-based wealth management process, comprises three different phases, two of which are of an internal nature with respect to the advisor's firm, and the other is totally external. The wealthy should understand how these phases differ from one another and where they should be concerned, versus when the issue should be secondary to them.

The first step relates to the ultimate goal of *developing goals-based modules*, based on a set of macro-economic and capital market assumptions and a determination of the generic kinds of goals we believe we are prepared to handle. Each module is meant to be the "model sub-portfolio" used to meet a certain kinds of goal and, collectively, the set of modules is meant to cover the range of goals that we think we need to consider. This is not to say that an advisor would reject clients who have goals that do not fit that format, but increasing as it would the cost of servicing that client, one would need to be careful with respect to serving that client or to how to compute the fee that will be charged.

The second step is totally external in nature. The ultimate goal is to develop the dollar allocation to each of the various modules so that their combination provides a *good description of the client's investment policy*. This can only be done with a detailed analysis of the individual goals, or the horizons that characterize them, and of the required probabilities of success that relate to each goal. This does not require any significant focus away from the client, other than making sure that he or she is aware of the likely market implications of each choice.

The third step is almost totally internal, as it relates to the *implementation of the investment policy* and of its being periodically tilted

---

[6]By "different country" we mean that they seem totally different from ours. There is no intention to suggest a geographical difference!

toward or away from certain asset classes and strategies in response to perceived tactical opportunities. Although advisors who operate on a non-discretionary mandate must bring the client on-side with any of their recommendations, the generation of these recommendations should be principally internal. In my opinion, an important mistake advisors often made is to modulate their tactical views to reflect client preferences. Although it is by definition inevitable that the ultimate decision must incorporate the client, the best service to give to these clients is to offer an unvarnished and clearly articulated view of current beliefs and to calibrate the extent to which these views are reflected into each portfolio, given the comfort client has with the recommendation. Clients do not hire advisors to hear the sound of their own voices or the echo of their own opinions.

SUMMARY AND CONCLUSIONS

The major challenge in this chapter was to articulate the main implications associated with the process without spending too much time anticipating the contents of subsequent chapters, in which we will look at each of these steps in more depth. At this point, it should be clear to readers that moving to a goals-based process is almost guaranteed to require changes, which may be significant at times. In short, this decision must be taken with a great deal of care, rather than by default.

The key part of the process, from an advisory firm's standpoint, has to be the mapping of assets, strategies, and goals, as one cannot hope to achieve any client's objective without clear expectations associated with the various asset classes and strategies. Dealing with clients' objections is an important element of the process as, although this is in clients' interests, whatever we offer is distinctly different from what clients have experienced in the past. Thus, helping them over the hump is a critical success factor. Our final point is the need for humility on the part of advisors. No process is perfect and goals-based wealth management is no exception.

From the point of view of the client, the key is to be quite clear as to goals and their various characteristics and to require that the advisor explain how some eventual outcome serves to meet these goals. That it often pushes the wealthy into a level of detail that has rarely been required of them beforehand is the unfortunate truth; that this may create some measure of initial surprise, if not outright discomfort, is the reality. In the end, recalling a variant on our Yogi Berra quip: What are the chances you will meet your goals, dear client, if you are not ready and prepared to articulate them in detail?

CHAPTER 8

Creating Goals Modules

Goals modules are the first crucial element of the process. They have required us to identify generic goals we believe we might know how to address, to ensure that we have mapped the various asset classes and strategies that are consistent with meeting them and to have a sense of the return and volatility expectations associated with each of the modules we created.

DEVELOPING GENERAL CAPITAL MARKET EXPECTATIONS

Using the process that was described in Chapter 3, our first step must be to create expectations for return, volatility, and correlations for those assets and strategies we believe ought to be a potential part of our clients' investment policies. Crucial to this process and slightly upstream is the development of the list of assets and strategies we feel will be appropriate. This involves answering three key questions.

The first question relates to the degree of detail required in my asset class list. This decision is driven by two radically different considerations. The first consideration has to do with the trade-off between simplicity and complexity. Who would not want simplicity? The answer is that, although simplicity is desirable, it can also be self-defeating. Would you rather use an abacus or a computer? I suspect almost everyone will agree that a computer is more user-friendly than an abacus. However, would you rather have to build an abacus or a computer? I suspect that everyone would rather build an abacus. The point is that complexity is needed at times and settling for simplicity at all costs can be a mistake. The key is to consider the trade-off between complexity and simplicity on the one hand and achieving client goals on the other.

The second consideration has to do with the topic we covered in Chapter 2: tax-efficiency. All else being equal, having the broadest possible definition of an asset class or strategy—and the narrowest list of asset classes and strategies—will maximize the number of uncorrelated or partially correlated sources of volatility, which in turn will increase the likelihood that the resulting volatility can be captured to enhance the tax-efficiency of the portfolio.

The second question involves assessing how my manager selection effort maps to the overall list of asset classes or strategies. Although this may initially look like putting the cart before the horse, it is an important dimension. For instance, there is a clear difference between U.S. and non-U.S.–developed fixed income markets, even if currency risks in the latter are hedged back to the base currency. Yet, a U.S. individual investor who does not have the means to allocate tens of millions of dollars to separate account managers will often find it extremely hard to execute a strategy focused regionally within the non-U.S. developed fixed income market universe. Similarly, although large investors will be able to create their own diversified portfolios of hedge fund–type strategies, quite a few investors will at times find it difficult to qualify for non-all-encompassing funds of funds. Both examples suggest that it is not worth complicating the problem with more strategies if one cannot execute an investment in all of the strategies being considered. An honest analysis of one's manager selection universe is a crucial component of the strategies incorporated in the asset class and strategy universe.

Finally, I must ask how detailed a list will be required by or acceptable to my client universe. Although some might argue that this should be the first question, I beg to disagree. As stated at the end of the previous chapter, I believe that client customization is necessary and appropriate, but should only be performed after I have arrived at what I think is the right solution from a theoretical—or professionally specialized—standpoint. In many ways, I view this as one of the principal tests needed to assure me that I am discharging my fiduciary responsibilities appropriately. Once I have that "rock," represented by what I think is "right," I will always have the time to see how that rock must be changed to go from theoretically correct to practically implementable from a client standpoint. An example illustrates this point. Most investors seeking tax-efficient strategies should not worry, as suggested earlier, about sub-asset classes and strategies, such as large, mid- and small capitalization equities. As mentioned in Chapter 2, David Stein and Cliff Quisenberry both explained why it might be more optimal to look at the whole domestic equity universe.[1] Yet, many clients have been used

---

[1] Although families who can afford to consider derivative-based approaches to portfolio rebalancing may find Stein and Quisenberry's logic less compelling, also assuming that they can deal with the tax, accounting, and operational implications of these more complex instruments.

to that differentiation and, more to the point, a few of them might actually think that the concept of the "market portfolio" we first encountered in Chapter 3 is flawed. They might believe that some structural overweighting to mid- or small capitalization stocks, for instance, might be desirable. This might be a case in which one might consider deviating from the "rock" that was designed with a focus on the total U.S. equity market.

Once the list of eligible and appropriate asset classes and strategies has been formulated, one can then apply whatever capital market forecasting model one chooses to generate the appropriate expectations. I believe that such expectations ought to be based on some solid forecasting tool and not simply developed on the basis of historical data. Yet, there are many variants on the forecasting theme, and the forecasting needs are obviously dependent on the mode of portfolio optimization required. We will later see how the use of the Black-Litterman model, for instance, changes both the nature of the required inputs and the way in which one approaches the third phase of the process described at the end of Chapter 7.

DESCRIBING SUFFICIENTLY GENERIC AND SPECIFIC GOALS

Fundamentally, as discussed in Chapter 6, there are two different ways—or "doors" as we called them—to approach client goals. The first involves the use of labels, while the second depends on specific discounted cash flows. A first step in the process is for each advisor to determine how he or she, or the firm, will deal with client goals. Most advisors with a large list of small- to medium-sized clients tend to opt for a label-based process whereby one creates a list of those goals that are most likely to be those that clients seek to meet. Income replacement, capital preservation, growth, and a few others immediately come to mind. Before expanding on this version of the goal-derivation process, let me spend a minute introducing the alternative: cash flow–based goals. For these, one does not seek to feature a generic label, but rather works to create a series of time horizon/probability of success combinations that will drive an equivalent series of model portfolios.

Note that the wealthy also have a parallel choice to make. They must decide which of the two approaches works best for them. Do they have the willingness and ability to provide detailed cash flows to describe their goals? Do they feel more comfortable with the generic nature of the label approach? Can they afford the kind of advisor who will be most likely to use a cash flow approach? Is it necessarily true that all goals can be modeled with a cash flow process or are there certain wishes or dreams whose nature does not lend itself to specific cash flow predictions? In short, the decision to be made by both the wealthy and their advisors are similar and based on somewhat comparable criteria: What feels best and what is most affordable?

Returning to the "label" approach, a while back, working with a well-known multi-family family office, we elected to devise goals using a label approach and published our findings in the *Journal of Wealth Management*.[2] The process we put in place had three important bifurcations, and though not unique, it can serve as an illustration of a label approach to selecting potential client goals.

The first dichotomy required the identification of "internal" versus "external" assets. While the former were managed by the client—in financial markets, operating business, or real assets—the latter were delegated in part or in full to an advisor. By definition, the advisor did not need to define generic goals for internal assets and only focused on those that were "external." Yet, explicitly, the advisor ought to understand how these internal assets interplayed with the rest in terms of client goal achievement.

The second dichotomy differentiated between those assets that were needed by the family to support their lifestyle and those that were dedicated to other goals. Lifestyle assets were further sub-divided into short- and long-term time periods. The idea was to recognize that inflation is the hidden—or not so hidden—enemy of people who rely on financial capital to meet their lifestyle expenditures. Thus, we agreed to view the short term as the time period during which we felt that the risk of unexpected inflation was low or at least manageable. The period beyond that horizon was specifically considered as subject to changes in inflation, which required individuals, families, and their advisors to spell out a strategy to deal with it. As we saw in Chapter 6, the sub-portfolios designed to meet these goals will most often be of a declining-balance rather than endowment nature.

The last dichotomy related to the non-lifestyle assets and dealt with the difference between growth and capital preservation. At some level, I was not totally comfortable with these labels, as they mixed "financialese" and "everyday language." Said differently, there was the potential for misinterpretation, as what a word might mean to one individual could be quite different from what it meant to someone else. Also, one could argue that growth or capital preservation are means to some end rather than some end in itself Yet, this dichotomy allowed us to identify sub-portfolios whose principal goal was to grow the assets through time, while the others sought not to see a decline in their value over rolling periods of three years or more, in nominal or real inflation-adjusted terms.

---

[2]Brunel, Jean L.P., "Goals-Based Wealth Management in Practice." *Journal of Wealth Management*, Winter 2011, pp. 17–26.

In the end, we had a short list of four generic goals:

1. Short-term lifestyle, which typically covered clients' expected expenditures for the next five years or so;
2. Long-term lifestyle, which covered lifestyle spending needs from years six onwards, rarely extending beyond the next twenty-five years;
3. Capital preservation, which dealt with assets designed to meet goals that had at least a ten-year horizon where the tolerance for decline in portfolio values over any rolling period of three years was low; and
4. Growth was a bit of a catch-all and was meant for assets that were designed to meet goals that were either at least twenty years out or where the risk of a potentially meaningful decline in value was perceived to be less important than the chance of being able to meet some goal that was currently inaccessible given present asset levels.

The next trick, which we will cover later, was to help clients allocate their assets among these goals.

An intellectually more satisfying and academically more robust alternative was to create true discounted cash flow streams for each of the client goals. Although we will cover this exercise in detail below, this does not eliminate the need for the advisor to create a few "prototypical" goals. Indeed, one will eventually need to match goals with specific sub-portfolios that can be viewed as highly likely to allow the client to meet each goal. So the focus is not to identify a specific goal, but rather to create a family of sub-portfolios that are sufficiently different from one another to offer a meaningful difference in terms of return and return volatility patterns and still are, collectively, sufficiently exhaustive to cover a wide enough swath of capital market alternatives.

In our current practice, we prefer this cash-flow-based approach and have developed six such generic sub-portfolios to meet a wide range of combinations of time horizon and required probability of success:

1. We define short-term lifestyle in very much the same manner as above.
2. We then define a long-term lifestyle goal, typically a time horizon of up to thirty years and a required probability of success of 80 percent or more.
3. We define a set of two goals that are the parallels of the capital preservation we saw above and view them as combining time horizons of ten to twenty years and required probability of success of 75 percent or less. I say a set of two such goals because we view one of them as being expressed in nominal terms, while the other is not only inflation-adjusted, but, more importantly, adjusted for cost-push inflation.

4. Similarly, we define a set of two growth portfolios that have time horizons in excess of twenty years and probability of success below 75 percent. Here again, we differentiate between inflation-adjusted and nominal goals.

We define these six generic sub-portfolios under four different sets of general client preferences reflecting the acceptability of non-traditional strategies, but will cover this point in more detail soon.

Irrespective of the thought process underpinning the formulation of the goals an advisor will handle, some thoughts are clear. First, in this business, as in many others, one cannot be all things to all people. Thus, there will be goals that one cannot or will not address. Focusing first on advisory firms that serve a small- to medium-sized clientele, it will always, at some point, be necessary to be able to say "no" to a client. Note that this is not strictly limited to lower wealth levels. We knew of a family who had set fairly lofty goals for future generations and thus found itself in a challenging position one day. Historically, the family had created its wealth through a series of almost ideally timed forays in operating business areas. As the patriarch started aging—although he was still totally fit and more than able to keep operating—he elected to invest some of his wealth in public markets. This put less pressure on future generations, as well as employees, to be able to replicate his savvy when it came to making profitable operating investments. He eventually was forced to return to the private investment world when it became very clear that the returns he needed for his perpetual trust to make the expected distributions were not achievable in public financial markets.

In short, honest advisors must know how far they can go before they must recommend against their own services. In some cases, this will be because the complexity of certain strategies would exceed the advisor's skill level. In other instances, it will be because the return expectations or required probabilities of success will be judged incompatible. In other cases still, the advisor has to preserve some measure of homogeneity within his or her practice to be both sufficiently profitable to justify the risk of being in business and sufficiently competitive in terms of price to remain in business.

CREATING CONSTRAINTS APPROPRIATE TO EACH GOAL

Having created capital market return and volatility expectations as our first step, our second and next activity relates to the fact that all possible potential capital market assets or strategies do not fit all goals. Generally speaking, one should think of three sets of constraints, which mirror the questions we asked in Chapter 6.

The most obvious and often binding constraint relates to *liquidity*. Particularly with respect to declining balance portfolios, it goes without saying that illiquid or partially liquid assets must be handled carefully. A portfolio designed to meet goals with a time horizon shorter than the full liquidation expectations of illiquid assets cannot take such a risk. Annual withdrawals would quickly increase the weight of assets that cannot be sold to the point of totally distorting the expected risk profile.

The second relates to the *way expected portfolio returns are generated*. The more meeting a goal requires material partial periodical liquidation of the portfolio, the more it will be necessary for certain assets or strategies to rely on income as their main return driver. By contrast, strategies that rely on capital appreciation as their main return driver will likely be most suitable for goals that have both a longer-term horizon and relatively limited need for annual cash outflows.

Finally, and this is different from the way we formulated the issue in Chapter 3, one will need to make decisions as to the balance one can and should maintain between *portfolio optimization* rather than relying on the "market portfolio." The market portfolio is defined as the universe in which one would typically invest and its composition is designed to mirror the market capitalization weights of each of the various components. The case for the market portfolio typically relies on two rationales: first, weights vary in the same way in the market portfolio and in any portfolio that is weighted in the same manner as the market portfolio; this minimizes the need for periodical rebalancing. Second, not having to rebalance a portfolio is typically viewed as enhancing potential tax-efficiency for jurisdictions where taxes are due on realized capital gains.

In the end, each advisor will choose the best way for him or her to translate the goals that he or she has set for an "average client" into capital market realities. For our part, the four key conceptual drivers to our constraint formulation process are:

1. *Liquidity*, which we define as one minus the number of days required for a position to be liquidated without affecting market prices, divided by the number of days in a year. Thus, illiquid strategies have an assumed liquidity of zero; alternative assets have assumed liquidities ranging between 100 percent for those that offer daily liquidity to zero for those that have minimum holding periods of more than a year.
2. *Volatility*, which we define in the classic manner as the standard deviation of expected returns. We typically seek for there to be more than 1 percent to 2 percent expected volatility differences between two adjacent modules to ensure that we have enough diversity.

3. *Market portfolio composition* for assets such as equities and fixed income to ensure that we do not make unintended geographical, credit quality, size, or style bets in the overall strategic allocation of goals-based modules.
4. *Suitability and client preferences* meant to ensure that clients are not surprised by the performance of certain assets or strategies with which they might not be familiar. This extends to a careful analysis of long-term price variation patterns, as expected return and volatility statistics do not always tell the whole story. Thus, experience suggests that certain individuals or families will feel comfortable with equities and uncomfortable with foreign currencies, and vice versa. I used to refer to this when at J.P. Morgan as the biases of "onshore" versus "offshore" clients.

Table 8.1 illustrates one such set of constraints for one set of goals, for clients for whom all strategies are broadly eligible (that is, they do not rule out illiquid or alternative investments when they are appropriate). It is divided into six horizontal categories of constraints and covers six possible modules.

1. The first horizontal section sets out the appropriateness of holding *cash* in the sub-portfolio.
2. The second sections sets out size and composition constraints for the part of the sub-portfolio, which we call the *lower half of the volatility spectrum*, to avoid falling into the all too common trap of viewing certain lower volatility alternative strategies as fixed income substitutes.
3. The third section sets out the size and composition constraints for the *equity portion* of the portfolio. The careful observer will note that the geographical allocation constraints are based on the market portfolio. This is a choice I made and it is not the only option. For instance, one could easily argue for a structural overweighting to emerging markets on the grounds that they should offer higher long-term opportunities.
4. The fourth section sets out the size and composition constraints for the *real asset*—or diversifying asset—part of the portfolio.
5. The fifth section deals with a single item: the liquidity parameters associated with illiquid assets. While certain observers will argue that a well-structured illiquid asset portfolio, with appropriate vintage year diversification, will eventually "self-finance", a cynical investor will note that this statement is true except when it is not. Thus, cautious investors often tend to want to hold some cash in reserve—in escrow—to account for instances when distributions and capital calls are out of sync.
6. The sixth and final section deals with the issue of the *volatility and liquidity* parameters for the portfolio as a whole.

TABLE 8.1 Example of Constraints for Goal-Based Modules

Constraints	ST Life	LT Life	Nom PP	Real PP	Real G	Growth
Minimum Cash	10%	0%	0%	0%	0%	0%
Maximum Cash	30%	5%	4%	6%	7%	6%
Minimum Lower Half Volatility Spectrum	70%	55%	20%	0%	0%	0%
Maximum Lower Half Volatility Spectrum	90%	100%	50%	25%	10%	20%
Minimum Investment Grade Fixed Income as a % of LHVS	75%	50%	50%	0%	0%	0%
Maximum Extended Market Fixed Income as a % of LHVS	25%	25%	25%	35%	0%	50%
Minimum EAFE as a % of Extended Market Fixed Income	35%	10%	10%	0%	0%	0%
Minimum U.S.H.Y. as a % of Extended Market F.I.	35%	30%	50%	0%	0%	50%
Maximum Liquid Fixed Income as a % of LHVS	100%	75%	80%	0%	0%	50%
Maximum LHVS Alternatives as a % of LHVS	0%	30%	35%	75%	50%	60%
Minimum RV Multi-Strategy as a % of LHVS	0%	0%	25%	0%	0%	0%
Maximum Global Macro as a % of LHVS	0%	50%	50%	50%	50%	40%
Maximum Illiquid Fixed Income as a % of LHVS	0%	30%	40%	50%	100%	100%
Minimum Equity Risk Spectrum	0%	0%	30%	0%	40%	70%
Maximum Equity Risk Spectrum	0%	15%	60%	35%	70%	100%
Minimum Public Equities as a % ERS	0%	0%	40%	0%	25%	60%

(continued)

TABLE 8.1   (*Continued*)

Constraints	ST Life	LT Life	Nom PP	Real PP	Real G	Growth
U.S. Public Equities as a % of Public Equities	0%	45%	45%	45%	45%	45%
E.M. Public Equities as a % of Public Equities	0%	20%	20%	20%	20%	20%
Maximum ERS Alternatives as a % of ERS	0%	50%	35%	25%	30%	30%
Maximum Illiquid Equities as a % of ERS	0%	0%	10%	25%	40%	30%
Maximum Managed Futures as a % of ERS Alternatives	0%	50%	20%	50%	50%	40%
Minimum Real Assets	0%	0%	20%	40%	30%	5%
Maximum Real Assets	0%	30%	40%	100%	60%	15%
Maximum Liquid Real Assets as a % of RA	0%	100%	90%	80%	75%	70%
Maximum Illiquid Real Assets as a % of RA	0%	0%	30%	40%	55%	60%
Minimum Income Producing RA as a % RA	0%	50%	20%	0%	0%	0%
Maximum Income Producing RA as a % RA	0%	75%	60%	50%	50%	50%
Minimum Precious Metals as a % of RA	0%	15%	15%	20%	20%	0%
Minimum Commodities as a % of Liquid RA	0%	0%	10%	30%	30%	0%
Escrow Cash	0%	5%	10%	10%	10%	10%
Maximum Partially Liquid Alternative Assets	0%	30%	30%	30%	30%	30%
Minimum Liquidity	100%	80%	75%	75%	70%	70%
Minimum Volatility	5.0%	5.5%	6.0%	7.5%	8.5%	11.5%
Maximum Volatility	5.5%	6.0%	7.0%	8.5%	11.5%	13.5%

The six types of goals (Short-Term Lifestyle, Long-Term Lifestyle, Nominal Purchasing Power Preservation, Real Purchasing Power Preservation, Real Growth, and Nominal Growth) fit with those discussed earlier in this chapter.

One final note on constraints: in our practice, we have four sets of constraints for the same six generic goals listed above. The first allows all assets and strategies and thus explicitly assumes that clients are prepared to invest in both illiquid and alternative strategies. The second goes to the other extreme and only allows traditional—that is, long only—strategies. The other two add either illiquid but not alternative or alternative but not illiquid strategies to the traditional-only list of eligible investments. A second look at Table 8.1 will show that the constraints for the short-term lifestyle module should not be expected to change across the four different categories of permissible strategies, as it uses long-only low volatility investments. In short, our practice runs twenty-one different modules, one short-term lifestyle and four sets of five others.[3]

OPTIMIZING THE COMPOSITION OF EACH MODULE

Once we have both defined the kinds of goals we are trying to deal with and the constraints we feel are appropriate, the creation of goals-based modules is only a simple step away: optimization of the composition of each of the sub-portfolios. There are, however, at least two conceptually valid and yet totally different approaches to dealing with portfolio optimization.

The first, the most traditional, relies on a simple mean-variance model, based on equilibrium return, volatility, and correlation expectations for the various asset classes and strategies. We know the process well; we know its inherent weaknesses. We know that it is a highly powerful and complex tool that is dependent on assumptions that are at times dicey; we know that the

---

[3]It is important to note that one should have two parallel sets of portfolio modules reflecting those that were optimized on the basis of pretax return and volatility assumptions and those that relied on after-tax capital market assumptions. Although this clearly complicates matters a great deal, it is necessary to reflect the extent to which taxes make the challenge quite a bit more complex. For instance, in the United States, it would not be unusual for pretax capital market expectations to rely on actively managed strategies, while after-tax assumptions are often based on tax-aware or passive strategies. Thus, a family's tax-exempt or tax-deferred holding structures might be constructed from modules based on pretax assumptions, whereas the taxable holding pockets would use modules based on after-tax capital market expectations.

short- to intermediate-term rarely look anything like the calm equilibrium assumptions we use. Yet, in the end, it is a framework to which the wealthy and advisors have become accustomed.

The second, based on the Black-Litterman framework, incorporates capital market expectations that are not based on "equilibrium" data, but reflect what these return expectations need to be to fit the current conditions observed in markets. In such a case, one would not be constructing optimal portfolios that are regularly "tilted," but rather would construct optimal portfolios regularly to reflect how markets are speaking to us and how that fits with or differs from our views.

For the balance of this book, we will rely on the traditional Markowitz optimization, but recognize that one could operate in a Black-Litterman framework just as effectively.

One of the challenges associated with traditional optimization is that it can be a bit of a self-fulfilling prophecy. Indeed, individuals who have sufficient capital market and modeling experiences can "game" the assumption and constraint formulation part of the process so that the optimization "happens" to generate exactly the kind of portfolio they had in mind in the first place. The process described here has a couple of important preventative measures to guard against that risk, although it is never truly absent.

The first is that the capital market assumption step is highly systematic. The structured approach to capital market forecasting we discussed in Chapter 3 virtually ensures that the assumptions generated in terms of return and volatility expectations are internally consistent and generally fair—which does not mean accurate! The correlation table used to describe diversification potential is strictly historical. Thus, although judgment is used to arrive at certain assumptions, these assumptions are set before they are brought together with constraints to determine optimal portfolios.

The second is that the capital market assumption and constraint formulation steps are wholly independent. Although it must be clear that constraints in one way or another reflect a few of the same biases that underpin capital market assumptions—for instance, in terms of the nature of return streams—it should be equally clear that these constraints are at best "inspired" by the same spirit. Ostensibly, experienced professionals participating in both sets of judgment calls can anticipate how variations in one—capital market assumptions—or the other—constraints—may affect the outcome of the optimization. Yet, the focus that should be placed on preserving as much independence as possible between the two activities should militate in favor of honesty and intellectual rigor.

In short, the firm or individual who follows this approach must make doubly sure that each of the steps is justified on its own rather than when the two are taken together. Capital market expectations also must stand on their own two feet with, as suggested in Chapter 3, clearly laid out structural assumptions—the way the various return and risk building blocks come together for each asset class and strategy—and clearly specified individual building block assumptions—the actual value that is given to each building block, taken on its own rather than as a component of a given return or risk forecast.

Once the integrity of the two sets of inputs into the optimization process can be reasonably assumed, the formulation of the various sub-portfolios—or goals-based modules—is mostly mechanical. One of the issues we had to face in our own process was the fact that constraints had to be checked for internal consistency. The list of constraints found in Table 8.1 is quite long and provides ample opportunity for internal contradictions. These constraints fall into three broad categories. The first relates to overall portfolio features, such as liquidity and return volatility, those which clients would most directly "experience." The second constraints set limits to the allocations to various groups of asset classes and strategies and are designed both to help achieve what experience might call "portfolio balance" and to counteract a few of the basic mechanical biases that we know are built into any optimization process. The third focuses on sub-asset class or strategy allocation and is meant to bring us as close as possible to the concept of market portfolio. It does not take a Rhodes scholar to realize that there is ample room for conflict among the objectives assigned to each group. It is not unusual for the first or second go-around of the process to lead to failure.

In the end, one of the lessons we have learned by going through this process many times in the last fifteen years or so is that one should keep the list of constraints as compact as possible. One should indeed try not to pre-order the eventual outcome and thus work to minimize the number of constraints. In practice, we typically start with the bare minimum and only add to the list as and when the model results in an outcome that seems odd. By "odd" I mean impractical, rather than different from expectations. Indeed, I only call "odd" an outcome that I understand and feel is unacceptable.

Take the example of long-only equities. You know and I know that whether focused on size or geographical dimensions, the typical return difference between small and large capitalization stocks or developed versus emerging equities will more than offset the increase in expected volatility, when looked at in a broad portfolio context. Unless correlations were to be materially different—and history suggests they are not—an optimization model will allocate to small capitalization or emerging equities rather than to large capitalization and developed market equities, respectively. If needed, it may provide for a bit more cash, fixed income, or some other diversifier to control overall portfolio risk. This is where some market portfolio derived constraint can and, in my opinion, should be used.

More importantly, it is crucial to remember what mean-variance optimization can and cannot do. The best way to illustrate this point is to focus on alternative assets. Numerous articles have pointed out that many so-called alternative strategies suffer from abnormal distribution features, often summarized in terms of skew and kurtosis; the former describe the fact that a distribution may not be symmetrical around its mean—statisticians know that the mean and the median are the same in a normal distribution. Kurtosis simply describes what we have come to call "fat tails." Combine negative skew and fat tails and you have just increased the probability of a nasty surprise.

Now, assume with me that markets are generally somewhat efficient. If it is true that a negative skew with or without excess kurtosis is an unattractive feature, should it not also be true that the other dimensions characterizing the return distribution of such a strategy should adjust or compensate for that unattractiveness? In practice, we know that this is probably the reason why such strategies have either higher returns or lower volatility than more traditional variants. Note that my optimization model only knows of mean and variance for each of the variables. Thus, the risk is real that the model will max out the allocation to strategies where means and variances are "abnormal" because of the need to adjust for equally "abnormal" skew and kurtosis. Without specific constraints to prevent such an over-allocation, one knows that the model will provide a solution that is sub-optimal. Davies, Kat, and Lu[4] discussed the challenge and showed that one can deal with it using a more complex optimization process that incorporates these additional dimensions. They also pointed out that the optimization problem becomes so complex that it loses feasibility when the list of assets and strategies expands.[5]

In short, we are still stuck with the idea that constrained optimization may well be—paraphrasing the words of Sir Winston Churchill[6]—the worst form of portfolio construction except for all others. Just as we emphasized the need for what we called the triple "clarity" criteria in Chapter 3 when dealing with capital market forecasting, we need to remind ourselves here

---

[4]Davies, Ryan, Harry M. Kat, and Sa Lu. "Fund of Hedge Funds Portfolio Selection: A Multiple-Objective Approach." AIRC Working Paper No. 20, 2004. (www.cass.city.ac.uk/airc).

[5]A careful commentator will make sure that this is left open-ended, as enhancements in computing power are not only predictable but virtually guaranteed; thus, what may be practically not feasible today could become commonplace tomorrow.

[6]"Democracy is the worst form of government, except for all those other forms that have been tried from time to time" (House of Common speech on November 11, 1947).

that the outcome of our optimization is crucially dependent on our inputs, is a direct function of the structural assumptions that we build into it, and is, therefore, a general indication of where one should be, rather than a specific solution that is correct to the third decimal![7]

A POSSIBLE EXAMPLE

The best way to illustrate the kind of outcome we feel is appropriate is probably to show what set of modules is generated by the combination of the constraints set out in Table 8.1 and our capital market expectations, which are presented in Table 8.2. Please remember that these forecasts for returns and volatility of returns are crucially dependent on the assumptions on which they are based. They should not be used unless one fully understands and agrees with these assumptions. Also, they are U.S. dollar–based. Finally,

TABLE 8.2 Example of Equilibrium-Based Capital Market Forecast[8]

Passive Management Except for Alternative and Illiquid Strategies	Return	Volatility	Liquidity
Cash	2.3%	3.2%	100.0%
U.S. Fixed Income Inv. Grade	4.1%	7.5%	100.0%
U.S. Fixed Income HY	6.1%	12.0%	100.0%
EAFE Fixed Income Hedged	5.1%	8.1%	100.0%
EM Debt	8.0%	11.0%	100.0%
Relative Value Multy Strategy	7.8%	5.5%	65.0%
Global Macro	8.2%	7.3%	65.0%
Illiquid Fixed Income	7.6%	5.6%	0.0%
U.S. Equities	7.0%	15.2%	100.0%
EAFE Equities	7.1%	17.1%	100.0%
EM Equities	11.0%	18.2%	100.0%
Directional Hedge Eq L/S	7.8%	7.1%	65.0%
Managed Futures	8.1%	7.9%	100.0%
Illiquid Equities	12.0%	23.3%	0.0%
REITs	9.8%	13.6%	100.0%
Precious Metals	6.0%	12.8%	100.0%
Commodities	6.5%	10.5%	100.0%
Illiquid Real Assets	11.6%	15.5%	0.0%

[7] I cannot resist mentioning that I do "cringe" when I see advisors presenting their portfolio allocations to the second or third decimal, as if capital market forecasting or mean-variance portfolio optimization were exact sciences.

[8] In this table and in subsequent tables, REITs as a category also include MLPs, which are both considered income producing real assets.

TABLE 8.3 Resulting Goals-Based Modules

Asset Class/Strategy	ST Life	LT Life	Nom PP	Real PP	Real G	Growth
Cash	25.7%	0.6%	1.8%	2.1%	3.0%	2.7%
U.S. Fixed Income Inv. Grade	55.7%	27.5%	17.9%	0.0%	0.0%	0.0%
U.S. Fixed Income HY	6.5%	0.0%	0.0%	0.0%	0.0%	0.2%
EAFE Fixed Income Hedged	6.5%	0.0%	0.0%	0.0%	0.0%	0.0%
EM Debt	5.6%	0.0%	0.0%	0.0%	0.0%	0.2%
Relative Value Multy Strategy	0.0%	8.3%	6.3%	4.5%	0.0%	0.4%
Global Macro	0.0%	8.3%	6.3%	4.5%	0.0%	0.2%
Illiquid Fixed Income	0.0%	11.0%	5.4%	3.0%	0.0%	0.0%
U.S. Equities	0.0%	3.3%	7.6%	2.5%	11.3%	21.9%
EAFE Equities	0.0%	2.5%	5.9%	2.0%	8.8%	17.1%
EM Equities	0.0%	1.4%	3.4%	1.1%	5.0%	9.8%
Directional Hedge Eq L/S	0.0%	3.6%	8.4%	1.4%	0.0%	7.8%
Managed Futures	0.0%	3.6%	2.1%	1.4%	0.0%	5.2%
Illiquid Equities	0.0%	0.0%	2.6%	2.8%	16.0%	19.6%
REITs	0.0%	22.5%	15.6%	26.4%	18.1%	7.5%
Precious Metals	0.0%	4.5%	4.9%	14.9%	11.2%	0.0%
Commodities	0.0%	3.0%	2.3%	17.7%	12.6%	0.0%
Illiquid Real Assets	0.0%	0.0%	9.7%	15.6%	14.0%	7.5%
Overall Total	100.0%	100.0%	100.0%	100.0%	100.0%	100.0%

please note that they are expressed with only one decimal, which is probably even more specific than should be the case, as I would be nothing short of delighted if the digit to the left of the decimal point was correct!

Table 8.3 shows the set of resulting goals-based modules—or sub-portfolios. Again, these are only a sub-set of what a firm might want to produce and they only fit circumstances when:

1. The six types of generic goals are collectively exhaustive and thus liable to meet the needs of a majority of the firm's clients;
2. The fact that they allow the use of alternative and illiquid strategies is consistent with both the firm's philosophy and capabilities and the willingness and ability of the firm's clients to use these investments;
3. They are meant for clients who express their needs in U.S. dollars; and

4. Capital market assumptions and optimization constraints are appropriate from the point of view of the firm and are explainable to and understandable by its clients.

Two final comments are required:

1. Note that, again, the various outcomes are only shown on the basis of a single digit to the right of the decimal point. One does not want to project too high a degree of precision.
2. In fact, it has been our practice to work from this output and simplify it both by reallocating overly small positions so as to avoid the obvious lack of practicality and to make the eventual policy allocation sensible and by presenting the resulting data in round numbers only.

SUMMARY AND CONCLUSIONS

The first detailed step in the goals-based wealth management process is mostly indigenous to the firm that is providing advice. It involves creating the modules that will eventually be assembled into a whole to make up the individual and specific investment policy for each and every client. Although, in an ideal world, one would wish to be able to deal with every possible prospect and thus be prepared to offer building blocks to meet all possible goals, this is not practical for most advisors. They must, therefore, set out on a process to specify which goals they feel they will be able to help meet and those they cannot. This first step comprises three distinct phases.

First, the individual advisor or the firm must be able to specify a set of capital market assumptions that fairly describe expectations for long-term return and risk for the various asset classes and strategies the firm proposes to use or recommend. Second, the firm or the individual must be able to come up with a set of generic client goals that is sufficiently exhaustive, when all goals are taken collectively, to cover most eventualities and yet compact enough to be actionable in practice and in a for-profit environment. Although these goals will eventually be presented to clients in plain vernacular, they will be primarily described, internally, in terms of what asset classes or strategies are suitable and of constraints that ensure that portfolios will be both reasonable and acceptable. Finally, combining capital market assumptions with goals and constraints, the firm must be able to create sub-portfolios—or modules—each of which is designed to defease one or another of the goals that were initially specified.

As always, a measure of intellectual honesty and rigor on the one hand and humility on the other is required here. It is important to remind oneself that models are used in large measure because reality is too complex to be readily captured. Yet, whenever any simplifying assumption is made—and many must be made at this point—the cautious individual will remember that such an assumption is taking him or her away from reality. This injects a need to be humble in that, although best efforts are deployed to achieve a goal, they may not always be sufficient. It is useful to remember two of the most important tenets of the scientific process: first, be prepared to be totally transparent in terms of assumptions and process, as one does not have the monopoly on brains or knowledge. Allowing others to replicate your experiment with the same model and the same data goes a long way toward providing the required credibility; those who do not very often are accused of using the classic "black box!" Second, make sure that whatever is being recommended has been empirically tested and proven successful in the past, in at least half of all instances. How can one trust any model that has not even managed to "forecast the past" when the inputs that can be used are facts rather than assumptions? Remember that clients are not asking us to explain to them how to make a watch; they are asking us the time. Thus, one must be prepared to share anything and everything but should not impose it on clients who are not interested or even concerned with the inner workings of our watch.

CHAPTER 9

Working to Understand Client Goals and Goal Allocations

I t is worth thinking of a restaurant analogy here. Dishes which are served to each patron hopefully reflect all the skills of the chef and what the diner ordered. Yet, back in the kitchen, each dish is rarely prepared fully from scratch each time and for each patron that orders it. Each of the various ingredients has been prepared, whether this simply involve peeling and dicing vegetables or concocting a fancy sauce that will eventually be delicately poured into the plate and on which the various elements of the dish will be artistically placed. Chapter 8 really dealt with the process that, in our restaurant analogy, takes place in the kitchen. It is generic to the restaurant and applies to all patrons, at least to the extent that they order the same dish. Chapter 9 takes us upstream of this process in that it deals with sitting down with our diner and discussing what he or she wishes to eat. Chapter 9 must, in our own mind, come after Chapter 8, even though one could argue that client needs come first, because we must, keeping with our analogy, know what kind of restaurant and what kind of cuisine we are serving. Sushi shops rarely serve spaghetti dishes, and it is rare—although fusion cuisine is gradually making this dichotomy somewhat arbitrary—to see Chinese restaurants offer French cuisine and vice versa. In some way, we can argue that Chapter 8 dealt with capital market realities subject to client needs, while Chapter 9 will deal with client needs subject to capital market realities.

IDENTIFYING CRUCIAL INITIAL CLIENT CONSTRAINTS

We must return to the issues covered in Part 1 of the book. Asset or investment management is only one of the many disciplines that come together when one deals with wealth management. Thus, before moving forward with the process of advising an individual or a family of the investment management part of the exercise, one needs to develop as full an understanding of the issues surrounding the management of financial capital as possible. Ostensibly, the depth to which one is allowed to go is crucially dependent on each client's willingness to share. Some elements are indispensable; without them, it is hard, not to say impossible, to proceed. Others, although desirable, are not critical. Thus, the smart advisor knows when to press and when to lay off when trying to get that information,[1] and the smart client knows what must absolutely be disclosed and what can be reserved for a later time when the relationship has evolved to a greater degree of intimacy.

What constraints are we discussing here? Broadly speaking, they fall into three categories: constraints created by the nature of the structures within which the assets are held; constraints related to the diversity and complexity of the number of stakeholders in the wealth; and constraints resulting from individual preferences that are viewed as non-negotiable.

The first set of constraints falls squarely under the broad "asset location" header. Four types of possible holding structures for any individual or family are listed below:

1. Those that maintain the beneficial ownership in the hands of an individual or group of individuals and that are subject to regular income taxation. These own the assets outright and can receive the income they generate or the proceeds of any sale; personal accounts would qualify here, for instance.
2. Those that look very much like the structures above, but that provide some form of sheltering against income taxes or at least some measure of tax deferral; retirement or pension accounts or life insurance structures could fit that bill in certain jurisdictions.
3. Those that result from some measure of generational or charitable transfer; there, individuals might be beneficiaries of income flows, which may or may not be specifically described, or might be the eventual owners of the assets upon some qualifying event occurring (time-related or associated with the passing of some beneficiary). These structures may or may not be taxable, as such, or in the hands of set beneficiaries or grantor.

---

[1] I cannot fail to mention the onerous regulatory processes that are popping up in quite a few jurisdictions—with the United States leading the way. These impose important duties on advisors in terms of knowing their clients, which may in effect force them to ask questions to which clients would prefer not to reply. Our main point here is that, beyond factual or regulatorily required information and data, there are many nuances that, although desirable, may not initially be so crucial that the risk of alienating the client is worth taking.

4. Those that result from an actual transfer, for instance, to a family foundation, where the benefactor no longer has any ownership right; although many such structures are exempt from taxes in most circumstances, there may be instances when certain residual taxes apply.

The second set of constraints is more complex, because it cannot be as neatly codified. It principally concerns families whose assets are held in a variety of multi-generational or individual structures that tend to be aggregated for management purposes and yet are distinctly different. A family we know has over 1,000 trusts, a few of which hold assets worth quite a bit more than $100 million, while others have assets of less than $1 million. Here, the need to understand which set of assets can be considered collectively as one pool and which cannot is very important. In another family we know, there are more than one hundred different accounts and more than forty different investment policies. Although aggregated into four broad pools, the constraints related to each account or structure are real. A final dimension of this particular set of constraints is the possible limitation associated with the fact that one or several of these pockets might have issues with respect to minimum investment requirements. This type of issue can arise both because certain investments require some minimum commitment and as a result of regulatory mandates that state that one must have some minimum asset or income level before being allowed to participate in certain investment programs.

The final set of constraint is simultaneously much easier to explain and understand—and virtually limitless. It deals with the preferences clients—both direct and indirect—want to impose on themselves or their managers. I mention indirect clients here because certain decision influencers can have more influence than the client himself or herself. I remember dealing with a family for which a senior family advisor thought he knew investment management and really did not, at least in my opinion; yet, he had a number of somewhat odd biases that he presented as a matter of plain logic and experience, when in fact he was dead wrong. One lesson I learned early on is that the advisor or consultant stays in the room after I leave, and there is no point antagonizing him or her. Thus, irrespective of where any bias might originate, advisors are confronted with a clear dichotomy: Is this bias something I can educate the client to avoid, or it is something that is here to stay? The follow-on question is equally important: Can I live with that bias or is it professionally—and fiduciarily—required that I should simply step away?

Our point in each of the three foregoing categories of constraints is to understand the specific client situation so that any solution we develop together is sensible. On a totally unrelated note, I cannot resist mentioning the poor corporate finance soul who was once advising a client on the other side of the Iron Curtain, while it still existed. Upon facing a client objection to a bond structure he suggested the client should use, he simply offered to transform it into some variation on a convertible bond! Too bad they had no stock market there!!! The analog for us, in the wealth management sphere, would be to offer to use some structure to meet the income needs of a person when that structure is one to which he or she does not have access.

DETERMINING WHETHER ANY CONSTRAINT IS A SHOW-STOPPER

We alluded to this issue in the prior section when we discussed the choice any advisor should feel he or she ought to make: Can I deal with the constraint the client is imposing? Let's also accept that the constraints that can be show-stoppers principally come in the form of investor preferences. Indeed, regulatory or structural issues such as the ones that would be imposed by asset locations tend usually to be manageable on their own, unless a client seeks the kind of return pattern that is only produced by investments that are prohibited by location requirements. At the other end of the spectrum, there is the easy case of the client who does not fully recognize the complexities imposed upon him or her by the structures within which the assets are held and asks the advisor to, effectively, commit fraud. In that situation, the need for the show to stop is not only professional and ethical, but it is also a regulatory mandate.

One important variation on the theme relates to structural constraints that prohibit certain investments, chiefly on the ground of minimum bite size—minimum investment requirement—but also to the extent that they may require disclosures that are viewed by the family or its trustees as inappropriate. Certain forms of commingling may provide partial solutions, but, again, cost and practicality issues may simply rule them out. Other such constraints might apply to cases when trustees or custodians refuse to deal with certain investments without which the needs of the clients cannot be met. It may be that one would like to help the prospect deal with the challenge, but that route is closed or much too complex to be practical in a for-profit business environment.

Turning back to the issue of investor preferences and our third set of constraints, it is worth revisiting an example mentioned in Chapter 8. There, we discussed the case of a wonderful family who had to move away from financial assets and back toward operating businesses because the returns they needed were simply not achievable in our view in financial markets. I suspect that certain advisors, at the time, might have thought that the returns the family sought were achievable; in that case, one should simply assume that different opinions are what make markets. But there may also be advisors who did not think that the goals were achievable. Yet, they would have chosen to humor the client, work to keep the mandate, and in the end fail to achieve the goal of the client. To me, the appropriate approach was simply to "tell it like it is." The client might not be happy, and I might lose the mandate, but at least I can continue to look at myself in the mirror each morning!

Staying with this example for a moment, we can imagine variants on the theme that make it more difficult or, conversely, easier to handle. One could imagine that the returns the client needs are in fact achievable, but require the use of strategies the client rejects. The client only wants to use liquid fixed income strategies and requires equity-like returns, for instance. That is an easy case of constraints being binding. But there may also be cases when the issue is not the return target, but rather the return needs in the face of risk-taking tolerances. Equity-like returns might be needed for some current sum of money to grow to the level that is desired at some future point in time, but the client is unwilling—or has proven unable—to deal with equity-like return volatility. This is a harder case to settle, as there are instances when some sensitive education—and the passing of time—will help alleviate the challenge.

In short, although this is always a very delicate issue, advisors must know what mandates they can accept and those they should not. Years ago, I remember being in an internal meeting at JPM when a client advisor told me: "After all, it is his money!" The advisor was referring to a client who wanted something done which, as the person ultimately responsible, I felt was not sensible. I replied: "Yes, but it is our mandate!" The point was immediately settled, as the advisor was an incredibly perceptive young woman who, years later, thanked me for having drawn that distinction for her. She had understood that she had a responsibility to the client, first, to tell him or her whether the goal was achievable within the constraints he or she set and, second, to walk away from the business opportunity if the client could not be convinced that something has to give when goals and constraints conflict.

TIME HORIZON AND REQUIRED PROBABILITY OF SUCCESS

Our semi-ultimate goal in the process addressed in this chapter is to match client assets with the goals the client aims to achieve. Thus, we must allocate the appropriate amount of asset to each goals-based module (so that each goal can be appropriately "funded") to be able to create an overall aggregated policy that has a real chance of meeting the needs of our client. Irrespective of whether the process revolves around what we called "label-based" goals in Chapter 8, or is more complex and deals with cash flows, time horizons, and probabilities of success, as we described it in Chapter 7, an important decision is to identify the appropriate discount rate, that is, the rate that should be used to translate future cash flows into a current amount of money that should, when judiciously managed, allow the client to meet that goal, over that time frame with a probability of success that reflects its a priori requirement.

Early on, I—and others—fell into the trap of choosing the given module's expected return as the discount rate we applied to the anticipated cash outflows—most often, but not always, the client's anticipated expenses, appropriately indexed to some measure of inflation. The key error in this approach is that it did not recognize the interaction between required probability of success and time horizon. In truth, I had initially overlooked the probability of success issue, at least directly, as I only dealt with it indirectly. For goals I had identified as more crucial than others, I postulated that one could not take excessive investment risk. Yet, I would use the same "label-based" module whether the expenditure stream was expected to last for ten or for twenty years; thus, I would apply the same discount rate to either set of cash flows.

The fact that I arrived at solutions that did not seem to make sense naturally led me to find the error, and this is when I "discovered" the interaction between time horizon and expected return at some required probability of success. I use quotation marks, as this was almost as obvious a step as the proverbial discovery of warm water! Figure 9.1 illustrates the idea that, even assuming that returns are normally distributed and thus can be represented by a bell curve, one must be careful to differentiate between the median return—which, in a normal distribution, is the same as the mean or the average—and the return such that there is a set probability that it will be either met or exceeded. In the example in the figure, we show the difference between the mean and the return that should be met or exceeded 90 percent of the time. It stands to reason that a return that will be met or exceeded 90 percent of the time is considerably lower than the median, which should be met or exceeded exactly 50 percent of the time.

Certain people initially objected to this formulation of the discount rate, as, by definition, the return that we use will be met or *exceeded*. Thus, it is likely that the sum of money that is set aside will turn out to be more than actually needed. Yet, the objection quickly crumbles in the face of the behavioral finance principles we discussed in Chapter 5: individuals are worried

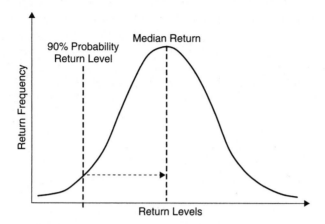

FIGURE 9.1 Illustrating the Difference Between Median and Probability-Based Discount Rate[2]

about shortfall, not about exceeding their goals.[3] The real challenge would be to under-budget for a goal rather than to budget too much. Anticipating an issue we will discuss later, this leaves us some room to revisit certain decisions—in terms of sizing the assets needed to meet a goal—for those clients whose total assets appear insufficient to meet all goals. At times,

---

[2]Certain readers will find the depth and detail in this table and the discussion that follows either excessive or simply too hard to follow. The main idea is that, even with a portfolio with a given expected return and expected return volatility, various actual outcomes are not only possible, but in truth probable. Thus, the probability of achieving a return that meet expectations is just 50 percent. The more I seek to be sure that the return I expect will be met, the lower than return must be with that same portfolio.

[3]In fact, it may be worth discussing this in more depth. Mental accounts are a crucial behavioral finance foundation and are defined as the "pockets" that are mentally set aside by someone to deal with some goal or set of transactions. Schlomo Bernatzi and Richard Thaler (Bernatzi, Shlomo, and Richard H. Thaler. "Myopic Loss Aversion and the Equity Premium Puzzle." *Quarterly Journal of Economics*, February 1995, pp. 73–92.) used that concept to justify their idea that the avoidance of short-term losses—ergo the term "myopic"—was an individual challenge; incurring a loss resulted from "closing a mental account" while allowing that loss to run was less painful as the mental account remained open. Thus, any approach that breaks the link between a goal and the module or mental account that serves to fund and defease it is fraught with danger, even if meant with all the best intentions, such as raising the overall expected return of the overall portfolio.

simply cutting the required probability of success from 95 percent to 85 percent might suffice to go from an asset deficit to some small surplus. Is it truly crucial for you, dear client, that this goal be viewed as a need that must be met versus a want that should be met?

In general, one can formulate two simple rules to help one understand the dynamic of time horizons and required probabilities of success. First, it stands to reason that the longer the time horizon, the more risk can be taken at any given level of required probability of success. Although short-term volatility of returns would be higher, time would help smooth that volatility out. Second, it is also clear that, for any given time horizon, the higher the required probability of success, the lower the investment risks that can be taken. Except for advisors whose firms have chosen to have "label-based" goals-based modules, the challenge when deciding which module to choose for which goal revolves around looking for the module that produces the highest expected return at a given time horizon with a set required probability of success[4].

Tables 9.1 and 9.2 illustrate this issue and help make the simple point that settling on the appropriate module does not have to be terribly complicated. Table 9.1 requires some initial explanation. It shows the maximum return available across all modules over the given time horizon and at some given level of required probability. These data are obtained by applying to all modules the process that is illustrated in Figure 9.1. As return distributions are assumed to be normal, we can calculate what the return is that will be met or exceeded, over each of the various time horizons, with each of the required given probabilities of success.[5] The data in each of the cells of Table 9.1 represents the maximum return available across all modules for each given probability of success[6] and over the relevant time horizon. The only exception to this rule is an arbitrary decision we make to force the

---

[4]Note an important consideration: success is defined here in terms of meeting a set of cash flow needs *during* or *over* a time horizon rather than meeting each and every cash flow in each and every year comprising that horizon. It should thus be clear that certain goals where cash flow requirements *must* be met each and every year may necessitate that each yearly requirement be set as a separate goal rather than aggregated with other similar requirements over the horizon when that category of obligation persists.

[5]For those readers who are used to the Excel software, this is achieved using NORMINV function that specifies mean, variance, and probability of success. Further, the estimated mean return for time horizon x is derived from the average annual return times x, while the estimated standard deviation of return is derived from the annual standard deviation times the square root of x.

[6]Although Table 9.1 shows a distribution of possible probabilities that is quite detailed—probabilities change by increments of 5 percent—it may actually be more

TABLE 9.1 Maximum Expected Return at Given Horizons and Success Probability[7]

Goal: to Seek to		Success						
Achieve	Avoid	Probability	5	10	15	20	25	30
Dreams	Concerns	50%	8.9%	8.9%	8.9%	8.9%	8.9%	8.9%
		55%	8.2%	8.4%	8.5%	8.6%	8.6%	8.6%
		60%	7.5%	7.9%	8.1%	8.2%	8.3%	8.3%
Wishes	Worries	65%	7.0%	7.4%	7.7%	7.9%	8.0%	8.0%
		70%	6.4%	7.0%	7.3%	7.5%	7.6%	7.7%
		75%	5.9%	6.6%	6.9%	7.1%	7.3%	7.4%
Wants	Fears	80%	5.2%	6.2%	6.6%	6.8%	7.0%	7.1%
		85%	4.5%	5.6%	6.2%	6.5%	6.7%	6.8%
Needs	Nightmares	90%	1.1%	5.0%	5.6%	6.0%	6.2%	6.4%
		95%	0.3%	4.2%	4.8%	5.3%	5.6%	5.9%

return of the lowest risk module into the table, for the 90 percent and 95 percent probability levels and the five-year time horizon. The insight is that we fear that the five-year time period may not fit the conditions of the law of large numbers—which we covered in Chapter 5—on which probability theory is partially based.

---

practical to consider making changes in larger increments. We need to be able to look at four "steps"—the ones corresponding to needs, wants, wishes, and dreams—but we may also need to recognize that nobody really knows the difference between a 60 percent and a 65 percent probability of success! Thus, using the example here, one might look for the average probability of success associated with each of the four categories: 55 percent for dreams, 70 percent for wishes, 82.5 percent for wants, and 92.5 percent for needs, and calculating the respective maximum expected returns across the various modules for these probabilities! The fundamental point must be that the process is more systematic than quantitative: clients and advisors should focus on the rigor of a systematic approach more than on the precision of a quantitative result.

[7]Just as was the case with Figure 9.1 and will be the case with Table 9.2, the point may be too complex for certain readers. Suffice it to say that the interactions among expected return, expected return volatility, time horizon, and required probability of success drives the actual return that can be expected for a given portfolio at some given time horizon with some required probability of success. Given the fact that we have constructed six modules in the example, Tables 9.1 and 9.2 simply inform us of what the highest reasonable expected return should be under the given conditions and what module is most likely to generate it.

TABLE 9.2 Modules Expected to Generate the Highest Expected Return at Given Horizons and Success Probability

| Goal: to Seek to | | Success Probability | 5 | 10 | 15 | 20 | 25 | 30 |
Achieve	Avoid							
Dreams	Concerns	50%	G	G	G	G	G	G
		55%	R G	G	G	G	G	G
		60%	R G	R G	R G	R G	R G	G
Wishes	Worries	65%	R PP	R G	R G	R G	R G	R G
		70%	R PP	R PP	R G	R G	R G	R G
		75%	R PP	R PP	R PP	R PP	R G	R G
Wants	Fears	80%	R PP	R PP	R PP	R PP	R PP	R PP
		85%	LT L	R PP	R PP	R PP	R PP	R PP
Needs	Nightmares	90%	ST L	R PP	R PP	R PP	R PP	R PP
		95%	ST L	LT L	R PP	R PP	R PP	R PP

SETTLING ON THE APPROPRIATE MODULE

Taking this to the logical conclusion of this part of the goals-based wealth management process, the advisor, who will by now have a sense of what his or her client's goals are, will be able to select the module best suited to each goal by looking in the table at the cell that has the correct time horizon and the correct required probability of success. For instance, in Table 9.1, one would expect a discount rate of 0.3 percent for a goal that runs over five years and is required to be achieved with a 95 percent probability; conversely, one might chose a 7.7 percent discount rate for a goal that is required to be achieved with a 70 percent probability at the end of a thirty-year time horizon. In this context, Table 9.2 simply completes the sequence by showing which module provides the highest possible return at each time horizon and for each given probability of success.[8] Because the yardstick here is the highest reasonable appropriate return and because this return will often be used to discount the expected cash flows to determine the size of the pool of assets that must be applied to each goal, you can think of the choice of this or that module as the selection of the lowest possible funding cost to achieve a particular goal.[9]

---

[8]Here, we limit our module choice to the six modules that fit a client's asset class and strategy preferences, assumed in this case to extend to all forms of traditional, alternative, and even illiquid strategies.
[9]I am indebted to Robert E. Mallernee and W. Jackson Parham for this insightful formulation.

At this point, a reader who is not an advisor might wonder why he or she needs to process through all this detail. The answer is simple: "You do not need to, but it should be useful for you to know how the various advisors make their sausages!" Understanding how they determine the advice they will eventually give to their clients should help the wealthy feel comfortable with the solution and the integrity of the process used.

An important note of caution required before we turn to advisors whose firms use label-based modules: for the two modules that have a real—that is, inflation-adjusted—return goal, it may be necessary to exercise special care. Indeed, we implicitly accept the notion that we are seeking a different risk/return trade-off to benefit from the inflation protection provided by real assets; yet, the truth is that, although this postulate might be valid over time and on average, there may well be instances, for example, when there is persistently low inflation, when the heavy real asset—commodities in particular—portfolio exposure will cause returns to be both more volatile and lower, which is not what we expected. So with respect to the purchasing power protection modules, it may make sense to overrule the model in these circumstances when the inflation risk is perceived to be particularly low and to replace the real purchasing power module with either nominal purchasing power or nominal growth, as the case may be. Similarly, but in reverse, the real growth module trades lower returns and lower volatility for a chance to earn higher returns when inflation—particularly cost-push inflation—is severe; again, it might be a good idea to question the output of the model if inflation is not an issue and replace the recommended real growth module with the nominal capital preservation alternative.

For advisors whose firms use label-based modules, the process of settling on the appropriate module is simpler in that the choice is not really dependent on either time horizon or required probability of success, both of which are hypothetically subsumed into the definition and formulation of the modules.

I would highly recommend that advisors in these circumstances still develop the same kind of matrix as in Table 9.1, except that, rather than looking for the highest return among all the modules, they simply develop an array of expected returns at each probability level and over each time horizon for each module. At the very least, they should do so with respect to the two modules—in our earlier example in Chapter 8—which are designed to defease lifestyle expenditures. It is indeed less necessary to conduct the exercise for the growth and capital preservation modules, particularly when they are used to invest assets whose amount is set initially as an absolute number or as a percentage of total wealth rather than in reference to the goal of achieving some minimum terminal value. For those cases when the goal is indeed to achieve some terminal value, then it will be necessary to have a sense of what the expected return is that we should use to size the capital that must be set aside today, given the time horizon and required probability of success. For instance, echoing back to the earlier comment about the fallacy of using the mean expected return as the discount rate, and assuming the goal of wanting to leave $10 million in today's purchasing power terms to the next generation in twenty years' time with a 70 percent probability of success, one would need to know first whether this is best achieved with a capital preservation or a growth strategy and, second, what the expected return is for the module chosen at the twenty-year time horizon and with the 70 percent required probability of success.

SIZING ASSETS NEEDED TO MEET EACH GOAL

Although the topic must be covered here to preserve the logical chronology of our effort, it will by necessity be a short reference: we have looked into the topic twice before in the foregoing paragraphs.

Fundamentally, we are addressing here the final goal of the second step of the process described in Figure 6.1: sizing the assets required to meet each of our client goals. Three issues must be addressed.

First, for goals that involve specific cash flows, whether addressed via label-based or probability/time horizon-based modules, the process simply involves discounting the specific cash flow with the appropriate rate so that a declining balance portfolio invested today in the appropriate module would have the correct probability to meet or exceed the client's goal over the required time horizon.[10] This has been the meat of the last two sections we discussed in this chapter.

Second, for goals that involve achieving some form of desired terminal value, again at some set time horizon and with some set required probability of success, the process is similar to what we would follow in the preceding paragraph. This can indeed be considered a special case of the one we handled there, with the desired cash flows represented by one single terminal pay-off rather than a series of yearly expenditures.

Third, for goals that are set either in absolute terms or in relation to the asset base—either a single amount of money in today's dollars or as a percentage of current asset levels—the issue is somewhat moot: the starting

---

[10]Again, there are a few circumstances when an endowment portfolio makes sense, usually because of wealth transfer or another asset location issue. The general case, as argued in Chapter 6, remains that such portfolios most often tend to be of a declining balance type.

point of the client's thinking is, in fact, the terminal point of ours. The issue can become a bit more complex if a client desires that some share of future assets be used to meet some goal, with an additional minimum required amount. For instance: "I would like 50 percent of our assets in thirty years' time to go to the next generation, but this should not be less than $10 million, with a 75 percent required probability of success." This effectively requires some measure of iteration in order to arrive at a decision as to how the assets should be managed.

A POSSIBLE EXAMPLE

The foregoing discussion may have been a bit theoretical or esoteric. Therefore, a simple case study may help put things in the proper perspective. I hope that the combination of the description of principles and processes and their actual practical application will allow me to deal with all readers, whether they have a theoretical or a practical set of intellectual preferences, and whether they are in the client or the advisor category.

Let me set the stage with a hypothetical client. Let us assume a family with a total financial wealth of $50 million. The family spends $1,000,000 each year, and agrees with our assumption that inflation will average around 3 percent per year for the foreseeable future; income taxes are currently paid out of these funds. The family states that it wants to meet its annual expenditures with a 95 percent probability over the next five years. They want their lifestyle expenses provided for with an 80 percent probability for the next twenty-five years after that, which corresponds roughly to the couple's life expectancy, as they are both fifty-five years old. Upon further discussion, the family reveals that $10 million of their current assets are set aside in grantor trusts for their four children and that they have been paying the taxes on the income earned by these trusts. They also indicate that they have $5 million in generation-skipping trusts that were recently set up, and on which they are also paying taxes. They assign growth goals to each of these pools of assets. Assuming that all goes well, the family would like to set up a family foundation in ten years, and they have mentally set $10 million as the initial funding size. The family also indicates that, although they recognize it may not make the most sense in financial terms, they want to keep $3 million in cash or near cash, as what they call "pillow money." For whatever assets that are surplus to these requirements, the family indicates that it would like to invest in an equal mix of growth and capital preservation; these funds are earmarked for distribution to future generations and to charity in, at present, unspecified shares. The family finally tells the advisor that $10 million of their total assets are held in retirement accounts, which the husband

and wife know they cannot expect to use to meet their expenses for at least fifteen years.[11]

My first request of you, dear readers, is that, if you are wealth advisors, you stop reading now and use the data in the case study to come up with you own suggested allocation. For readers who are among the industry's potential clients, and if this looks remotely like circumstances that might fit your own, please take the time to compare both process and outcomes to your experience. The point is certainly not to stick someone's proverbial nose in it, but to show that our section entitled "It Changes Everything" in Chapter 6 was not sheer hype.

How do we handle this case in the goals-based wealth management process? The first step is for us to create "accounts" reflecting instances for which we have different ownership or beneficiary structures. Initially, it would seem that there are at least four and possibly five "accounts," although an additional account will need to be created in ten years' time to reflect the initial funding of the family foundation. What are the initial accounts?

1. The "pillow money" portfolio stands by itself, as it has little or no interactions with the rest of the family's money;
2. The two grantor trusts might stand by themselves, as they are both designated as future growth vehicles. Yet, experience suggests that they will probably have to be split into two different accounts. Why? Simply because, at some point, the taxes on the income earned by the non-GST trusts might become so onerous that the family will choose not to pay them anymore and thus require that the trusts pay them.
3. The retirement accounts also stand by themselves, at least for the next fifteen years, as they cannot be used to defease lifestyle expenses until then and because they can earn tax-free returns that can be compounded within the accounts until it becomes mandatory under U.S. tax laws to draw some income from them.
4. The balance of the wealth represents the sums that both need to be invested so as to defease lifestyle expenditures and to grow assets, both for the initial funding of the family foundation and for future transfers to the next generations and to philanthropy.

Having identified these individual "accounts," we are now ready to set them up separately and to see how the goals assigned to each of them should

---

[11]For non-U.S. readers, this restriction reflects the rule that certain private pension accounts may remain untapped until one reaches 70.5 years of age.

determine how they might be invested. A critical step in this process will be to keep watching that the fourth account above, the one from which the first generation supports its living and a part of its future goals, is sufficiently funded.

1. The size of our first account is given to us in the text: $3 million.
2. Whether the grantor trusts and the GSTs are split into two accounts or not, we do know that, combined, they are worth $15 million.
3. Again, the size of our third account—or fourth if the grantor and generation-skipping trusts are split into two accounts—which represents the retirement assets, is also given: $10 million.
4. Our fourth account is thus equal to the balance, $22 million.

Unfortunately, our challenge is not completed here. We must ascertain whether $22 million is sufficient to cover the goals the first generation has set, assuming first that there is no need to defease any expense from the retirement accounts. The analysis shows that the family can achieve its goals, although the first generation will likely find that it is constrained in its ability to finance much of a generational or philanthropic transfer from funds other than the retirement accounts.

1. Our analysis suggests that the first generation needs $5.2 million to meet its $1 million expense coverage for the next five years. This simply reflects the assumption that inflation will average 2 percent initially—during the first five years—and then trend back to 3 percent thereafter, and that portfolio returns will only be 0.3 percent at the 95 percent confidence level.
2. The first generation will need $11 million to finance its expenses from years six through thirty, the apparently low amount reflecting the fact that the longer horizon and the lower required certainty (80 percent versus 95 percent for the first five years) will allow one to assume a higher discount rate (7.1 percent versus 0.3 percent).
3. The family will need to set aside $6.6 million to have a 95 percent chance of funding a $10 million private family foundation in ten years.
4. Having done all of this, the family will only have $2.1 million left over from the original $25 million—inclusive of the "pillow money"—after having funded their expense defeasance and their family foundation. Ostensibly, the $10 million held through the retirement accounts has the potential to grow to $80 million at the end of thirty years, assuming no withdrawal. However, there clearly will have to be withdrawals, as tax laws in the United States require minimum withdrawals from retirement accounts once the beneficiary reaches age 70.5! We will address this contradiction later.

Our final step is to match each of these accounts with the appropriate goals-based module. This is where things can become a bit more complex. Indeed, we must note that each of the various "accounts" we defined earlier may actually comprise more than one goal. The first account has a sole goal—pillow money—and is thus likely to require the use of the lowest risk module, which we call here "short-term lifestyle." All the others may actually require the use of more than one module. We explicitly just saw that, in the case of the $22 million the first generation has total control over—after having set aside the assets representing the pillow money—we actually have at least four different modules:

1. The assets designated to defease family lifestyle expenditures for the next five years will also require the use of the short-term lifestyle module.
2. The assets needed to defease family lifestyle expenditures for the twenty-five years starting in year six will require the use of the "real purchasing power" module, for the reasons stated earlier.
3. The assets designed to grow into the initial funding for the family foundation will require the use of the "nominal purchasing power" module, because of the high required probability of success only partially offset by the ten-year time horizon.
4. Finally, the limited "surplus assets" will require the use of two modules "nominal purchasing power" and "growth," in line with the family's stated risk profile for that part of their assets.

One could also argue that the retirement assets must meet more than one goal. In this current iteration, we see them as "surplus" because they are not called upon to help meet lifestyle spending. We are explicitly assuming no withdrawal from these accounts despite the legal requirement to do so, but will correct that "mistake" later, when the additional complexity can be more easily understood by readers who will, by then, have a better sense of the full process. So they will probably also require the use of two nominal purchasing power and growth modules in line with the family's stated risk profile (with a corresponding decline in the size of the assets from the $22 million) dedicated to defease expenditures.

In short, we can see that different amounts, from different accounts, will have to be invested across most of our modules to allow the family to meet their goals.

We will come back to this case study in our next chapter, when we bring these various module allocations together to create an investment policy for the family. Indeed, the point we just reached is not the final iteration, because one should do some sensitivity analysis on at least two fronts. First, one should see whether having the grantor trusts pay their own taxes starting five years from now frees up a substantial amount of potential capital to be used to make generational and charitable transfers. Second, more importantly, one should also look at the investment policy for the retirement accounts in more depth to evaluate the impact on the taxable family account of not having to support their full expense defeasance. We will cover this deeper analysis in our next chapter, as our purpose here was simply to illustrate how one would proceed to match goals and modules.

SUMMARY AND CONCLUSIONS

One can honestly argue that the steps covered in this chapter represent the crux of the goals-based wealth management process. Clearly, one could not perform any of the tasks in Chapter 9 without having done the work covered in Chapter 8. We need the capital market forecast and generic goals-based modules to assess which module is required for which goal and what discount rate should be used to evaluate the assets that should accrue to each goal. Anticipating Chapter 10, matching client goals and modules is only useful and sensible if one takes it to the next step of combining these modules into an aggregate investment policy.

The critical take-away from this chapter is the trade-off between time horizon and required probability and the way this should drive both the choice of the kind of risk profile appropriate for each individual goal and, by helping determine the appropriate discount rate, the dollar amount of assets that must be dedicated to each goal. Remembering what we said in Chapters 5 and 6, it is a crucial element of individual wealth management to recognize that the investor's risk profile is built from the bottom up rather than the top down, as would typically be done in an institution. Thus, matching each of an investor's goals with the module—a different way of talking of a risk/return trade-off for each goal—that will achieve the goal at the lowest cost (with the highest expected return, since the required probability of success and the time horizon are input and not output variables) is the essence of what we are trying to achieve.

The process is not complex, although it involves rather cumbersome computations at times, but it is delicate. It requires intellectual honesty and rigor and a willingness to go through several iterations if one finds that the assets of the clients are insufficient or simply borderline sufficient or if small changes in required probabilities of success could move from asset sufficiency to asset insufficiency. It must be deliberate and acceptable to explain assumptions, but not to debate them. This why I separated the contents of Chapters 8 and 9. I wanted to illustrate that these are distinct steps and that, although obviously related, they should be carried out as independently as possible.

CHAPTER 10

Finalizing a Goals-Based Policy Allocation

This chapter is the final phase of the troika that together constitutes the strategic goals-based asset allocation process. We will still need to cover two important issues when we are through with this chapter, but our starting point was the need to develop an investment policy. We postulate that one cannot develop a goals-based investment policy without first creating the basic architecture within which we want to operate—this is what we covered in Chapter 8, with the various steps leading to the creation of goals-based modules. Our second step required us to match individual client needs and the assets required to meet them with the various modules we had thus created; this we did in Chapter 9. This final step involves pulling the modules together and proceeding from a series of modules to which some various assets amounts had been dedicated to an overall strategic asset allocation, which will form the basis of the ongoing management of the assets.

TWO POSSIBLE APPROACHES

Before going further, it is worth taking a side-step to discuss an important variant on the theme. One can imagine two completely different designs within which one can handle family assets: the first is a single portfolio, a separately managed account, while the second is a combination of commingling structures, whether family dedicated—goals-based family partnerships would be an example—or commercially available, such as registered investment companies or something similar. Cultural as well as economic factors combine to influence the decision to use one or the other approach.

Culturally, many families, particularly in the United States, but also in a few Asian countries, would find it difficult to see a report on their portfolio that only comprised a handful of lines: one for each module, effectively. Thus, those who tend to agree to go that route tend to be those who cannot afford anything "better" and who dream of the day when they can actually move "up" to a "more customized solution." Here, in short, economics trump cultural preferences.

Yet, in other cultures, particularly in Europe, where certain investors have less difficulty with the idea of a portfolio of mutual funds, the idea of creating goals-based structures aligned with the various modules is actually quite tempting. Luxembourg, for instance, with their world-leading Undertakings for Collective Investment in Transferable Securities (UCITS) platform,[1] is a logical locus for many of these funds to be created, and many firms have used it to commingle client assets. Unfortunately, this commingling has hitherto not been focused on goals-based modules, but transitioning to that new modus operandi would not present much of an operational challenge. It is probably worth adding here that such an approach has significant favorable attributes when it comes to reporting, particularly at the module—or goal—level.

An important drawback of commingling structures is that they do not always provide the required tax transparency so that each investor is able to take maximum advantage of provisions that allow one to offset capital gains with losses. Numerous partnerships offer this ability with both "inside tax basis" and "outside tax basis;" yet, for smaller investors for whom limited partnerships are not feasible, the use of traditional registered investment companies may prevent them from fully maximizing their own tax-efficiency, although they would implicitly still be optimizing, as the latter requires us to deal with practicalities.

Operational advances have actually made commingling structures more palatable to many from a cultural standpoint, to the extent that they involve "core and satellites" designs under the terms of which each satellite investor is able to see his or her proportional share of all the underlying line-item investments in the core. Although it is not always possible, currently, to combine this with the tax transparency that one would wish to have, one can surmise that the time is not too far away when this issue will be tackled, too.

Interestingly, the economics can change dramatically for families that are large enough to devise family-dedicated goals-based module structures. There, the cultural issue fades into the background and it becomes a case of being better able to execute the myriad transactions that might be required

---

[1]According to Investopedia, these funds are a European Union "creation" in that a UCITS is a "public limited company that coordinates the distribution and management of unit trusts amongst countries within the European Union ... These funds can be marketed within all countries that are a part of the European Union, provided that the fund and fund managers are registered within the domestic country. The regulation recognizes that each country within the European Union may differ on their specific disclosure requirements."

when there are many individual asset pools, with their own individual break-down into goals-based modules.

In the balance of this chapter, we will assume that all individual assets are held separately and will therefore discuss the process that leads to a single investment policy formulated based on the combination, in the appropriate proportion, of the various modules into a single portfolio. Ostensibly, the thought process is no different than the one we would use with commingled structures: it simply goes one step further in that investments that may be held in different modules are aggregated into a single line in the overall portfolio, rather than being listed in their distinct smaller individual amounts in each module. In short, we will be discussing the most complex version of the process, with the use of commingled structures simplifying certain aspects with selected new or additional costs in certain instances.

WORKING FROM ASSETS AND MODULES TO A WHOLE

As Chapter 9 progressed, we could see that two things were developing:

1. Specific goals within specific holding structures were being matched with one or several goals-based modules.
2. The assets needed to defease those goals were ascertained, using either appropriately discounted cash flows or set dollar amounts.

It is worth recalling our restaurant analogy here. We discussed the difference between the dishes as they are served and the ingredients, sauces, and the like as they are brought together to create these dishes. We saw that Chapter 8 really dealt with the process which took place in the kitchen, whereas Chapter 9 invited us—as restaurant owners—to sit down with our diner and discuss what it is that he or she wanted to eat. In Chapter 10, we now focus on the whole meal, to stick with this restaurant analogy.

We have the building blocks we need: the set of goals-based modules we want to use and the dollar allocation each goal requires to be invested in the appropriate module to meet our client's needs. We have checked that the total assets required is less than or equal to the total financial wealth available. The investment policy that is to be proposed to each client thus brings together our building blocks.

Yet, before reaching this step, it is worth noting that each "account" (in the parlance of this chapter) has its own set of goals, each of which requires allocating some of its assets to the goals it is intended to meet. Thus, in the example proposed in Chapter 9:

1. The "Pillow Money" account allocates all of its assets to the short-term lifestyle goal. Its own "sub-investment policy" is thus the asset allocation of the Short-Term Lifestyle module.

2. The "Grantor Trusts" account is allocated 30/70 to the Real Growth and Growth modules. Its sub-investment policy is a 30/70 weighted average of the allocations of these two modules.

3. The "GSTs" account is allocated 5/95 to the Real Growth and Growth modules. Its sub-investment policy is a 5/95 weighted average of the allocations of these two modules.

4. The "IRAs" account is initially allocated 30/70 to the Real Growth and Growth modules. Its sub-investment policy is a 30/70 weighted average of the allocations of these two modules.

5. The allocation of the "Family" account is more complex, as it reflects its focus on several goals. We will return to this in more detail when we revisit the example of this family at the end of this chapter.

Thus, the overall investment policy is a weighted average of the individual sub-policies, where the weights are the ratios of the actual dollar values of each "account" relative to the family's total wealth. Table 10.1 illustrates this process, showing each account's individual sub-policy in each vertical column and the overall policy in the right-most column of the table. Note that this example illustrates one of the most important benefits associated with the goals-based wealth management process: each policy is unique. It would indeed be quite an unusual occurrence to see two families have exactly the same amount of financial wealth, distributed among the same structures, weighted in exactly the same proportions. Add to this the requirement that their actual goals—those that are used to allocate assets within each of the various structures to meet these goals—be exactly the same and one realizes that the odds of two policies eventually being the same are certainly not tempting. And this is so, despite the fact that the advisor they both use is the same and would thus use the same set of goals-based modules! Simple arithmetic suggests, as mentioned in Chapter 6, that there would be 1,001 possible policies, assuming that each goal—or account—has dedicated assets that represent a set fraction of total family financial wealth expressed to the first decimal point. Mass customization can be quite an impressive process!

DESCRIPTION OF DEVIATION RANGES

For those who feel that tactical portfolio tilting—or changed portfolio weights to reflect anticipated out- and under-performance for certain asset classes or strategies in response to anticipated market conditions—can add value, it is still important to set limits to how far from home they can move. My first boss at J.P. Morgan—the late John A. Weed—used

TABLE 10.1 Example of Family Investment Policy Process

Asset Class/Strategy	6.0% 3,000,000 Pillow Money	20.0% 10,000,000 Grantor Trusts	10.0% 5,000,000 GSTs	20.0% 10,000,000 IRAs	44.0% 22,000,000 Family	100.0% 50,000,000 Family Total
Cash	25.7%	2.8%	2.7%	3.0%	7.6%	7.6%
U.S. Fixed Income Inv. Grade	55.7%	0.0%	0.0%	0.0%	18.3%	18.3%
U.S. Fixed Income HY	6.5%	0.1%	0.2%	0.0%	1.5%	1.5%
EAFE Fixed Income Hedged	6.5%	0.0%	0.0%	0.0%	1.5%	1.5%
EM Debt	5.6%	0.1%	0.2%	0.0%	1.3%	1.3%
Relative Value Multy Strategy	0.0%	0.3%	0.4%	0.0%	4.0%	4.0%
Global Macro	0.0%	0.2%	0.2%	0.0%	4.0%	4.0%
Illiquid Fixed Income	0.0%	0.0%	0.0%	0.0%	3.0%	3.0%
U.S. Equities	0.0%	18.8%	21.4%	11.3%	3.0%	3.0%
EAFE Equities	0.0%	14.6%	16.7%	8.8%	2.3%	2.3%
EM Equities	0.0%	8.3%	9.5%	5.0%	1.3%	1.3%
Directional Hedge Eq L/S	0.0%	5.4%	7.4%	0.0%	2.9%	2.9%
Managed Futures	0.0%	3.6%	4.9%	0.0%	1.2%	1.2%
Illiquid Equities	0.0%	18.5%	19.4%	16.0%	1.7%	1.7%
REITs	0.0%	10.7%	8.0%	18.1%	17.5%	17.5%
Precious Metals	0.0%	3.3%	0.6%	11.2%	8.8%	8.8%
Commodities	0.0%	3.8%	0.6%	12.6%	9.5%	9.5%
Illiquid Real Assets	0.0%	9.4%	7.8%	14.0%	10.4%	10.4%
Overall Total	100.0%	100.0%	100.0%	100.0%	100.0%	100.0%

to tell us young analysts: "You should have enough discretion to hang yourselves, but not enough to hang portfolio managers." I have modified this wonderful insight a number of times to reflect the idea that there are always both a primary purpose and secondary or intermediate targets. Thus, with respect to the management of an individual's financial wealth, the primary purpose must be to reach the various goals set out by the client. At the same time, a secondary or intermediate target might be to try to do better than the passively applied policy, if and when one thinks one has insights into how various asset classes and strategies might perform in the nearer term. Paying appropriate attention to the primary goal requires the investor—whether he or she is the client or an advisor—to retain the broad risk profile inherent in the policy—the profile that was appropriately determined from the bottom up. Taking advantage of potential market insights involves being prepared to move enough away from the policy that the trade does make a difference—the local equivalent of "enough room to hang ourselves"—but not so much that one ends up taking too much risk relative to the policy—the local equivalent of "the rope that could lead one to hang the client."

Whether in the institutional or the private wealth management world, deciding how much rope should be given—which is principally in the realm of overall risk control—typically involves setting ranges around each of the policy positions that determine minimum and maximum positions in each of the various asset classes and categories.

Personally, I take this one step further in that I like to set ranges both for individual strategies or asset classes, but I add to them ranges for what one might call the "mega" asset classes. In the example in Table 10.1, there are eighteen different asset classes and strategies and, arguably, four mega asset classes. In many ways, these directly map back to the constraints we discussed in Chapter 8:

1. Cash, which is the only asset for which there is likely no narrower a range than from 0 percent to 100 percent. Ostensibly, other ranges will prevent the extremes of this cash range from being reached, but one needs to have some area that serves to balance the portfolio out to 100 percent.
2. Lower half of the volatility spectrum: this comprises all the fixed income strategies, liquid and illiquid, together with the three non-traditional strategies which, typically, provide return patterns that are in the lower half of the volatility spectrum, but have characteristics that are quite different from those of fixed income assets.
3. Equity spectrum, which comprises long-only equities, liquid and illiquid, and non-traditional strategies such as long/short equities and managed futures.

4. Diversifiers, or real assets, which comprise a variety of commodities, real estate, and related investments, liquid or illiquid, which often have lower correlations with financial assets than what prevails within financial markets and offer certain hedging benefits in certain environments.

Once these categories are established, one can then proceed to establish ranges for both asset classes and strategies and mega asset classes. I have traditionally recommended to clients that the ranges for mega asset classes be wider than those set for individual asset classes or strategies, but not so much as to allow each and every individual asset class to be at its maximum or minimum simultaneously. I believe that mega asset classes, to the extent that they do reflect an aggregation of strategies that have certain common features, must still be tightly controlled, as they are the place where it is easiest to change dramatically the overall risk profile of a portfolio, unless one is careful not to. For instance, it is not unusual for me to specify ranges that allow asset class or strategy weights to vary up to 10 percent on either side of their policy position, all the while limiting the overall resulting mega asset class variations to only 15 percent on either side of their policy norm. It is also a good idea, in my opinion, to consider using narrower ranges for strategies that tend to have lower liquidity. There are two reasons for this. The first, which stands to reason, is that it makes little sense to "decide" to allow a large variation in a position that is insufficiently liquid for that variation to be executed. The second is a second-degree variation on the same theme: while it may be possible to execute a trade that takes a position away from its neutral allocation, one is never sure that the reverse trade will be feasible when the time comes to execute it. In a similar vein, there may be a delay between the time a decision is made and the time it is executed, because of liquidity considerations; thus, being humble and only allowing modest moves recognizes the practical limitations under which one will labor.[2] Finally, we prohibit shorting any strategy or asset class and thus have all lines showing a minimum of zero, just as we do not allow leverage and thus do not have any line with a maximum greater than 100%.

Ostensibly, one can add several dimensions to this concept of deviation ranges, just as we had a few of them in the optimization process. One could create "super" strategies that aggregate asset classes or strategies across mega asset classes—alternative assets would be an easy one. Passive versus active management could be another, as could the creation of "alpha"

---

[2]Following this point to its ultimate logical conclusion might suggest that variation ranges for partially liquid strategies—such as alternative assets that may mandate notice periods and specified redemption dates—might also be narrower than those used for traditional, long-only strategies.

versus "beta" strategies, which would group together those strategies that have possibly high manager risk versus those that should have low to minimum manager risk.

In the same vein, but expressed differently, many investment policies go beyond asset allocation ranges. Traditionally, these reflect various security or operational level constraints, such as credit quality in the fixed income world or deviation from market portfolio capitalization weights in both fixed income and equity arenas. Certain families can set limits to those managers who are expected to be tax-inefficient or to managers whose fees exceed some industry average. Others set limits in terms of a maximum percentage of their assets to be entrusted to a single manager, or to how much of a manager's total assets under management their own mandate could be. In the end, policy constraints can be viewed as a reflection of the family's need for control.

Whether focusing on deviation ranges or on individual portfolio constraints, the primary goal of this phase of the policy formulation process is to set out, ahead of time and away from the heat of the moment, generic guidelines that should govern the way the portfolio is managed on a continuing basis. Many advisors, principally those who are also money managers, would like to have as much of a free hand as possible, often arguing that diversification and guidelines amount to shooting for mediocrity. At some level, they may be intellectually correct. Yet, they often miss two important points. First, delegating discretion is a difficult task and lack of control brings stress; one thing that wealthy people often feel they do not need is more stress. Just as many commercial airline pilots silently long for the days when their flight plans were much less rigid, those who are most successful and responsible gladly admit that the main task of a commercial pilot is to manage a trajectory! Success is measured in having exactly the same number of take-offs and landings, not in how quickly one could climb or descend! Second, besides the obvious comfort dimension, there must also be the recognition that no part of the portfolio stands on its own: each sub-portfolio is part and parcel of a greater whole and success or failure are felt and measured at the overall portfolio level at least as much as at the manager level! Individual managers may not have that necessary piece of the puzzle.

OUR ORIGINAL EXAMPLE, MODIFIED AND COMPLETED

When we first dealt with our family case study in Chapter 9, we elected to keep things as simple as possible. Our goal was to focus on the move from individual goals to goals-based modules. Now, it is time to consider the issue in more depth. As discussed earlier in this chapter, the principal change is that we must recognize that each "account" may have multiple goals. Thus, we

TABLE 10.2 Sub-Investment Policy for Pillow Money

| | Account Size | | 3,000,000 |
Asset Class/Strategy	100% STL	Actual Allocation STL	Sub-Investment Policy
Cash	25.7%	771,717	25.7%
U.S. Fixed Income Inv. Grade	55.7%	1,671,212	55.7%
U.S. Fixed Income HY	6.5%	194,975	6.5%
EAFE Fixed Income Hedged	6.5%	194,975	6.5%
EM Debt	5.6%	167,121	5.6%
Relative Value Multy Strategy	0.0%	0	0.0%
Global Macro	0.0%	0	0.0%
Illiquid Fixed Income	0.0%	0	0.0%
U.S. Equities	0.0%	0	0.0%
EAFE Equities	0.0%	0	0.0%
EM Equities	0.0%	0	0.0%
Directional Hedge Eq L/S	0.0%	0	0.0%
Managed Futures	0.0%	0	0.0%
Illiquid Equities	0.0%	0	0.0%
REITs	0.0%	0	0.0%
Precious Metals	0.0%	0	0.0%
Commodities	0.0%	0	0.0%
Illiquid Real Assets	0.0%	0	0.0%
Overall Total	100.0%	3,000,000	100.0%

shall look at the investment sub-policy of each account, accepting that each account can use more than one module, as we already discussed in broad terms, and proceed from there to the investment policy for the family.

Table 10.2 shows that our first "account" remains very simple, as it really only involves a single goal: "protect my money!" Our module choice is therefore equally simple: we must select the module that involves the lowest possible risk (if risk is defined here as a decline in the nominal value of the principal—note how this explicitly accepts the risk that the capital might have lost a significant portion of its purchasing power, for instance because of the potential raveges of inflation), which in this case is the Short-Term Lifestyle module. A word of caution is required here: one might discuss with the family the one alternative that is not covered by our modules. One can imagine a case in which the family might think that "no risk" should be understood to mean that the only acceptable investment should be a short-term treasury bill portfolio, with these treasury bills being issued by the "home country" and, given the general perception that short-term home government paper is the only risk-free asset, the truly risk-free portfolio might indeed be allocated solely to these instruments. Those following this line of logic would point to the credit risk associated with bank deposits when their amount exceeds deposit insurance and to the mark-to-market risk that would be present in any treasury bond with a maturity exceeding a few months. Experience suggests that families generally accept the implicit 21 percent probability of a negative return in any given year from the portfolio represented by the Short-Term Lifestyle module; yet, the very fact that the probability of such negative returns means that one could have a decline in the value of the portfolio one year out of five makes the alternative choice of investing these "absolute" safety assets 100 percent in short-term treasury bills totally reasonable.

Table 10.3 illustrates the fact that the sub-investment policy for the Grantor Trusts is a bit more complex, as it requires the use of two modules.

TABLE 10.3   Sub-Investment Policy for the Grantor Trusts

Asset Class/Strategy	Account Size		10,000,000			Sub-Investment Policy
	30% R G	70% G	Actual Allocation			
			R G	G	Total	
Cash	3.0%	2.7%	90,000	189,459	279,459	2.8%
U.S. Fixed Income Inv. Grade	0.0%	0.0%	0	0	0	0.0%
U.S. Fixed Income HY	0.0%	0.2%	0	14,510	14,510	0.1%
EAFE Fixed Income Hedged	0.0%	0.0%	0	0	0	0.0%
EM Debt	0.0%	0.2%	0	14,510	14,510	0.1%
Relative Value Multy Strategy	0.0%	0.4%	0	26,119	26,119	0.3%
Global Macro	0.0%	0.2%	0	17,412	17,412	0.2%
Illiquid Fixed Income	0.0%	0.0%	0	0	0	0.0%
U.S. Equities	11.3%	21.9%	339,298	1,535,757	1,875,055	18.8%
EAFE Equities	8.8%	17.1%	263,898	1,194,478	1,458,376	14.6%
EM Equities	5.0%	9.8%	150,799	682,559	833,358	8.3%
Directional Hedge Eq L/S	0.0%	7.8%	0	543,366	543,366	5.4%
Managed Futures	0.0%	5.2%	0	362,244	362,244	3.6%
Illiquid Equities	16.0%	19.6%	481,332	1,369,586	1,850,918	18.5%
REITs	18.1%	7.5%	544,269	525,000	1,069,269	10.7%
Precious Metals	11.2%	0.0%	334,935	0	334,935	3.3%
Commodities	12.6%	0.0%	376,802	0	376,802	3.8%
Illiquid Real Assets	14.0%	7.5%	418,668	525,000	943,668	9.4%
Overall Total	100.0%	100.0%	3,000,000	7,000,000	10,000,000	100.0%

Although this will also be true for the Generation Skipping Trusts (GSTs), the family wanted to allocate a growth goal to this account. Yet, although the longer term horizon of the GSTs allows them to choose to be principally concerned with nominal growth—because time will allow any inflationary spurt to filter into equity prices—they prefer to have a more conservative allocation for the Grantor Trusts, as these are expected to mature in thirty years or less. Thus, they asked that 30 percent of the allocation be invested in a real growth module, while the balance would follow the nominal growth path.

Table 10.4 shows the sub-investment policy for the GSTs; it only differs from the Table 10.3 for the Grantor Trusts in that the allocation to nominal growth goals is 95 percent, rather than 70 percent.

TABLE 10.4   Sub-Investment Policy for the GSTs

| Asset Class/Strategy | Account Size | | 5,000,000 | | | Sub-Investment Policy |
| | 5% R G | 95% G | Actual Allocation | | | |
			R G	G	Total	
Cash	3.0%	2.7%	7,500	128,561	136,061	2.7%
U.S. Fixed Income Inv. Grade	0.0%	0.0%	0	0	0	0.0%
U.S. Fixed Income HY	0.0%	0.2%	0	9,846	9,846	0.2%
EAFE Fixed Income Hedged	0.0%	0.0%	0	0	0	0.0%
EM Debt	0.0%	0.2%	0	9,846	9,846	0.2%
Relative Value Multy Strategy	0.0%	0.4%	0	17,723	17,723	0.4%
Global Macro	0.0%	0.2%	0	11,816	11,816	0.2%
Illiquid Fixed Income	0.0%	0.0%	0	0	0	0.0%
U.S. Equities	11.3%	21.9%	28,275	1,042,121	1,070,396	21.4%
EAFE Equities	8.8%	17.1%	21,992	810,539	832,530	16.7%
EM Equities	5.0%	9.8%	12,567	463,165	475,731	9.5%
Directional Hedge Eq L/S	0.0%	7.8%	0	368,713	368,713	7.4%
Managed Futures	0.0%	5.2%	0	245,808	245,808	4.9%
Illiquid Equities	16.0%	19.6%	40,111	929,362	969,473	19.4%
REITs	18.1%	7.5%	45,356	356,250	401,606	8.0%
Precious Metals	11.2%	0.0%	27,911	0	27,911	0.6%
Commodities	12.6%	0.0%	31,400	0	31,400	0.6%
Illiquid Real Assets	14.0%	7.5%	34,889	356,250	391,139	7.8%
Overall Total	100.0%	100.0%	250,000	4,750,000	5,000,000	100.0%

The higher degree of complexity starts with the IRA—or pension savings—accounts in that we now account for the fact that the first generation must start to draw a minimum annual amount for them once they reach 70.5 years of age. We thus needed to provide for a steady flow of withdrawals starting fifteen years from now. The fact that these cash flows only start fifteen years from now, despite the requirement that this goal be met with a 95 percent probability, led us to select the Real Purchasing Power Protection module, rather than a Lifestyle alternative, which might have been the intuitive choice. Ostensibly, it would be useful at this point to have a conversation with the family discussing what might happen if the actual capital market performance they experience is materially different from our projections. One can observe the actual equity market pattern of Japan over the last twenty-five years and note that it fell outside of all norms hitherto observed. There are a number of safeguards built into the process here, as the amount that must be withdrawn is conditional upon the market value of the retirement accounts in fifteen years, rather than some appropriately inflated dollar amount set today. Thus, where capital market behavior can be tricky, if it differs from expectations, might be with respect to the family's personal assets, which would need to adjust to any withdrawal shortfall from the IRAs to meet ongoing lifestyle expenditures—we will cover this in the next paragraph. The balance of the assets in the IRAs, as requested by the family, are assigned a growth goal, with the same 30/70 split between real and nominal growth as applied to the Grantor Trusts given the couple's life expectancy. Table 10.5 displays the details behind the IRAs' proposed sub-policy.

Before bringing everything together to arrive at the family's overall investment policy, we need to work on the one account that is likely to be the most complex in the vast majority of cases—as it is here—in large measure because this account comprises the greater variety of goals. Indeed, one can argue that the other accounts are set up for some specific purpose and are thus reasonably straightforward, even though computations might be tedious and somewhat complex. This account, by contrast, brings together both clear and less clear needs, wants, wishes, and dreams.

Table 10.6 presents this analysis. It requires four modules to meet the family's goals, and this number might actually have to be boosted if one assumed, for instance, that the family prefers to stop paying taxes on behalf of the Grantor Trusts at some point over the next thirty years. Note that, as one would expect, we must provide for certain assets to be invested in the Short-Term Lifestyle module to take care of expenses over the next five years; this is in keeping with my general observation that a family's worst

TABLE 10.5 Sub-Investment Policy for the IRAs

	Account Size			Actual Allocation 10,000,000				Sub-Investment Policy
Asset Class/Strategy	23% R PP	23% R G	54% G	R PP	R G	G	Total	
Cash	2.1%	3.0%	2.7%	48,185	69,695	146,715	264,595	2.6%
U.S. Fixed Income Inv. Grade	0.0%	0.0%	0.0%	0	0	0	0	0.0%
U.S. Fixed Income HY	0.0%	0.0%	0.2%	0	0	11,237	11,237	0.1%
EAFE Fixed Income Hedged	0.0%	0.0%	0.0%	0	0	0	0	0.0%
EM Debt	0.0%	0.0%	0.2%	0	0	11,237	11,237	0.1%
Relative Value Multy Strategy	4.5%	0.0%	0.4%	101,643	0	20,226	121,869	1.2%
Global Macro	4.5%	0.0%	0.2%	101,643		13,484	115,127	1.2%
Illiquid Fixed Income	3.0%	0.0%	0.0%	67,762	0	0	67,762	0.7%
U.S. Equities	2.5%	11.3%	21.9%	56,704	262,748	1,189,273	1,508,726	15.1%
EAFE Equities	2.0%	8.8%	17.1%	44,103	204,360	924,990	1,173,454	11.7%
EM Equities	1.1%	5.0%	9.8%	25,202	116,777	528,566	670,545	6.7%
Directional Hedge Eq L/S	1.4%	0.0%	7.8%	31,502	0	420,777	452,279	4.5%
Managed Futures	1.4%	0.0%	5.2%	31,502	0	280,518	312,020	3.1%
Illiquid Equities	2.8%	16.0%	19.6%	63,005	372,738	1,060,592	1,496,335	15.0%
REITs	26.4%	18.1%	7.5%	596,670	421,476	406,554	1,424,700	14.2%
Precious Metals	14.9%	11.2%	0.0%	336,972	259,370	0	596,341	6.0%
Commodities	17.7%	12.6%	0.0%	400,132	291,791	0	691,923	6.9%
Illiquid Real Assets	15.6%	14.0%	7.5%	351,085	324,212	406,554	1,081,851	10.8%
Overall Total	100.0%	100.0%	100.0%	2,256,111	2,323,167	5,420,722	10,000,000	100.0%

TABLE 10.6 Sub-Investment Policy for the Family Account

Asset Class/Strategy	Account Size				22,000,000 Actual Allocation					Sub-Investment Policy
	24% STL	40% R PP	30% N PP	7% G	STL	R PP	R G	G	Total	
Cash	25.7%	2.1%	1.8%	2.7%	1,344,372	185,815	117,275	39,648	1,687,110	7.7%
U.S. Fixed Income Inv. Grade	55.7%	0.0%	17.9%	0.0%	2,911,340	0	1,182,276	0	4,093,616	18.6%
U.S. Fixed Income HY	6.5%	0.0%	0.0%	0.2%	339,656	0	−576	3,037	342,117	1.6%
EAFE Fixed Income Hedged	6.5%	0.0%	0.0%	0.0%	339,656	0	0	0	339,656	1.5%
EM Debt	5.6%	0.0%	0.0%	0.2%	291,134	0	−576	3,037	293,594	1.3%
Relative Value Multy Strategy	0.0%	4.5%	6.3%	0.4%	0	391,964	413,797	5,466	811,226	3.7%
Global Macro	0.0%	4.5%	6.3%	0.2%	0	391,964	413,797	3,644	809,404	3.7%
Illiquid Fixed Income	0.0%	3.0%	5.4%	0.0%	0	261,309	355,835	0	617,144	2.8%
U.S. Equities	0.0%	2.5%	7.6%	21.9%	0	218,667	503,822	321,387	1,043,876	4.7%
EAFE Equities	0.0%	2.0%	5.9%	17.1%	0	170,074	391,862	249,967	811,903	3.7%
EM Equities	0.0%	1.1%	3.4%	9.8%	0	97,185	223,921	142,839	463,945	2.1%
Directional Hedge Eq L/S	0.0%	1.4%	8.4%	7.8%	0	121,482	555,138	113,710	790,329	3.6%
Managed Futures	0.0%	1.4%	2.1%	5.2%	0	121,482	138,785	75,807	336,073	1.5%
Illiquid Equities	0.0%	2.8%	2.6%	19.6%	0	242,963	169,109	286,612	698,684	3.2%
REITs	0.0%	26.4%	15.6%	7.5%	0	2,300,919	1,029,275	109,866	3,440,061	15.6%
Precious Metals	0.0%	14.9%	4.9%	0.0%	0	1,299,453	321,649	0	1,621,102	7.4%
Commodities	0.0%	17.7%	2.3%	0.0%	0	1,543,017	150,103	0	1,693,119	7.7%
Illiquid Real Assets	0.0%	15.6%	9.7%	7.5%	0	1,353,877	643,297	109,866	2,107,040	9.6%
Overall Total	100.0%	100.0%	100.0%	100.0%	5,226,158	8,700,170	6,608,787	1,464,885	22,000,000	100.0%

nightmare often is to have to change their lifestyle.[3] The balance of the following twenty-five years is split into two sub-periods, as we do assume that the family will start withdrawing from its retirement accounts in fifteen years. We then have the following ten and the subsequent fifteen years. Both of these fit well with the Real Purchasing Power Protection module, but we might come to a different conclusion—because of different required probabilities of success—if the family elected to stop covering the Grantor Trusts' income taxes at some point. The assets dedicated to the Nominal Purchasing Power Protection module indeed reflect the monies needed to fund their family foundation with $10 million in ten years, with a 95 percent required probability. The one element that might lead them to the conclusion that it would be prudent to stop paying these taxes at some point is the relatively small size of their "Growth" portfolio, which reflects their "surplus assets." Add to this that the differential between the expected returns of the Grantor Trusts—which hypothetically do not require any cash outflow—and of their personal family assets makes it highly likely that the trusts will exceed the value of those personal family assets in very short order, particularly when the foundation is funded.

These last observations illustrate an important truism: the process must be iterative for several reasons, two of which dominate. The first is that it is the rare exception when a family has thought out all of its needs, wants, wishes, and dreams at the onset of the process. After all, this should not surprise to the extent that they need a financial interpreter to help them understand what assets are required to meet each goal. The second is that it is quite common for families to dream larger than their means: this is not meant to be a critical comment, but rather recognition that wealth opens doors to many opportunities and eventually requires families to arbitrate among personal, dynastic, and philanthropic goals. An important conclusion is that the phase of the process that matches assets and goals is crucially important, because it is often the first time a family is confronted with the fact that it may have to make choices, either in terms of the nature of their goals or of the risk they are prepared to take that one or another goal may not be met.

Table 10.7 brings this analysis to the final dimension: the actual formulation of a family's investment policy, assuming that they wish their portfolio to

---

[3] I cannot resist mentioning an anecdote of a family in London who once phrased this a bit differently: "We do not want to have to change our lifestyle in a way that our neighbors might notice." The patriarch was referring to certain expenses—principally of a philanthropic nature—he did not want to have to cut, as they were a good part of the reason why the matriarch chaired an important public charity! Any risk that she might lose that position was simply unacceptable to him.

TABLE 10.7 Family Goals-Based Investment Policy

Asset Class/Strategy	6.0% 3,000,000 Pillow Money	20.0% 10,000,000 Grantor Trusts	10.0% 5,000,000 GSTs	20.0% 10,000,000 IRAs	44.0% 22,000,000 Family	100.0% 50,000,000 Family Total
Cash	25.7%	2.8%	2.7%	2.6%	7.7%	6.3%
U.S. Fixed Income Inv. Grade	55.7%	0.0%	0.0%	0.0%	18.6%	11.5%
U.S. Fixed Income HY	6.5%	0.1%	0.2%	0.1%	1.6%	1.1%
EAFE Fixed Income Hedged	6.5%	0.0%	0.0%	0.0%	1.5%	1.1%
EM Debt	5.6%	0.1%	0.2%	0.1%	1.3%	1.0%
Relative Value Multy Strategy	0.0%	0.3%	0.4%	1.2%	3.7%	2.0%
Global Macro	0.0%	0.2%	0.2%	1.2%	3.7%	1.9%
Illiquid Fixed Income	0.0%	0.0%	0.0%	0.7%	2.8%	1.4%
U.S. Equities	0.0%	18.8%	21.4%	15.1%	4.7%	11.0%
EAFE Equities	0.0%	14.6%	16.7%	11.7%	3.7%	8.6%
EM Equities	0.0%	8.3%	9.5%	6.7%	2.1%	4.9%
Directional Hedge Eq L/S	0.0%	5.4%	7.4%	4.5%	3.6%	4.3%
Managed Futures	0.0%	3.6%	4.9%	3.1%	1.5%	2.5%
Illiquid Equities	0.0%	18.5%	19.4%	15.0%	3.2%	10.0%
REITs	0.0%	10.7%	8.0%	14.2%	15.6%	12.7%
Precious Metals	0.0%	3.3%	0.6%	6.0%	7.4%	5.2%
Commodities	0.0%	3.8%	0.6%	6.9%	7.7%	5.6%
Illiquid Real Assets	0.0%	9.4%	7.8%	10.8%	9.6%	9.0%
Overall Total	100.0%	100.0%	100.0%	100.0%	100.0%	100.0%

be managed as one rather than in terms of individual accounts. The process is simple: we must compute the weighted average of the sub-policies, weighing each asset or strategy position by the respective sizes of each account.

One might want to take a quick look back at Table 10.1 and compare the policy that would have been chosen had it been possible not to withdraw any funds from the IRAs for the whole time period relative to the alternative shown in Table 10.7. Table 10.8 provides the information, looking at the differences between the two overall investment policies and between the "accounts" in each policy. It illustrates how the need for the IRAs to provide for the potential for withdrawals and the reduction in the need for the personal family assets to support the whole of the lifestyle spending requires both to deemphasize real assets and allows then to add to the equity sector. One can go back to the assumptions used in each "account" model and to the conclusions that came out of the process and understand how and why each element of the process contributed to the change. This is one of the most attractive elements of the model[4]; it allows one to follow from assumptions to conclusions in complete transparency; and, because that transparency is at the level of each goal in each account, the process is much easier to follow and understand. A final note of caution: the policy reproduced in Table 10.9 comprises a few individual line item allocations that are extremely—and probably too—small; the final iteration of the process would require the advisor to work with the client to round many of these, perhaps by consolidating or eliminating certain lines. We will not go through this step here in a bid to preserve the model's technical integrity and to illustrate it in its full theoretical incarnation.

The final step in this process geared to formulate a family's strategic asset allocation is to incorporate deviation ranges that will limit the discretion afforded to deviate from the policy on a periodic and tactical basis. Table 10.9 shows a possible such solution, with permissible ranges varying between plus or minus 5 percent, 10 percent, or 15 percent, depending on the three variables discussed earlier in this chapter.

SUMMARY AND CONCLUSIONS

Ostensibly, no model is better than the assumptions that are fed and the decision rules that are codified into it. Back in Chapter 3, we discussed the three "Cs" I believe ought to be a part of any model: clarity of assumption,

---

[4]Again, I do not mean this to be a commercial for this model. Rather, I mean to point to the benefit associated with such a conceptual framework that makes all assumptions clear and thus allows the most successful "wedding" of "My Wealth" and "My Life."

TABLE 10.8 Difference to Family Goals-Based Investment Policy Due to IRA Withdrawals

Asset Class/Strategy	Family Investment Policies			Delta Individual Accounts				
	No IRA Withdrawal	IRA Withdrawals	Delta	Pillow Money	Grant or Trusts	GSTs	IRAs	Family
Cash	7.6%	6.3%	-1.3%	0.0%	0.0%	0.0%	-0.4%	0.0%
U.S. Fixed Income Inv. Grade	18.3%	11.5%	-6.7%	0.0%	0.0%	0.0%	0.0%	0.3%
U.S. Fixed Income HY	1.5%	1.1%	-0.4%	0.0%	0.0%	0.0%	0.1%	0.0%
EAFE Fixed Income Hedged	1.5%	1.1%	-0.5%	0.0%	0.0%	0.0%	0.0%	0.0%
EM Debt	1.3%	1.0%	-0.3%	0.0%	0.0%	0.0%	0.1%	0.0%
Relative Value Multy Strategy	4.0%	2.0%	-2.1%	0.0%	0.0%	0.0%	1.2%	-0.3%
Global Macro	4.0%	1.9%	-2.1%	0.0%	0.0%	0.0%	1.2%	-0.3%
Illiquid Fixed Income	3.0%	1.4%	-1.6%	0.0%	0.0%	0.0%	0.7%	-0.2%
U.S. Equities	3.0%	11.0%	8.0%	0.0%	0.0%	0.0%	3.8%	1.8%
EAFE Equities	2.3%	8.6%	6.2%	0.0%	0.0%	0.0%	2.9%	1.4%
EM Equities	1.3%	4.9%	3.6%	0.0%	0.0%	0.0%	1.7%	0.8%
Directional Hedge Eq L/S	2.9%	4.3%	1.4%	0.0%	0.0%	0.0%	4.5%	0.7%
Managed Futures	1.2%	2.5%	1.3%	0.0%	0.0%	0.0%	3.1%	0.3%
Illiquid Equities	1.7%	10.0%	8.3%	0.0%	0.0%	0.0%	-1.1%	1.4%
REITs	17.5%	12.7%	-4.8%	0.0%	0.0%	0.0%	-3.9%	-1.8%
Precious Metals	8.8%	5.2%	-3.7%	0.0%	0.0%	0.0%	-5.2%	-1.5%
Commodities	9.5%	5.6%	-3.9%	0.0%	0.0%	0.0%	-5.6%	-1.8%
Illiquid Real Assets	10.4%	9.0%	-1.3%	0.0%	0.0%	0.0%	-3.1%	-0.8%
Overall Total	100.0%	100.0%	0.0%	0.0%	0.0%	0.0%	0.0%	0.0%

TABLE 10.9 Family Goals-Based Investment Policy with Deviation Ranges

Asset Class/Strategy	Policy Target	Minimum	Maximum
Cash	6.3%	0.0%	100.0%
U.S. Fixed Income Inv. Grade	11.5%	1.5%	21.5%
U.S. Fixed Income HY	1.1%	0.0%	11.1%
EAFE Fixed Income Hedged	1.1%	0.0%	11.1%
EM Debt	1.0%	0.0%	11.0%
Relative Value Multy Strategy	2.0%	0.0%	12.0%
Global Macro	1.9%	0.0%	11.9%
Illiquid Fixed Income	1.4%	0.0%	6.4%
Total Lower Half of Volatility Spectrum	20.0%	5.0%	35.0%
U.S. Equities	11.0%	1.0%	21.0%
EAFE Equities	8.6%	0.0%	18.6%
EM Equities	4.9%	0.0%	14.9%
Directional Hedge Eq L/S	4.3%	0.0%	14.3%
Managed Futures	2.5%	0.0%	12.5%
Illiquid Equities	10.0%	5.0%	15.0%
Total Equity Spectrum	41.3%	26.3%	56.3%
REITs	12.7%	2.7%	22.7%
Precious Metals	5.2%	0.0%	15.2%
Commodities	5.6%	0.0%	15.6%
Illiquid Real Assets	9.0%	4.0%	14.0%
Total Real Asset Spectrum	32.5%	17.5%	47.5%
Overall Total	**100.0%**		

clarity of structures, and clarity of expectations. These rules are at work in the model presented in this and the prior two chapters. Unfortunately, this does not guarantee that the output will always be better than the simple flipping of a coin. Yet, it would be a probabilistic impossibility for there to be many such instances; more to the point, the effort we have described does not solely seek to achieve the "best" investment policy for an individual, however "best" is defined. Rather, it is meant to create a suitable investment policy that is likely to be sustained through time because each individual can, through the process, experience a "bonding" with his or her wealth. Equally importantly, and we will revisit this in Part 4 of the book, it ensures that the same process, with the same assumptions—where it is important for assumptions to be the same—will be used across the whole of an advisor's clientele. Each and every client will thus be able to benefit from the whole of the advisor's expertise.

An important point is worth repeating: the process and its architecture are somewhat like the developer agent in non-digital or even X-ray photography: it transforms a latent image into one that becomes visible and permanent. Remember that the family has not necessarily spent a great deal of time thinking about its goals and objectives, or the risk it is prepared to take. Going back to our photography analogy, the role of the advisor and the mission of the process that he or she uses are straightforward: they must help the family reveal its goals to itself. Thus, one needs to be prepared to follow iterative steps so that the various trade-offs which will inevitably come up can be resolved in a way with which the family is and remains comfortable. By focusing this analysis of the required trade-offs where it belongs—that is among goals, the risks one is prepared to take to achieve them and the hierarchy that one assigns to these goals—one maximizes the chances that any decision will be made based on the right criteria rather than in a bid to "game" the system. A last point before we move on: it is not uncommon for families to appear to agree to some early iteration of the process, only to change their minds when the formal, written investment policy is illustrated. This highlights the need for this investment policy statement to be written in plain language rather than language reflecting the business and compliance—or legal—needs of the advisor. Chapter 13 of the second edition of my earlier book actually provides the outline I generally use and, importantly, makes the point that I prefer to write all these policies in the first person, indeed as a letter that each family writes to itself. Seeing their goals, time horizons, required probabilities of success, choices, and preferences on paper and written by them often makes families take a breather and realize that selections they might have made earlier in the process may not be appropriate in the end. Being prepared to help the family iterate is an important dimension of the interpreter role each advisor should see as his or her central responsibility.

A final point is in order. It relates to the time horizons that we have been discussing. Although one might wish that they were strictly correct, there are at least two reasons why they are not; the implications of this simple observation is that the wealthy and the advisors who serve them is that they should be viewed as guides rather than specific dates. Why is that? First, humans tend to set certain time frames in some rough manner: I am sure, in my own case, that my view of my life expectancy today is not exactly ten years shorter than it was ten years ago! Any target horizon which is broadly governed by life expectancy, for instance, will tend to shift over time, except in instances where a fiduciary structure—a trust for instance—has a specific maturity date. Second, certain short-term horizons will come to pass—or be viewed as being too close now—and will need to be extended. This helps explain why I strongly advise the wealthy and advisors whom we serve to plan to review their goals-based policy process and its outcome at least every other year, if not yearly.

CHAPTER 11

Managing the Portfolio Tactically

We mentioned this a couple of times already, but reading the contents of Chapter 10 must have brought the point home powerfully: a goals-based strategic asset allocation process is indeed quite tailored to the needs of each client; *but* it also introduces a potential nightmarish amount of complexity when it comes to managing each portfolio actively, from the point of view of the advisor, whether he or she is the chief investment officer of a single-family family office or an employee of a larger advisory firm. The need to deal with this central issue is the main theme of Part 4 of this book, but this chapter introduces a systematic approach to tactical portfolio allocation or rebalancing; without it, it is unrealistic to expect each advisor to be able to reflect, faithfully and in full, his or her views or those of the firm for which he or she works. Yet, it is a clear Securities and Exchange Commission (SEC) requirement that all clients benefit fully and fairly from the insights of their advisor. Similarly, the problem is the same for the office of a larger family, with multiple members and asset holding structures, although regulatory requirements may or may not differ.

Before moving to the detailed discussion of this point, it is worth setting out the limits of what we seek to achieve here. First, a definition: tactical management or portfolio rebalancing is the act of modifying the allocation to any of the various asset classes, strategies, or mega-categories comprising the portfolio's strategic asset allocation. Within this definition, portfolio rebalancing involves taking steps to return any asset class, strategy, or mega-category to its neutral position after diverging market returns among them moved them away from the normal allocation. In this context, the activity is not driven by investment insights, but by investment discipline. Tactical management assumes that the manager or advisor has insights—or thinks he or she has insights—as to the likely future relative performance of each asset class, strategy, or mega-category; the manager or advisor will thus want to tilt the portfolio toward investments that he or she expects to do better than average and away from those he or she anticipates will underperform.

Tactical portfolio management, theoretically, would extend to selecting managers within each line item. A purely passive approach would lead the advisor to select broad market indices or strategies that aim to minimize the tracking error with those indices—but which might not match them exactly if, for instance, tax-efficiency is the reason why certain security weights differ from those of the index. A passive approach may be used in one of two circumstances: first, the advisor does not believe that tactical value added is feasible or worth its cost—in terms of management fee or of tax-inefficiency. Second, the advisor might believe that most liquid, traditional strategies are operated in markets that are too efficient for there to be value added, but recognize that some value added is still available in the non-traditional, alternative world, be it liquid, partially liquid, or broadly illiquid. Whether the advisor believes that active management value added is limited to non-traditional strategies or not, he or she must select managers who can implement the strategies that comprise each portfolio's strategic asset allocation.

In this chapter, we will ignore manager selection issues, although we recognize that they are very important. Therefore, we explicitly assume that each advisor will have developed an approach to deal with the issue. Traditional practices have advisors selecting one or several managers, using qualitative or quantitative processes. At the most quantitative end of the spectrum, advisors develop a series of "manager modules" that can be used by all clients when the allocation to the strategy represented by each of these modules is finalized. At the other, more qualitative end of the spectrum, advisors select managers alone or in consultation with their clients, either from some firm-wide list of approved managers or from the full universe. Our focus here will be solely on how allocations to strategies or asset classes are formulated when the advisor and the client agree that some tactical portfolio tilting makes sense.

THE COMPLEXITY IN THE ABSENCE OF A SYSTEMATIC TOOL

Now, while it is practically not terribly complex to tilt the policy of a single client (or a single portfolio in a family where all assets reside under one "roof" and have the same investment policy), imagine how the tilting process must be run across a number of clients or distinct investment portfolios in a family. In fact, even with a single client, the challenge can be real if the family, rather than asking for all "accounts" as we defined them in Chapter 10 to be consolidated in a single portfolio, desires for each account to be managed distinctly and separately. To me, the complexity comes from two different—and somewhat complementary—angles.

What I might call "financial hygiene" requires any decision-maker to be able and willing to measure the effectiveness of his or her activity. In short, one should not be willing to keep making certain decisions unless one is able to verify that those decisions add value *a posteriori*. In the context of tactical portfolio tilting, one should want to be able to test the extent to which the views one held with respect to this or that asset class or strategy did pan out as expected or not. While this should not be the most challenging thing on earth, it becomes quite complex when one recognizes that no portfolio is managed in a vacuum and to a specific immutable time horizon. Measuring the effectiveness of my decisions would not be too hard if I could state that they have a one-year time horizon and that I will not touch the portfolio between now and a year from now. But, in reality, this is hardly the way things work. In practice, one develops views of markets, usually with a time horizon that is anything but specific, and one allows these views to evolve over time. Thus, while the first iteration of the tilting process might reflect the views I had when I started managing a portfolio; each time that allocation is modified as time passes, there is a change that would require one of two actions:

1. I should measure the impact of the first decision over the period between the first and the subsequent decision, or
2. I should measure how the generic class of tilting decision helped or hurt the portfolio's performance over the full horizon.

Note how following the first avenue would be silly and complicated, as it would effectively require measuring the performance of the real portfolio, together with as many steady-state portfolios as there are decision periods, plus one.[1] Thus, the performance of the first iteration would be measured against the base; the second against the first; the third against the second; and so on until the most recent allocation. Assuming that decisions are made quarterly, this would mean keeping track of at least five portfolios for the first year, and there is no reason why one should stop at one year, as the effectiveness of a decision might not be visible until sometime later. The second approach is considerably more practical and it is covered in most investment textbooks under the header of performance attribution. Yet, although there is a well-known and effective performance measurement algorithm to deal with the attribution issue, it only measures the variations that were

---

[1]This is the classic "interval problem," where the number of poles will be equal to the number of intervals, plus one, because there must be a pole at the beginning and at the end of each interval.

actually implemented in the portfolio, as it is based on the actual allocations as compared to the policy targets. We will come back to this next.

The second challenge is more insidious, but it relates to the actual extent to which the "investment view" that represented the key insight is faithfully and totally reflected in the changes that are made in the portfolio. One could argue that a view can be expressed in terms of some sense of likely out- or underperformance, over some time horizon, and with some level of conviction. We already know that the actual performance we measure reflects the interaction of skill and luck. One way to reduce the impact of luck is to increase the number of decisions; aggregating the "same" decisions over multiple time periods can help generate more data points which, although never fully eliminating luck, can show skills a bit more convincingly. For this to be done, it helps to be able to codify—"standardize" is another word—the way in which these insights are expressed and translated into portfolio action. Having a systematic tool does indeed help separate pure luck from presumed skill.

When looking at how advisors seem to be making decisions, one is forced to admit that this is often the essence of the proverbial sausage factory. I was the chairman of J.P. Morgan Investment Management's Global Balanced Committee for a good part of the 1990s and can testify to the fact that, although all members were unquestionably moved by professional considerations and most often quite good at their trade, whatever came out at the end of the sausage machine was pretty soft and general rather than specific. Although we could measure the performance of one or another of the large commingled funds that faithfully sought to apply the committee's conclusions, we could not assess either how faithful the translation had been from the committee to any given portfolio or how successful any member had been at the whole effort or any dimensions within it. The moment one has a systematic process, each and every facet of any decision can be evaluated and feedback can be given to any individual within the decision chain as to what worked and what did not.

The term "systematic" can be misleading here as, at this point, we do not really need a true model in the quantitative sense of the term. We could certainly use a mix of the qualitative and the quantitative and capture material insights as to how we are doing. In fact, many multi-family family offices already do some serious performance measurement, usually to the extent that they have a number of "model portfolios" managed by the firm and among which clients choose whichever appears most suitable to their needs, with the help of a well-meaning advisor. But that process falls apart if each client portfolio is unique. The number of decisions multiplied by the number of portfolios creates a universe that simply defies analysis. The fact that the industry rarely conducts the type of detailed performance analysis that it should is not because of nefarious intentions, but rather because of the sheer complexity of measuring the performance of a multiplicity of portfolios, influenced as they are by a multiplicity of factors and individuals and where the output is much more of the dreaded average of conflicting views than an honest assessment of all those factors that went into each decision.[2]

INTRODUCING THE CONCEPT OF A TILT MODEL

As should have become clear by now, one needs both a standardization of the decision-making inputs and a tool that systematically translates these inputs into portfolio actions to be able to assess the extent to which a portfolio tilting activity is worth the effort.

Standardizing the inputs is actually the simple part of the exercise. The process involves replacing words that do not always mean precisely what they seem to mean with simple scores. The framework I prefer to use to is to request that each line item be scored on a −3 to +3 scale, with no use of decimal values permitted. Minus 3 means that I dislike a particular asset class or strategy about as much as I could, while the corollary is true for +3, where I cannot envision being more bullish. A 0 simply means that I currently do not have a view and that I would expect returns to fall pretty much around the capital market forecast. When I input a −3, I effectively say that I would like to allocate the minimum allowed position to that particular asset or strategy, while a +3 means the opposite in that I would like to have as much in that asset or strategy as permitted. A 0 means that I am quite comfortable with holding the neutral position prescribed by the strategic asset allocation for that investment category.

These individual line scores are only applied to each line, not to the asset class or strategy totals, to ensure that valuation insights are measured or communicated at the lowest possible action level—or granularity. Indeed, one does not buy "fixed income"; one rather buys U.S. investment grade bonds or high yield bonds or debt from non-U.S. or emerging firms or countries. So it makes sense to develop and communicate views at that level of detail. Although it could be interesting to point to inconsistencies—when they exist—if one were to score not only each line but also the asset total, it may not be a truly constructive item. This would happen if one were to score all fixed income strategies higher than 0 and yet score fixed income as a whole at 0 or less than that! While a lively debate might follow, I would rather use the time and intellectual energy of the decision-makers

---

[2]Again, one is allowed to dream that computing power will eventually make this so easy that firms will not hesitate doing it; that is what "big data" is all about!

to discuss the reason for their individual scores than to have them defend themselves . . . . Note, however, that the model I will discuss later generates an implicit asset class score that provides an opportunity for inconsistencies and discomfort to be addressed and changed without anyone having to spend time justifying his or her position.

Note that there is no magic to the −3 to +3 range chosen. The choice that one must make must incorporate two conflicting variables:

1. The range must be sufficiently wide to allow one to distinguish between like" and "love" or their corresponding values at the other end of the scale. A range that only included −1, 0 and +1 would force extreme position-taking, which might not be realistic and thus lead to too many "zeroes" if people could not contemplate the extreme trades a +1 or −1 would require.
2. The range must be sufficiently narrow so that one does not start to split hairs. A family we know has limited its range to −2 to +2 on the grounds that the wider range they used to use was not fully utilized by the members of its investment committee. This, they rightly noted, had the effect of narrowing the deviation ranges provided in the investment policy. Narrowing the range ensured that extreme values were selected and actual allocations could and would run the full gamut allowed by the investment policy.

Our choice reflects the observation that we should be able to differentiate between a buy, a strong buy, and a very unusually enthusiastic buy, as well as their symmetrical values on the other side of neutral.

A tilt model by this definition is a process that translates these scores into portfolio actions, based solely on the scores and the neutral allocation of each portfolio, together with the ranges that surround each central allocation.

Before moving on to the mechanics of such a possible model, we should spend a few minutes on another practicality. Most of the families we know work with some version of an investment committee, usually comprising the family's chief investment officer, often one or several external members, and a selection of family members. The scoring process we just described can add to the effectiveness of these committees along three lines:

1. It can serve to force views from people who do not agree on much. I have sat through many such discussions where the group was debating the sex of the angels rather than the issues at hand. In fact, the first iteration of the model I now use was created for one such family, working with a highly mathematically gifted family member.

2. It allows a straightforward aggregation of all votes with the use of a weighting system, under the terms of which each member receives a certain weight in the final decision. The only constraint here is that the total of all weights must add up to 100 percent. By providing certain members with more or less "quantitative clout" than others, one is able to recognize different levels of experience or family authority.
3. It can be used to train younger family members. Although they may be invited to participate in the discussions and the scoring, their votes might receive a 0 weight when aggregating all inputs from all members. The fact that their votes are recorded can help younger members have their performance measured, discover their own biases and preferences, and yet preserve them from the pressures of being asked to participate too early. I heard at least one younger member of a family say that it made it easier for him not to have to face other members of his generation when the committee's decisions proved uninspired.

Once the committee is established, I have found it useful to work along a three-step process to maximize the effectiveness of the decision-making effort and minimize the often disliked mechanistic nature of the process:

1. Invite all members of the committee to enter their scores once they have been exposed to the materials everyone agrees are important for the decisions to be made. This can involve written materials that are distributed ahead of time, in which case votes can be entered in the privacy of one's own office. Alternatively, there might be cases in which oral presentations are delivered to the whole assembled group and votes are entered during a short interlude provided for that purpose.
2. Have an initial compilation of all votes made, and use it to identify the outliers for each line item. Then conduct a thorough discussion where each outlier is invited to articulate—but not defend—the reasons for his or her vote. Note that the process is focused on clarification of the thoughts of each member, rather than a debate pitting one view against another.
3. Invite all members to revisit their votes—if they wish—given what they heard that might have led them to change their views. Often, people will forget one or another dimension of a problem. Hearing someone else argue that this or that element is critical to a decision for this or that reason might lead one to change his or her vote. This should be pressure-less and be focused on the idea that more information and a detailed discussion of a possibly arcane facet can move the group to a different decision.

Once these second votes have been recorded, the average scores are computed and become the view of the group, unless someone feels so compelled to debate it that further discussion is needed. A clear background belief here is that more eyes see better and more minds think better than one. Thus, the wish is for the chair of the committee to be prepared to welcome discussion for as long as it is constructive and thus respectful of other people's views and to cut it when it has become a case of "I am right and you must therefore be wrong!"

FIVE POSSIBLE VARIATIONS ON THE SAME THEME

We must now turn to the mechanics of how these average scores can be translated into portfolio actions. Remember that the reason why we want mechanics is that our ultimate goal is to present a way that can allow a myriad of different portfolios within a family or a firm to benefit from the same insights and to reflect them as much as allowed within each investment policy. Conceptually, there are two contradictory goals that must be sorted out:

1. One might shoot to maximize the implicit resulting score of the tilted portfolio based on the strategic asset allocation, the deviation ranges, and the individual line item scores from the investment committee. By definition, the higher a score, the higher the expected return, and vice versa. So, it is not illogical to aim to have the highest weighted portfolio tilt score as this should produce the highest expected return.
2. Alternatively, one might want there to be as much of a linear relationship as possible between individual inputs and the resulting allocation. This is also a logical goal, as the insight is that one is thinking of a movie and not of a still picture. As the portfolio, and the committee in some ways, are living creatures, the emphasis is one making sure that decisions can capture that gradual evolution rather than maximize the impact of today's views.

These goals are contradictory in that trying to maximize the resulting score will necessarily force certain assets and strategies toward the high or the low end of their respective ranges. Assume, for instance, that all but one of the strategies in the portfolio are rated a 0, while the last one is rated a +1 and it is within the fixed income area. A well-constructed optimization process will start by putting this latter asset at its maximum permissible level, as it is the only one with a favorable view. The asset class in which this strategy is classified—here, fixed income—will likely record an overweighting, but it may or may not be major, depending on the neutral policy weight of the lone favorably rated strategy. Also, all other strategies in the portfolio will be modestly to more seriously under-weighted, because the difference between the policy and the allocated weights of the +1 strategy will have to be made up by under-weights in strategies that were scored a 0. In short, a strategy with a score of 0 may be materially under-weighted. More to the point, what if the next time the committee votes, the same strategy that had a +1 the previous time is now scored a +2, while the scores of all the others remain at 0? The model will not come up with a different allocation, as it will already have maxed out its commitment to that sole positively rated strategy. This seems to contradict the goal that strategies be more and more over- or under-weighted as scores deviate more and more from 0.

Achieving some form of linearity such that this last sentence holds is feasible, but it may not produce an allocation that will necessarily maximize the overall expected resulting portfolio score. Indeed, if all strategies but one are scored at 0, the strategy with the different score will have an over- or under-weight proportional to its score, and therefore will only reach the upper or lower limit of its permissible deviation range if that non-0 score is +3 or −3. Note that, if as in the case above, the current vote is +1 and becomes +2 the next time the committee meets, the allocation to that strategy will increase—with corresponding offsets in all other strategies.

In short, we must consider at least two conceptual variants: one that uses overall portfolio optimization, with the goal of achieving the highest tilt score, and another that uses linear formulae to equate targeted allocations and scores. The problem becomes immediately more complex once one understands that there must be four variants of the second model, as illustrated in Figure 11.1. Indeed, the moment one moves away from a constrained optimization problem toward a formula-driven solution, it becomes obvious that a hierarchy is created among the various decision variables: each of the binary choices one has must be sequenced relative to the others, and the one that comes first effectively is the top priority.

In the formulaic design, one must make choices at two critical levels:

1. At the very top, one must decide whether the priority will be on selecting the asset class allocations based on their implicit score or the sub-asset classes based on their explicit scores.
2. One must then decide whether the asset class ranges (if one has selected the sub-asset class priority) or the sub-asset class ranges (if one has selected the asset class priority) will be absolutely enforced or not.

The first decision relies on an interpretation of whether alpha generation rather than risk management should play the more important role. Indeed, to the extent that the asset class score is derived rather than explicit, one could argue that one should aim to have the sub-asset class allocation drive

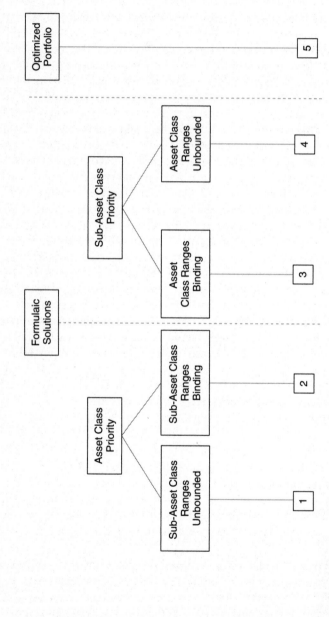

FIGURE 11.1 Five Possible Systematic Tilting Processes

the process, subject to an asset class risk control. In this design, each of the sub-asset class allocations would be as close as possible to the formulaic solution, subject to the need of the asset class total to remain controlled. By contrast, one could argue that significant variations within asset class allocations must carry the highest risk of tracking error relative to the policy. Then, one would set the asset class allocation as close as possible to that driven by its implicit score and allocate to sub-asset classes within that total as warranted, given individual sub-asset class scores.

The second decision relies on whether some modest violation of the policy ranges is truly problematic or not. From a practical standpoint, holding firm to those ranges associated with the second priority (sub-asset classes if the first allocation decision is focused on asset classes and asset classes if the first allocation is applied to sub-asset classes) increases the complexity of formulae in that it requires an additional series of iterations—through which excesses or shortfalls are redistributed as appropriate to force the allocation that violates a range back within that range. While families will not always feel the need to adhere to these ranges rigorously, registered investment advisors will have little choice but to insist that the ranges must hold.

Practically, my own preference is to prioritize the asset class decision and to force the ranges to hold. It fits better with my own view that controlling the risk taken on a tactical basis is crucial to the long-term success of an investment program. As mentioned in the Introduction, theoretical work does indeed suggest that the strategic asset allocation of a portfolio is the main driver of its risk. Thus, it seems to me that we should remain focused on controlling that risk, defined here as tracking error—or the volatility of excess return from tactical decisions relative to policy standards. I am also of the view that ranges should hold and am prepared to accept the added complexity. However, I should add that I am usually prepared to show to families both the tilted allocation that would fit with these constraints along with the results of the other four processes to ensure that they know how the portfolio might look if some other set of priorities or rules had been selected.

A MAJOR PITFALL

As is always the case with any model, no solution is better than the inputs and the rules that govern it. Here again, I think I can argue that the three "Cs" we already saw in Chapters 3 and 10 apply: the structure of the model is crystal clear, although complex; the assumptions that are used are equally clear and fully disclosed; and the expectations one has from the solution are also quite clear. One must recognize that tactical tilting is a discipline full of pitfalls, which divides the investment community in terms of the potential for real value added and is visibly subject to serious doubts when one measures that value added in after-tax terms.[3]

The biggest pitfall I have observed in the real world relates to "gaming the system." This happens when those who participate in the decision process adopt one of two unfortunate strategies. The first involves settling first on the allocation they would like, either at the asset or sub-asset class level, based on qualitative views and then literally backing into the tilt score that will produce that desired allocation. The second, which occurs only when there is more than one contributor to the overall voting, involves "loading" the vote to offset or out-power the position they expect from their associates on the committee.

Either and both of these actions are unfortunate, as they simply serve to violate the process. That they normally tend to occur when one or several members of the decision team effectively have not bought into the systematic nature of the process is obvious, but this does not address the challenge. Ostensibly, the promoter of the use of a systematic tilt model should make sure that people are philosophically onboard before adopting it. This can lead to serious human and organizational challenges when it becomes clear to that senior decision-maker that one of the most talented contributors may actually have to be taken out of the committee if he or she is more likely to frustrate the process than contribute to it. Here I am reminded of the first CEO of J.P. Morgan Investment Management, Inc., my boss and mentor, C. Nicholas "Nick" Potter. He taught me that no system was foolproof and that the only way to be comfortable with a process was to make sure that all members who participated in it were philosophically aligned. It proved an incredibly valuable piece of advice at several points during my career!

In the end, detailed performance attribution can help address the challenge and allow the senior decision-maker to contain any recalcitrant contributor. Earlier, we discussed the fact that an important secondary benefit of a systematic tool is that it can be audited. Thus, if I have the various tilt votes of all the members of a committee over a period of several quarters, possibly longer, I can construct the portfolio that the votes of each individual would have created. I can then track that portfolio against the policy portfolio. Thus, I can compute the value added—or subtracted—in the resulting individual portfolios and by each of the line-item—or sub-asset class—votes or decisions. I have found this analysis to be quite instructive and to serve to apply appropriate peer pressure on those members of the team who are

---

[3]For more detail on this, the following article assessed that factor as precisely as practicably then. Brunel, Jean L.P. "Revisiting the Fallacy of Market-Timing in an After-Tax Context." *The Journal of Private Portfolio Management*, Fall 1999, pp. 16–26.

not contributing as much as one would expect. In particular, the impact of "loaded" scores can quickly become so negative and obvious as to allow the senior decision-maker to gently suggest to that person that some moderation of excessive enthusiasm may be warranted. I used that process with encouraging success in a specific client circumstance when two of the most vocal members of an investment committee had not produced any value added for some time and whose contributions were, in fact, at the bottom among their peers. These discussions were surely not comfortable, but the results spoke for themselves.

A POSSIBLE EXAMPLE

The foregoing discussion may have been too theoretical for certain readers; so I propose that these readers follow the process in a practical sense, using the overall policy of the family whose case we have been using in the last three chapters.

Table 11.1 starts the process with a set of votes. I imagined a committee comprised of five members, one of whom has a 0 weight in the final decision, to show how the full process we described earlier might work. The only important column is the one that is boldface, as it represents the weighted average of the various scores, and the vector—or list of scores—that will drive the tactical tilting process.

Let's assume that the discussion of the votes focused on the various outliers and did not lead to a major change of opinions, despite material divergences. Let's say it was agreed that these divergences were driven by views of the relative importance of fundamental valuations in a liquidity-driven market; thus, rather than argue that one approach was better than the other, the group was simply satisfied to note that differences of opinions pointed to greater than usual risks and that the averaging associated with the process had erased the most significant "bets." Finally, let's imagine it was therefore agreed that the bets were all sufficiently modest to be reasonable at this point and to constitute a not totally comfortable, but yet acceptable average of the different points of view.

Table 11.2 illustrates the output from the tilting process, using the one tilting algorithm I prefer, with priority to asset class weights and a requirement that all line items be kept within their deviation range boundaries. Note that the net positive tilt scores in the fixed income and real assets asset classes lead to an implied bet that in both cases is positive and about twice as large in absolute value as the negative bet in the equity asset class, where the tilt score is negative, and about half the absolute value of the tilt scores of the other two asset classes. This observation confirms the expectation that asset

TABLE 11.1 Example of Tilt Scores Summary

Member Weight Asset Class	Proposed Tilts (−3 to +3)					
	CIO 35%	G-1 25%	G-1 25%	G-2 0%	Adviser 15%	Average
Cash						
Fixed Income and Related						
U.S. Fixed Income Inv. Grade	1.0	0.0	−1.0	0.0	1.0	0.0
U.S. Fixed Income HY	0.0	−1.0	−1.0	0.0	−1.0	0.0
EAFE Fixed Income Hedged	0.0	0.0	0.0	0.0	0.0	0.0
EM Debt	0.0	0.0	0.0	1.0	0.0	0.0
RV Hedge Multi Strategy	1.0	2.0	1.0	1.0	1.0	0.0
Global Macro	1.0	1.0	0.0	1.0	1.0	0.0
Illiquid Fixed Income	2.0	2.0	1.0	0.0	1.0	0.0
Public Equity and Related						
U.S. Equities	−2.0	1.0	−1.0	1.0	−1.0	0.0
EAFE Equities	0.0	0.0	0.0	1.0	−1.0	0.0
EM Equities	0.0	1.0	0.0	1.0	−1.0	0.0
Directional Hedge Eq L/S	−2.0	1.0	0.0	0.0	−2.0	0.0
Managed Futures	0.0	−1.0	0.0	0.0	0.0	0.0
Illiquid Equities	1.0	0.0	0.0	1.0	1.0	0.0
Others						
REITs	0.0	0.0	−1.0	1.0	1.0	0.0
Precious Metals	2.0	0.0	2.0	1.0	1.0	0.0
Commodities	1.0	−1.0	1.0	1.0	1.0	0.0
Illiquid Real Assets	1.0	0.0	0.0	0.0	1.0	0.0
Overall Total						

allocation tilts be proportional to their tilt scores. Further visual inspection reinforces this perception when looking simultaneously at the implied bets for individual sub-asset classes relative to their tilt scores; the "fit" is not perfect, as the model needs to balance a variety of what are, at times, conflicting positions, but the direction generally is exactly what we would expect.

Table 11.3 shows the "preferred tilts" together and alongside the other options. It clearly illustrates the general rule that the "optimized" tilt almost always yields the most potential value added, with allocations that are much more extreme than those recommended by the other, formulaic algorithms. Note that the allocation to equity is at its absolute minimum level, 21.9 percent, despite a relatively low −0.2, tilting score. By contrast, the real assets and fixed income allocations are very close to their own maximum, despite

TABLE 11.2 Example of Tilted Asset Allocation

	Policy Allocation	Deviation Ranges Minimum	Maximum	Tilt Inputs	*** Preferred Tilt	Implied Bet
Cash	6.3%	0.0%	100.0%		3.1%	−3.2%
Fixed Income and Related						
U.S. Fixed Income Inv. Grade	11.5%	1.5%	21.5%	0.3	11.1%	−0.4%
U.S. Fixed Income HY	1.1%	0.0%	11.1%	−0.7	0.0%	−1.1%
EAFE Fixed Income Hedged	1.1%	0.0%	11.1%	0.0	0.0%	−1.1%
EM Debt	1.0%	0.0%	11.0%	0.0	0.0%	−1.0%
RV Hedge Multi Strategy	1.9%	0.0%	11.9%	1.3	4.8%	2.9%
Global Macro	1.9%	0.0%	11.9%	0.8	3.1%	1.3%
Illiquid Fixed Income	1.4%	0.0%	6.4%	1.6	2.8%	1.4%
Total	19.9%	4.9%	34.9%	0.4	21.9%	2.1%
Public Equity and Related						
U.S. Equities	9.8%	0.0%	19.8%	−0.9	7.8%	−2.1%
EAFE Equities	7.7%	0.0%	17.7%	−0.2	7.9%	0.3%
EM Equities	4.4%	0.0%	14.4%	0.1	5.5%	1.1%
Directional Hedge Eq L/S	3.5%	0.0%	13.5%	−0.8	1.7%	−1.7%
Managed Futures	2.0%	0.0%	12.0%	−0.3	1.9%	−0.1%
Illiquid Equities	9.6%	4.6%	14.6%	0.5	11.2%	1.6%
Total	36.9%	21.9%	51.9%	−0.2	35.9%	−1.0%
Others						
REITs	13.8%	3.8%	23.8%	−0.1	12.4%	−1.5%
Precious Metals	6.4%	0.0%	16.4%	1.4	9.7%	3.4%
Commodities	6.9%	0.0%	16.9%	0.5	7.5%	0.5%
Illiquid Real Assets	9.7%	4.7%	14.7%	0.5	9.4%	−0.3%
Total	36.9%	21.9%	51.9%	0.4	39.0%	2.1%
Overall Total	100.0%			0.2	100.0%	
Tilted Score				0.2	0.3	

TABLE 11.3 Comparing Preferred Tilt to Other Algorithms

	Tilt Inputs	*** Preferred Tilt	Primacy AC SAC		Primacy SAC AC		Opti-Mized
			Outside Range Eligible	Stay Within Range	Outside Range Eligible	Stay Within Range	
Cash		3.1%	2.9%	3.1%	0.0%	0.0%	0.0%
Fixed Income and Related							
U.S. Fixed Income Inv. Grade	0.3	11.1%	11.2%	11.1%	11.9%	11.9%	1.5%
U.S. Fixed Income HY	−0.7	0.0%	0.0%	0.0%	0.0%	0.0%	0.0%
EAFE Fixed Income Hedged	0.0	0.0%	0.0%	0.0%	1.0%	1.0%	0.0%
EM Debt	0.0	0.0%	0.0%	0.0%	0.9%	0.9%	0.0%
RV Hedge Multi Strategy	1.3	4.8%	4.9%	4.8%	5.9%	5.8%	11.9%
Global Macro	0.8	3.1%	3.2%	3.1%	4.2%	4.2%	11.9%
Illiquid Fixed Income	1.6	2.8%	2.9%	2.8%	3.9%	3.9%	6.4%
Total	0.4	21.9%	22.2%	21.9%	27.8%	27.8%	31.7%
Public Equity and Related							
U.S. Equities	−0.9	7.8%	7.8%	7.8%	6.7%	6.7%	0.0%
EAFE Equities	−0.2	7.9%	7.9%	7.9%	6.9%	6.9%	0.0%
EM Equities	0.1	5.5%	5.5%	5.5%	4.5%	4.5%	7.3%
Directional Hedge Eq L/S	−0.8	1.7%	1.7%	1.7%	0.9%	0.9%	0.0%
Managed Futures	−0.3	1.9%	1.9%	1.9%	1.1%	1.1%	0.0%
Illiquid Equities	0.5	11.2%	11.2%	11.2%	10.1%	10.1%	14.6%
Total	−0.2	35.9%	35.9%	35.9%	30.3%	30.2%	21.9%
Others							
REITs	−0.1	12.4%	12.4%	12.4%	13.0%	13.0%	3.8%
Precious Metals	1.4	9.7%	9.7%	9.7%	10.5%	10.5%	16.4%
Commodities	0.5	7.5%	7.5%	7.5%	8.3%	8.3%	16.7%
Illiquid Real Assets	0.5	9.4%	9.4%	9.4%	10.2%	10.2%	9.5%
Total	0.4	39.0%	39.0%	39.0%	41.9%	41.9%	46.4%
Overall Total	0.2	100.0%	100.0%	100.0%	100.0%	100.0%	100.0%
Resulting Overall Tilt Score	0.2	0.3	0.3	0.3	0.4	0.4	0.8

relatively modest favorable, positive tilt scores. In short, both within the asset classes and the sub-asset classes, a few extreme allocations are recommended that have the potential to provide for a much more successful capture of the dichotomy between favorable and unfavorable investment views. Unfortunately, this is not very visible here, because the individual votes shown in Table 11.1 result in a somewhat "bland" average. Although certain individuals appear to have strong convictions with respect to there being material opportunities (this is when one has votes of −2 or +2 or even −3 or +3), other people take the opposite view. In short, extreme individual views did not attract unconditional and unequivocal support. With overall scores near the middle of the −3 to +3 range, the allocation differences between an optimized rather than a formulaic tilt model remain modest.

Within the formulaic variants of the tilt model, decisions based on sub-asset rather than asset classes allow some higher potential value added capture, but the difference between the proposed allocations when decisions prioritize sub-asset classes and those that start with asset classes remains somewhat minor. A detailed analysis of the data presented in Table 11.3 demonstrates that decisions based on sub-asset classes simply appear to be more "aggressive" than those based on asset classes. Clearly, the differences here are more manageable and it is worth having the family—or client—look at them and confirm that the more controlled decisions make more sense on risk management grounds. A simple simulation of decision rules over some intermediate-term, historical time period can help identify the extra tracking error involved in the more aggressive strategy.

Table 11.4 presents the final iteration of the process: the determination of required trades in the portfolio, given the current starting positions and the just agreed-on tilted allocation. For the sake of simplicity, I assumed that the starting portfolio was smack on policy, as there was no reason to be more complicated and assume anything different. Yet, one should certainly note that the current allocation, in practice, will rarely match the policy mix. Table 11.4 demonstrates that, given the current allocation and the preferred tilt, one can draw up a list of purchases and sales by sub-asset class or strategy. Ostensibly, this will require cash to be added to or subtracted from managers as appropriate. This is where we would need to address manager selection and the formulation and management of manager modules. Indeed, one could imagine at least two different ways of dealing with the required cash flows. The first would be to re-create the actual manager allocation found in the various modules, adding or subtracting in effect from all existing positions. The second would be not to rely on formal modules—but rather to rely on minimum and maximum individual manager allocations, for instance—and add to an asset class or strategy by investing in a new

TABLE 11.4 Transactions Resulting from a Tilting Cycle

	Percent Allocations		Dollar Amounts			
					Required Trades	
	Policy Allocation	Preferred Tilt	Current Allocation	Target Allocation	Purchases	Sales
Cash	6.3%	3.1%	3,154,848	1,571,155		−1,583,693
Fixed Income and Related						
U.S. Fixed Income Inv. Grade	11.5%	11.1%	5,764,828	5,562,375		−202,453
U.S. Fixed Income HY	1.1%	0.0%	561,448	0		−561,448
EAFE Fixed Income Hedged	1.1%	0.0%	534,631	0		−534,631
EM Debt	1.0%	0.0%	485,072	0		−485,072
RV Hedge Multi Strategy	1.9%	4.8%	956,712	2,420,925	1,464,213	
Global Macro	1.9%	3.1%	940,276	1,571,155	630,880	
Illiquid Fixed Income	1.4%	2.8%	684,906	1,399,120	714,213	
Total	19.9%	21.9%	9,927,874	10,953,575	1,025,701	
Public Equity and Related						
U.S. Equities	9.8%	7.8%	4,921,859	3,880,715		−1,041,144
EAFE Equities	7.7%	7.9%	3,828,112	3,953,636	125,523	
EM Equities	4.4%	5.5%	2,187,493	2,729,683	542,190	
Directional Hedge Eq L/S	3.5%	1.7%	1,733,910	859,433		−874,477
Managed Futures	2.0%	1.9%	975,627	934,484		−41,144
Illiquid Equities	9.6%	11.2%	4,824,539	5,616,729	792,190	
Total	36.9%	35.9%	18,471,541	17,974,680		−496,861
Others						
REITs	13.8%	12.4%	6,912,524	6,176,237		−736,287
Precious Metals	6.4%	9.7%	3,185,485	4,865,865	1,680,380	
Commodities	6.9%	7.5%	3,474,089	3,737,802	263,713	
Illiquid Real Assets	9.7%	9.4%	4,873,639	4,720,686		−152,953
Total	36.9%	39.0%	18,445,737	19,500,590	1,054,853	
Overall Total	100.0%	100.0%	50,000,000	50,000,000	0	0

manager or adding to one or two of the existing members of the stable, or to reduce partially or totally a single manager when an allocation needs to be cut.

Before we conclude this topic, consider Table 11.5. It presents the result of the investment committee performance measurement effort I conducted with a particular client, as referenced earlier. The investment committee had seven members. The table shows the value added—or detracted—by each member and by the committee as a whole,[4] together with the best and worst individual contributions for each particular line. The table shows that all but one member failed to add value—a euphemism for the fact that individually and collectively the committee detracted value! Not only can we look at the overall contribution of each member relative to his or her peers, but we can also focus on how each member contributed along each of the line items. For instance, note that member A was the only member with a positive contribution and contributed positively across all mega asset or strategy categories; yet, within each mega category, he or she had material differences, for instance, ostensibly getting U.S. equities quite right and emerging market equities terribly wrong. Is this a case of having been lucky with bets that might have been too aggressive? Further, considering the negative contribution for both emerging equities and debt, was there an unfortunate emerging market bias? By contrast, members F and G detracted quite a lot each and, in both cases, 50 percent or more of their negative contributions resulted from getting precious metals badly wrong; a detailed analysis of these votes would show that they used the most extreme score available for that line and stayed there for the full period, despite markets moving against them.

This is where educational insights can be gleaned both for the committee chairman and for each member. Not shown in the table is how these contributions moved over time (what we show here is the total contribution of each individual over an almost two-year period); these individual data, together with the full period results, help show each member where success or failure resulted. Was it the case of one bad period or a succession of unsuccessful decisions? Was there a clear bias that persisted in the face of adversity and when one might have paused to make sure one understood why one was wrong? Or was it due to gyrations in the face of adversity? In short, was it a case of being a momentum player in a trading market environment or too much of a mean reversal type when markets are trending? A review of meeting minutes that noted the most significant and strongest comments can also be used to add to this quantitative exercise. A key point

---

[4]Note that the I C scores may be—and in fact are—different from those of the average of the scores.

TABLE 11.5 Example of Investment Committee Performance Evaluation

	Investment Committee Members								IC		
	Full I C	A	B	C	D	E	F	G	Average	High	Low
Cash	0.00%	0.00%	0.00%	0.00%	0.00%	0.00%	0.00%	0.00%	0.00%	0.00%	0.00%
Fixed Income and Related											
U.S. Fixed Income Inv. Grade	-0.10%	-0.15%	-0.08%	0.04%	-0.08%	-0.16%	0.07%	0.07%	-0.04%	0.07%	-0.16%
U.S. Fixed Income HY	-0.06%	-0.10%	-0.04%	-0.01%	0.01%	-0.01%	-0.22%	-0.23%	-0.09%	0.01%	-0.23%
EAFE Fixed Income	0.04%	0.26%	-0.04%	0.01%	-0.08%	-0.06%	0.12%	0.12%	0.05%	0.26%	-0.08%
EM Debt	0.24%	-0.06%	0.19%	0.00%	0.30%	0.27%	0.28%	0.28%	0.18%	0.30%	-0.06%
RV Hedge	-0.08%	-0.12%	0.00%	0.03%	0.01%	-0.18%	-0.03%	-0.01%	-0.04%	0.03%	-0.18%
Global Macro	0.02%	0.34%	0.10%	0.01%	0.09%	-0.15%	-0.18%	-0.19%	0.00%	0.34%	-0.19%
Total	0.06%	0.17%	0.13%	0.08%	0.24%	-0.30%	0.04%	0.04%	0.06%	0.24%	-0.30%
Public Equity and Related											
U.S. Equities	0.22%	0.52%	0.16%	-0.03%	0.34%	0.18%	0.25%	0.22%	0.23%	0.52%	-0.03%
EAFE Equities	0.04%	0.12%	0.02%	-0.06%	-0.01%	0.05%	0.07%	0.01%	0.03%	0.12%	-0.06%
EM Equities	-0.09%	-0.47%	-0.36%	-0.04%	0.06%	-0.13%	0.29%	0.09%	-0.08%	0.29%	-0.47%
Long/Short Equities	-0.22%	-0.09%	-0.11%	0.01%	-0.14%	-0.34%	-0.23%	-0.23%	-0.16%	0.01%	-0.34%
Managed Futures	-0.10%	0.06%	0.25%	0.02%	-0.52%	-0.09%	-0.39%	-0.35%	-0.14%	0.25%	-0.52%
Total	-0.15%	0.14%	-0.04%	-0.10%	-0.27%	-0.33%	-0.02%	-0.25%	-0.12%	0.14%	-0.33%
All Equity and Related											
MLP	-0.08%	-0.12%	-0.12%	0.03%	0.00%	-0.14%	-0.09%	-0.11%	-0.08%	0.03%	-0.14%
REIT	-0.01%	0.33%	0.00%	0.00%	-0.22%	0.31%	-0.17%	-0.21%	0.00%	0.33%	-0.22%
Precious Metals	0.02%	0.59%	0.62%	0.00%	0.12%	0.11%	-0.83%	-0.61%	0.00%	0.62%	-0.83%
Commodities	-0.43%	-0.63%	-0.62%	-0.12%	-0.34%	-0.47%	-0.16%	-0.16%	-0.36%	-0.12%	-0.63%

that must be made before moving on: these analyses should be principally used to make the process better and help individuals improve rather than as short-term performance measure affecting compensation. A long succession of poor numbers may have meaning, but a two-year record—as shown in Table 11.5—does not provide sufficient perspective to make any definitive decision.

A final note is in order. Although we do not demonstrate it here, most families would require there to be an asset location exercise alongside the asset allocation effort. Indeed, as is the case in the family in our example, certain pockets may attract full income taxation, while others might benefit from tax exemptions or deferrals. Thus, when one is looking at the fixed income component of the portfolio, one would certainly need to choose between taxable and tax-exempt bonds so that the correct position tax status is found in the appropriate account or location. This can require the family to conduct two distinct tilting processes, one for the taxable accounts and one for the others. In this case, one will likely have formulated two different investment policies to ensure that tax issues are appropriately handled. We elected not to burden our readers with this complexity for two reasons. The first is simply that we did not feel that the demonstration of the complexity added much to the learning experience. The second anticipates the issue of readers who do not live in the United States and for whom tax considerations and their solutions are different from those we might apply in the United States. In their case, the complexity might have actually been counterproductive, as it would have pointed to solutions based on implicit assumptions that do not apply to their circumstances. How do you deal with the question I just raised with respect to fixed income in countries where the concept of tax-exempt—or municipal—bonds does not exist?

In short, the tilt model as presented here is a work in progress to the extent that it is still totally conceivable that someone will find a more sophisticated way of looking at the algorithms we propose and come up with some solution that will take more of a "consensus" approach if it is mathematically possible. My own view is that the choice between the various priorities is, unfortunately—or fortunately, depending on your point of view—relatively clear. One must decide whether to go for added return at all costs or to choose an approach that recognizes that there can be some measure of reasonable value added, but that any move designed to capture it must be controlled so that risk is appropriately managed.

SUMMARY AND CONCLUSIONS

The foregoing was an example of a systematic process designed to allow a manager—or advisor—who believes that some measure of tactical portfolio tilting value added is available. Ostensibly, this premise must be tested, and work that has been done thus far suggests that the endeavor is not risk-free. Although the jury is still out on the basis of pretax return, the historical and theoretical body of evidence does not provide huge comfort to those who must worry about after-tax value added. Yet, the thought is that we must remember that advisors are in the business of assisting clients and that clients come to the "party" with quite a number of preferences and biases. Thus, it may be true that it is better in the end to help a client systematize the way he or she makes tactical tilting decisions than to argue that tactical tilting simply makes no sense. The point is that it is important to retain the "right" to come back to the conference table and discuss the issue. Thus, being overly forceful and dismissive of a view a client has and to which he or she holds strongly may serve neither the advisor nor the client. It may not serve the advisor to the extent that the client might simply move on until he or she meets someone who will allow him or her to make the decisions that appear to be appropriate. It may not help the client either, as moving to some other manager may deprive the client from the balance and open-mindedness that will eventually bring him or her to realize that hypotheses might have been erroneous. Again, this does not mean that there are not certain cases when a disconnect with a client is such that walking away is the best strategy; the point is that one should be absolutely sure of one's view before taking such a step.

The one element of the issue that keeps coming up is the need for an auditable process that will allow both client and advisor to measure the value added actually generated. Only with hard data that show that the exercise might have been successful in absolute—and pretax—terms but actually hurt on an after-tax basis will the advisor help the client move away from activities that, although well-intended and appropriately executed, eventually cost after-tax dollars. Only then will it be possible to begin to tackle the question of how those insights can be captured and reflected in the portfolio in a profitable after-tax manner. This will be the eventual question and represent the current frontier of the tactical portfolio tilting process.

Although we do not know what this process actually looks like yet, we can begin to guess at a few of its most important features. Indeed, just as systematic loss harvesting allowed tax-focused managers to generate value added in many—but not all—circumstances, it is reasonable to suppose that a measure of systematic tax-loss harvesting focused on asset class or sub-asset class random price fluctuation could be combined with a systematic "coding" or "scoring" of investment views and some systematic formulaic or optimized portfolio tilting process to generate long-term tactical tilting value added. At one end of the spectrum is the idea that value added might solely be comprised of the realization of random short-term asset class or sub-asset class capital losses to allow gains to be taken elsewhere in the portfolio in a tax-protected manner, for instance, when the need to rebalance to the neutral allocation arises. At the other end, one might be able to devise a process that allows both the capture of random short-term losses and the benefit of short- to medium-term relative valuation insights.

Finally, focusing again on the wealthy client portion of our readers, although it may have been tedious to labor through something that is definitely within the mechanism of the watch, the point was to show that: first, without a systematic process, it is doubtful that an individual portfolio will reflect the same insights as any other, given the uniqueness of each investment policy; and second, a lot of insight can be coaxed from data if one takes the time to do it. The implication is that one should be able to begin to assess how individual members of each client's decision team has contributed.

CHAPTER 12

Portfolio Reporting

Portfolio reporting, in the definition I use here, is meant to comprise both the regular compilation of an organized list of assets together with their historical costs—tax basis where applicable—and current values, and the dissection of these line items to allow the investor to assess exposures to various "risk factors." This naturally leads to the computation of various performance measures and the compilation of the data required in order for the client or the advisor to assess that performance.

THE CURRENT CHALLENGE

At present, portfolio reporting in the individual—or private client—world has become almost as developed as in the institutional market. This should not surprise as—taxes aside—the actual process architecture should not be different from one market to the other; one of the most complex tasks, securities pricing, has been highly mechanized and securities codes or CUSIP numbers remain the same irrespective of the identity of the investor or whether he or she owns one share or one million shares. Tax-aware reporting presents more of a mixed picture to the extent that compiling all the various bits of information required is absolutely available, but performance computation and assessment rarely are.

The current environment becomes orders of magnitude more complex once the problem is expressed in the goals-based framework, rather than simply envisaged in terms of a single aggregate portfolio. The challenge chiefly revolves around the fact that certain investments overlap across several individual "modules." Returning to Table 8.3, which we reproduce here as Table 12.1 so readers do not have to flip back and forth to follow, you can clearly see that several asset classes or strategies are included in the neutral allocation of several modules (note that this becomes an even more prevalent fact when one starts to allow tactical variations in the various strategic

TABLE 12.1 (Reproducing Table 8.3) Resulting Goals-Based Modules

Asset Class/ Strategy	ST LIFE	LT LIFE	NOM PP	REAL PP	REAL G	GROWTH
Cash	25.7%	0.6%	1.8%	2.1%	3.0%	2.7%
U.S. Fixed Income Inv. Grade	55.7%	27.5%	17.9%	0.0%	0.0%	0.0%
U.S. Fixed Income HY	6.5%	0.0%	0.0%	0.0%	0.0%	0.2%
EAFE Fixed Income Hedged	6.5%	0.0%	0.0%	0.0%	0.0%	0.0%
EM Debt	5.6%	0.0%	0.0%	0.0%	0.0%	0.2%
Relative Value Multy Strategy	0.0%	8.3%	6.3%	4.5%	0.0%	0.4%
Global Macro	0.0%	8.3%	6.3%	4.5%	0.0%	0.2%
Illiquid Fixed Income	0.0%	11.0%	5.4%	3.0%	0.0%	0.0%
U.S. Equities	0.0%	3.3%	7.6%	2.5%	11.3%	21.9%
EAFE Equities	0.0%	2.5%	5.9%	2.0%	8.8%	17.1%
EM Equities	0.0%	1.4%	3.4%	1.1%	5.0%	9.8%
Directional Hedge Eq L/S	0.0%	3.6%	8.4%	1.4%	0.0%	7.8%
Managed Futures	0.0%	3.6%	2.1%	1.4%	0.0%	5.2%
Illiquid Equities	0.0%	0.0%	2.6%	2.8%	16.0%	19.6%
REITs	0.0%	22.5%	15.6%	26.4%	18.1%	7.5%
Precious Metals	0.0%	4.5%	4.9%	14.9%	11.2%	0.0%
Commodities	0.0%	3.0%	2.3%	17.7%	12.6%	0.0%
Illiquid Real Assets	0.0%	0.0%	9.7%	15.6%	14.0%	7.5%
Overall Total	100.0%	100.0%	100.0%	100.0%	100.0%	100.0%

asset or strategy weights). Note, for instance, still based on strategic allocations, that:

1. Cash can be held in all modules;
2. Fixed income can be held in the three modules with the lowest expected volatility;
3. Relative value or lower volatility alternative strategies can be found in all but two modules, while illiquid fixed income can be found in three of the six shown;
4. Long-only equities are found in all but the lowest expected return volatility module;

5. Alternative and illiquid strategies within the equity risk spectrum are also found in at least four of the six modules; and
6. Liquid real assets are found in all but the lowest return volatility module, while illiquid real assets can be held in four out of six.

Thus, without some additional information entered into the database when a security—or some commingled investment—is bought, the task of allocating different investments to each module is next to impossible.

As we saw in the section of Chapter 6 entitled "It Changes Everything," one of the two main attributes of the goals-based process is that "it creates a visible and real link between "My Wealth" and "My Life." We also noted there that, "by providing an opportunity to see how various portions of the wealth were doing through time, families begin to appreciate how markets interact with their own wealth and well-being." We concluded: "at a minimum, this feedback loop helps families live through nasty market conditions by experiencing at least some success."

It is necessary that portfolio reporting be feasible at both the overall portfolio level and with respect to each goal for the goals-based process to be fully effective—or for families and advisors to capture as many of its potential benefits as possible. Ultra-affluent families, particularly those with multiple family members or investment structures, do not always experience this problem as acutely as the merely affluent or wealthy. The creation of "goals-based" limited partnerships, for instance, can mitigate the challenge to the extent that each "goal" has its own module in the form of a separate and distinct commingled investment vehicle. Each member of the family or investment structure within the family group can own the appropriate proportional share of its total assets in each of the relevant partnerships. Similarly, in jurisdictions where it is a feasible solution, master/feeder arrangements can also achieve the same purpose, with lower investment thresholds. In both cases, full instrument transparency can even be provided so that one can actually see the full listing of the individual investments owned in one's portfolio, although they may be owned through intermediate structures.

The fact that the same security—or commingle vehicle—may be owned in more than one module—and thus be "used" to defease or meet more than one goal—requires a change in the typical architecture of most portfolio reporting systems. This has two important implications:

1. One must be able to "break" dealing lots—or minimum investments— into "sub-lots" to reflect the fact that the investment may be shared across multiple modules. This is particularly relevant when dealing with commingled structures, particularly when they involve minimum investments. Consider three simple cases. First, mutual funds typically

have multiple classes of shares, often extending to an "institutional" class that requires a larger minimum investment but charges lower fees. Second, most alternative managers have minimum investments as well, a requirement dictated to them by the limited number of "slots" their partnerships often comprise. Finally, many individual account managers will also require some minimum asset level to accept a mandate. In each of these cases, it may be necessary to be able to show a "common face" to the outside, all the while having "individualized faces" for internal reporting purposes.

2. Second, in the multiple cases where there are various forms of corporate actions (these include dividends or interest income earned, to name the two most frequent cases only), the system must be able to allocate to each module its proportional share of that action.

In short, when any investment is made, one must not only enter all the relevant and usual parameters required by all reporting systems, but one must also include information as to which "module" owns that investment. Without such a feature, any reporting at the level of each goal is not only incomplete, but can be quite misleading, as one does not know exactly who owns what. Beyond the simple listing of actual portfolio or sub-portfolio assets, performance computation and assessment becomes totally impossible without the ability to tag individual investments back to each goal.

Table 12.2 helps illustrate this point. It reproduces Table 10.6, which presented the sub-investment policy of the personal account of the family we encountered in the case study used in the last few chapters and shows the dollar allocations to each asset class or strategy, for both each "goal" and the whole account. Consider the U.S. equity exposure, for instance. We can see that the account's total exposure, assuming that the portfolio today is on policy, is $1,043,876. Although an important data point in itself, reporting at the level of each of the four goals we have for that account requires us to see the equity exposures of the three goals that are allowed to hold equity: lifestyle expense defeasance beyond the next five years, the capital needed to fund a family foundation in ten years, and surplus assets managed for growth. Table 12.2 shows that these comprise U.S. equity exposures of $218,667, $503,822, and $321,387, respectively. With amounts so relatively small, one would probably assume that the family would choose only one manager for that exposure—whether that manager is appointed to run a separate account or hired through a mutual fund or an exchange-traded fund (ETF). Using the simplest assumption, a mutual fund or an ETF, there would be a simple CUSIP number to the holding, but we must be able to allocate the appropriate amount to each goal. Further, when that mutual fund or ETF distributes dividends or realized capital gains, these income items must

TABLE 12.2 (Reproducing Table 10.6) Sub-Investment Policy for the Family Account

Asset Class/Strategy	Account Size				Actual Allocation 22,000,000					Sub-Investment Policy
	24% STL	40% R PP	30% N PP	7% G	STL	R PP	RG	G	Total	
Cash	25.7%	2.1%	1.8%	2.7%	1,344,372	185,815	117,275	39,648	1,687,110	7.7%
U.S. Fixed Income Inv. Grade	55.7%	0.0%	17.9%	0.0%	2,911,340	0	1,182,276	0	4,093,616	18.6%
U.S. Fixed Income HY	6.5%	0.0%	0.0%	0.2%	339,656	0	-576	3,037	342,117	1.6%
EAFE Fixed Income Hedged	6.5%	0.0%	0.0%	0.0%	339,656	0	0	0	339,656	1.5%
EM Debt	5.6%	0.0%	0.0%	0.2%	291,134	0	-576	3,037	293,594	1.3%
Relative Value Multy Strategy	0.0%	4.5%	6.3%	0.4%	0	391,964	413,797	5,466	811,226	3.7%
Global Macro	0.0%	4.5%	6.3%	0.2%	0	391,964	413,797	3,644	809,404	3.7%
Illiquid Fixed Income	0.0%	3.0%	5.4%	0.0%	0	261,309	355,835	0	617,144	2.8%
U.S. Equities	0.0%	2.5%	7.6%	21.9%	0	218,667	503,822	321,387	1,043,876	4.7%
EAFE Equities	0.0%	2.0%	5.9%	17.1%	0	170,074	391,862	249,967	811,903	3.7%
EM Equities	0.0%	1.1%	3.4%	9.8%	0	97,185	223,921	142,839	463,945	2.1%
Directional Hedge Eq L/S	0.0%	1.4%	8.4%	7.8%	0	121,482	555,138	113,710	790,329	3.6%
Managed Futures	0.0%	1.4%	2.1%	5.2%	0	121,482	138,785	75,807	336,073	1.5%
Illiquid Equities	0.0%	2.8%	2.6%	19.6%	0	242,963	169,109	286,612	698,684	3.2%
REITs	0.0%	26.4%	15.6%	7.5%	0	2,300,919	1,029,275	109,866	3,440,061	15.6%
Precious Metals	0.0%	14.9%	4.9%	0.0%	0	1,299,453	321,649	0	1,621,102	7.4%
Commodities	0.0%	17.7%	2.3%	0.0%	0	1,543,017	150,103	0	1,693,119	7.7%
Illiquid Real Assets	0.0%	15.6%	9.7%	7.5%	0	1,353,877	643,297	109,866	2,107,040	9.6%

be allocated to the correct goal, assuming that they are received in cash and not in kind. Similar analyses must be made for each line.

A SIMPLE ANALOGY

Although this challenge has seemingly and somewhat amazingly to me trumped many in the industry so far, it is not the first time that a problem of this nature has affected investors.

Consider the issue of taxes. Whether one is talking of individual investors in many jurisdictions or of Australian pension funds, for instance, the need to be able to report income to the taxing authorities is primordial. Further, for all jurisdictions where realized capital gains are taxable, one must be able to keep track of all investments down to individual tax lots—defined as the bundle of a given security that was purchased at some common price on some common date. Note that most jurisdictions allow the averaging of such individual lots bought on the same day, even if they were not all purchased at exactly the same price. This is required to be able to determine whether a sale gives rise to a capital gain or not—as there may be a wide range of prices at which an individual security has been purchased over time. This is also needed, where applicable, to assess whether the gain qualifies for long-term treatment or not. Note that there may be instances when a security—or an investment—is held at an average cost that straddles today's price. In these cases, selecting which lot is sold, for example, can mean the difference between realizing a gain or realizing a loss!!! When the security is liable to distribute income in forms that may lead to a change in the tax basis of the average holding, there is the added requirement that the accounting system be able to cope with changes in the tax basis of any investment.

This challenge led the industry, both at local and global levels, to develop the now ubiquitous tax lot accounting systems. Each individual purchase of any given security is tagged with a date, which is the most frequent descriptor and differentiator between tax lots. Thus, when I look at my holdings of any individual security or commingled instrument, I can see either or both of two things:

1. My overall holding, providing an average book value and today's appropriate pricing, both of which allow me to see my aggregate unrealized gain or loss in that position, or
2. A series of individual sub-positions—aggregating to the overall holding—broken down by tax lot showing the book value and today's pricing for each lot, allowing me to see the actual unrealized capital gain

or loss for each lot. For investments that may be purchased over time, it is not infrequent that certain lots might show an unrealized gain while others show an unrealized loss.[1]

Practically, tax lot accounting simply requires capturing some additional information at the security level. Although this certainly contributes to additional complexity in the system and its overall architecture, it is really nothing much more than a basic database management problem that has become almost trivial as computer memory costs have fallen considerably.

It is hard so see why a similar concept could not be applied in terms of a goals-based module. The need would simply be to "tag" each investment with information as to which goal sub-portfolio might own it. The presence of goals-based modules—which exist both within the total portfolio and within each account, as we saw in Chapter 11—makes this relatively simple, as the "tag" in this case would simply be the identity of the module that owns the security or the commingled investment. Any and all corporate action that affected any such investment would be tagged with the same module label, in the proportion in which the investment is owned by the various modules. One might need to provide for a few "decision tests" to ensure that total exposure to any investment does not fall below some required minimum—this would not be too much of an issue at purchase time, as the counterparty would simply reject the trade if it was of an insufficient size, but it could become one when a partial liquidation is needed.

Just as it is possible to ask for a report in terms of, for example, all current tax lots that are held at an unrealized loss, it would be feasible to construct detailed portfolio reports for each of our client's goals.[2] With such reports, we could not only answer the first question: What is the value of the portfolio dedicated to this or that goal? We could also see how it has performed and compare that return, if appropriate, to some policy benchmark; we can even attribute performance along decision dimensions, such as the tactical tilting and manager selection, or more detailed risk factors, such as industry, geography, currency, credit, interest rate exposure, and many others.

In short, two important conclusions come to the fore. First, without the ability to report down to the level of the individual goal, the goals-based

---

[1]Note that this is precisely the feature that allows managers who seek tax efficiency by using a systematic tax loss harvesting process to operate. Wash sale rules—where they exist—represent an important constraint, but this is not germane to our point here.

[2]Many accounting systems do not hold asset reports but only keep track of individual transactions. Reports are created by combining all transactions from inception to the current date.

wealth management approach loses a lot of its appeal. The crucial feedback loop as to how "my assets" are working to meet "my goals" is missing. Ostensibly, it does still allow one to match more effectively each individual goal to the appropriate asset classes and strategies. Yet, being unable to verify progress on the way to each goal's horizon at best complicates the process: an alternative would involve re-computing the asset allocation at more frequent intervals, but even that would be insufficient and unsatisfactory as it would still not allow the client and the advisor to see how one is doing, through time. Clearly, certain goals—particularly those that require long-duration assets—take time to be achieved and effectively ironing out short-term fluctuations is both costly and unnecessary.

Second, measuring and assessing performance is another feedback loop that is crucial: we called it "financial hygiene" for good reasons in Chapter 11. Although the actual determination of what my return was last month, last week, or yesterday—and for each goal—is not truly relevant in the long term, tracking with some measure of precision, and across each goal, the attribution of my performance is much more critical. It may well be, for instance, that biases, preferences, or simply skills make me better or worse with respect to one or another dimension of the investment process. It is equally possible that certain modules might be more or less affected by these biases, preferences, or skills differences than others. Thus, it may well be that it makes sense to reduce the activity that is carried out in a module if that activity is very important in that module and seems to be an area in which some work is needed on the process.

I want to mention a final element of the reporting process here, although it is a relatively easy dimension to create and incorporate into any reporting system. There can really be two different causes to a program being successful: first, the investment performance can meet or exceed expectations; second the cash flows that are actually spent match earlier projections. A goals-based reporting process should be able to address both, not only because of the need to be clear, but more importantly because some excess spending, for instance, may be "accidental" or "structural." If the former, one simply shrugs the variance and moves on; if the latter, there may be a need for a complete review of the policy to ensure that the allocation reflects the individual's actual needs rather than some earlier misinterpretation.

ADDING TAXES MAKES THINGS EVEN MORE COMPLEX

Readers will not be surprised by these last few paragraphs. Taxes always make things more complex. The challenge here relates both to the issue of classical tax accounting and to the challenge posed in terms of portfolio reporting when certain structures do not pay their own taxes. We are assuming here that structures that are tax-exempt or tax-deferred will most of the time need to make different investments than "sister" structures that may still be used to defease similar goals. This applies to the example we carried through Chapters 9, 10, and 11: the retirement accounts were to be used to meet certain lifestyle goals once the couple reached 70.5 years of age. It is unlikely, in this case, that investments held in the tax-exempt pockets might be commingled with those held for taxable entities.

The complexity of the issues and my not being qualified to offer tax advice require me to punt, as I would not want to lead anyone astray with a statement that might only be half true, if not totally wrong, when not precisely specified. The point I do want to make is that changes in tax basis can occur through time for a variety of reasons and that the accounting system that is developed must either allow for occasional "shocks" needed to make adjustments or incorporate the detail of transactions or occurrences that might cause a change in basis.

A similar issue arises when partnerships are introduced into the picture, for example, to commingle certain family assets for ease of investment. Rules governing inside and outside tax bases for partnerships in the United States are very complex and arcane and require special focus.

In short, however, it may be worth remembering the old adage that the best can be the enemy of the good. Although a system that can comprehensively address all the challenges faced by all investors may be the most desirable, it may be better to break the problem into bites that are more easily chewable and digestible. So knowing what one's reporting priorities are, or simply what one needs or wants to achieve from a given series of reports, it might make sense to develop distinct solutions rather than look for and fail to find or create a truly holistic framework. One would hope that the various partial solutions would feed off some common database—if only to make sure that they are compatible—but it may not be necessary to combine back into an overall answer to any and all questions.

SUMMARY AND CONCLUSIONS

Portfolio reporting started as the easiest part of the investment process. It might have been time-consuming and highly involved, but it only required the simple accounting of investments in a single currency—the home currency. The move beyond a simple—and often short—list of securities to more diversified sub-portfolios made the challenge a bit more demanding, as one certainly had to move from simple, potentially hand-maintained ledgers to more sophisticated approaches. The advent of multi-currency accounting for investors who traded in securities across currencies and geographical boundaries created an important challenge, which the industry met over time. The multiple forms of specific accounting required for taxable portfolios or for assets held in certain forms of trust added yet another complexity and transformed what could initially easily be done manually to involved processes with multiple decision rules and dimensions.

Goals-based investing, with the creation of individual sub-portfolios designed to meet one goal, over one horizon and with a given required probability of success rather than a single return/risk trade-off, is yet another additional complexity. However, when viewed in the perspective of the massive changes history has required of systems designers focused on asset management issues, it looks almost trivial, to the extent that it seems simply to require the adaptation of a framework that has now been time-tested and is well-understood. Attaching to that new system the various performance measurement and assessment sub-routines also already in use by many facets of the industry also does not look like a daunting task.

Yet, even though it may not be the dimension of the goals-based management challenge that is the most complex or the most intellectually involved, it is the one without which it is hard to see the goals-based framework move decidedly forward and become the new norm. Indeed, without being able to show to clients how their assets are deployed differently to meet different goals and allow them to experience that relationship between their wealth and their lives, it is hard to argue that people will live through the other complexities associated with the process of breaking one simple portfolio into multiple sub-portfolios. While this could be seen by certain actors as a good reason to defer and procrastinate, it is worth remembering that families that have been exposed to the new approach—at least in this author's personal experience—do not want to go back to the past. Thus, it is highly likely that the demand from the marketplace will be there. There will, therefore, be a premium for the leaders and a risk of being passed by for those who do not embrace it and invest in the tools needed to make it work.

Four

Managing an Advisory Practice

(And How That Can Impact the Sustainability of Advisory Firms)

Before jumping into Part 4, I must offer a disclaimer. The book is intended for both the wealthy and their advisors, whether these are specialized in the investment world or not. The point of this last part of the book is to observe both that the current structure of the industry appears flawed and that it should change. At some level, the wealthy reading these next three chapters might initially wonder: Why does this concern me? The short answer is that it concerns them directly because they are stakeholders in the way the industry that serves their wealth management needs operates and evolves. Thus, discovering what I think is flawed in the way the industry is structured is important, as these flaws might simply kill practitioners who are trying to "do the right thing." Identifying what I think is needed for the industry to offer both a first-class service and one that is sustainable should also allow the wealthy to know which behavior or practice to support in their service providers and which to avoid. Making sure that those who are trying to do what is right are appropriately rewarded is one of the ways that the wealthy can play a role in the industry's evolution. I hope the wealthy among our readers will join me in this endeavor to help the industry reform itself so that it can truly and better serve their needs. After all, most wealthy families have multi-generational time horizons and making sure that the industry operates in a sustainable mode over that long term would seem to justify a short-term minor economic sacrifice if that is even required.

We concluded the Part 3 of this book with a comment that is the perfect lead-in to our fourth and final set of chapters: moving to a goals-based investment management framework injects a number of complexities into one's practice, but it is likely to be a requirement from the marketplace in the near future. I vividly remember how seasoned professionals resisted the change imposed by Modern Portfolio Theory and still saw it become the norm: it was more complicated, but it was also more compelling. I had a comparable experience of markets trying to avoid change when tax-awareness was injected into the private asset management world. Similarly, I view the lack of traction experienced so far by goals-based wealth management as the interplay between the natural inertia that often characterizes status quo and the somewhat radical nature of the change required. In due course, the compelling feature of a better solution with a better marriage of "My Wealth" and "My Life" will make the change inevitable and irresistible.

This process complexity is but a simple mirror of the complex nature of the situation faced by our clients. We will expand the discussion of this issue in Chapter 15, which introduces a different firm structure and will make the point that the many thoughts on which we have expounded so far are equally applicable, if not more so, to the other dimensions of the integrated wealth management process. Yet, in the first two chapters of this last part of the book, we want to focus on the way the industry generally operates and on the issues this raises. Ostensibly, the most important issue, from the point of view of the industry, is that our standard modus operandi leads to profit margins that would appear quite low; this may be why many advisors tend to gravitate toward variants on the theme that produce higher margins, such as offering products for which they either receive a manufacturer's price or some commission from the manufacturer. Yet, for clients, the current structure is at least as problematic, although many of them still do not know it, often because they have not truly experienced how much better their relationships might be with their advisors if those operated in a profitable and yet still conflict-free truly advisory mode.

We therefore start with a discussion of the typical advisory firm structure, with the important caveat that there are exceptions to the general observation offered here. It would indeed be beyond pretentious for me to claim that I am the only one who has thought about the problem and addressed it. In fact, the truth is that many of the thoughts I will be offering have come to me either directly or indirectly, through conversations with families and advisors. So I will accept the blame for all bad ideas and will be happy to share the credit for the good ones with those who were kind enough to enlighten me. The second chapter—Chapter 14—deals with the notion that one individual rarely is enough to satisfy all the needs of the wealthy. The chapter looks at the issue of individuals versus teams and should lead our readers to the conclusion that teams must be the answer, except for those who are not running a business, but focus on a small personal practice, probably built around a reputation and experience acquired over decades of working for others.

As previewed above, our last chapter—Chapter 15—outlines an alternative solution. While we focus on the investment process for the large bulk of the chapter, our last set of paragraphs expands the issue to the whole of the firm's disciplines: what is true in the asset management realm is equally true with respect to the multiple other dimensions of the wealth management challenge. We conclude with the idea that the critical individual in the whole process is truly the *client advisor,* whose role is to orchestrate the various capabilities of the firm to deliver to each client what he or she needs. He or she should not be a discipline specialist but rather a well-trained generalist who not only understands—although he or she may not be the best at—each of the disciplines, but, more important, is fully aware of how these various disciplines interact with one another. I should add here that with that enhanced visibility come both privilege and responsibilities; nothing is free in this world!

CHAPTER 13

The Currently Typical Firm Structure

In some ways, the title of this chapter is misleading: sticking to it and describing the "typical firm" is like *Mission Impossible*! Indeed, there are many firms today that are dedicated to meeting a few or all of the wealth management needs of individuals and families. Before proceeding with the point of this chapter, it is probably a good idea to highlight the main kinds of service providers currently at work in this space. Probably by far the most frequent are specialty shops that focus on a single aspect of the wealth management challenge. They include accountants, tax and estate lawyers, portfolio managers, financial advisors, philanthropic advisors, insurance brokers, educational consultants, family governance specialists, and many more. Certain ones offer services; others sell products. A smaller number of firms aim to offer many, and at times all, of the functions provided by a single-family family office, except that they cater to multiple clients rather than a single family. The focus of these so-called multi-family family offices is often on services more than products, with a strong emphasis placed on conflict-free open architecture. Finally, a small number of firms are created to cater to the needs of a single family.

Although our focus may appear to be more geared to advisors than to wealthy individuals and families, I feel that the latter will benefit from reading this book as well, if only to gain insights into how their service providers operate. The discussion in this chapter is purposely restricted to multi-family family offices and to those firms that offer financial advice to the affluent, which we will call fee-only financial advisors. Firms that compete in a single discipline and offer the product or service usually provided by their competition find themselves in an environment in which many of the decisions surrounding business model issues are, if not already made for them, mostly so. Competition has a way of restraining the number of options available. Those who choose to be different have to be exceptionally good, failing which they are rapidly destroyed. This applies to innovators who have not fully figured out how their business models should work; it also applies to those who try to be more profitable than others by skimping on certain product or service attributes; it also applies to those who try to raise prices without having a premium offering that justifies it. In short, single discipline players have to live within the confines of their narrowly defined industries.

Multi-family family offices and fee-only financial advisors are different in that they remain very much an industry in the process of being created. I can hear readers argue that this statement is stupid, as there have been players in these two fields for quite some time. My answer is that, while there have been players in the field for a while, the nature of the field and the needs of clients have changed enough that the discipline is still evolving. Both models started life under the impetus of highly enlightened individuals who were intent on changing the world. Many multi-family family offices were founded by former private bankers who grew jaundiced by what they saw as a cultural change from serving the client to flogging products to the client. Many fee-only financial advisors also grew tired of an environment in which they were asking their clients to buy products made by manufacturers who paid them a commission. Both sets of visionaries knew that their clients deserved better, but many of them did not know what would or would not work in practice.

MANY CHIEFS AND FEW INDIANS

The way in which the industry—both multi-family family offices and fee-only investment advisors—was founded made it almost a foregone conclusion that the new leaders, the innovators, started their new ventures on a very small scale, often as a single employee practice and at times with a small number of employees, who might be friends or former associates in a prior life. These new firms did not have a well-tested business model—other than in the minds of their founders. More importantly, they did not have the wherewithal needed to employ significant support staff; they had to first build a practice and then expand. In fact, many felt that their initial strength was their own reputations—or the reputations of the small team that came together—and they wanted the new firm first to succeed before they could think of appropriate staffing levels. Surely, the regulatory framework within which they had to operate would force them early on to adopt a certain number of rules. Yet, perversely, these added compliance costs almost assured that the initial employees beyond the first few wealth management professionals would not be other, more junior professionals in that same space, but rather people who would help them meet their regulatory compliance requirements.

Although a few of these initial ventures did very well and thus became businesses growing in an organic manner, the substantial business infrastructure expenses, including compliance costs, they faced led many innovators to elect to grow through acquisitions, without really thinking of building a self-sustaining business. Thus, innovators who had been more successful more quickly than others acquired other soul mates. This meant that firms grew in revenues and staff through a business model that did not attempt to increase operational efficiency, but rather to replicate "more of the same," at times even bypassing the development of badly needed infrastructure and fostering an unfortunate mentality of "jack of all trades" (and master of none), rather than establish a suitable mix of specialists and generalists, front, middle, and back office professionals and even shared corporate resources. The net result of this process is that many firms, even today, are more a collection of like-minded and similarly skilled men and women than businesses whose staffing models and policies were designed from the ground up. More precisely, each and every senior employee acts more as a personal practice than a member of a diverse staff with well-defined and complementary functions and roles.

THE ROOT OF THE CHALLENGE

This naturally leads to four different challenges that eventually prove difficult to address and correct. The first is that there is often precious little separation of duty or specialization. Each professional is a bit of a jack of all trades, with advisory skills that may not be as sharp as the specialized skills that got them there, or vice versa. There may be exceptional investors who have managed to keep clients because their investment performance is stellar despite debatable bedside manners. There may be exceptional lawyers whose clients so value their legal prowess that they are willing to overlook limited experience with asset management. There may be exceptional relationship managers who relied on first-class specialists within a large private bank, for instance, and may now miss these inputs possibly without even knowing it. One could go on, but the point is made: people are in their positions because they were exceptionally good at one thing, but not because they were top-flight generalists. Depending on the make-up of the firm's employees, one may or may not have all the skills required, and yet, top management may not be aware of the problem, as they often ostensibly rose to prominent positions without all the skills that individuals and wealthy families should expect from their wealth advisors.

Second, there is often minimal leverage. Firms are typically created by successful and thus relatively senior individuals, who are initially concerned with serving their client base and expanding revenues. It is not unusual for these individuals to seek new partners who come with their own client bases. Thus, the impetus to create relatively junior positions—associates—is limited, as, in their very early lives, associates typically cost more than they produce. In the longer term, they are the people who allow the more senior individuals—the rainmakers—to serve more clients, without any loss of personalization or client service.

Third, and somewhat predictably, clients are often not "institutionalized," but rather remain clients of one or several individuals rather than clients of the firm. It is not unusual to see more loyalty to the individual who "brought" the clients to the firm than to the firm as a whole. In fact, I once saw a firm that experienced an incredible situation: the head of one of the largest offices could honestly say that he did not know—and had never met, other than at firm-wide functions—more than half of the clients of the office. Besides the fact that this creates potentially unhealthy human resource management headaches, it can in and of itself be a major brake if top management wants to sharpen certain sets of firm-wide skills or to add leverage into the mix.

Finally, firm strategy is often more driven by the personalities—and the prior lives—of the founders than by client needs. In fact, this can be stated in a harsher manner: firms only learn of their shortcomings when they experience difficulties in the marketplace. Client losses may lead to some rethinking of key success factors, but little proactive-ness is present. Except in the rare cases when the founders actually get together to focus on client issues and are from various earlier disciplines, it is not unusual for the founders simply to wish to do a better job at whatever specialty they possess, in contrast to their prior place of employment, where they felt constrained. This alone explains why there are so many different forms of multi-family family offices or independent fee-only financial advisors: each one builds on the personal experiences of founders rather than on some commonly accepted "norm" of client needs.

Note that many of these "imperfect" firms still do a much better job than competing institutions from the point of view of clients. Many still see the focus on the client and his or her needs as an absolutely non-negotiable necessity. Founders often cite the conflicts of interests they experienced in their prior lives as the main reason for creating their own firms. Therefore, the need to have totally aligned interests between the client and the advisor helps cure one of the most insidious aspects of the service provided by firms that view clients as customers. The advent and proliferation of open architecture should have allowed the most egregious aspects of the service of certain large institutions to be corrected, but many, in fact, eventually reverted back to prior practice where open architecture became the buzz word for the sale of third-party products. Further, although substantial disclosure requirements should also have helped, they became a self-fulfilling pernicious prophecy[1]: clients believed that the disclosure of a conflict suggested that the advisor was more worthy of their confidence, but advisors still did not work to manage that conflict away. I personally remember an individual, who had several hundred million dollars in assets who could point to three large institutions—those among which he had meted out his liquid financial assets to manage—having all (a) favored their own products among competing alternatives and (b) broken down individual trades so that the client paid higher management fees and higher transaction costs. One had, for instance, managed for him not to be able to buy institutional class shares in mutual funds. Although the imperfect firms we discuss here are not totally protected against these exactions, their own histories and the personalities of founders more often than not protect clients against them.

The most difficult aspect of the foregoing challenges is that they make it difficult for these imperfect firms to earn an appropriate return. Ostensibly, most of them provide compensation packages that are at or close to markets for all employees, even the founders. Yet, the founders' invested capital should also earn some return, and current structures often do not allow that. It is not unusual for these firms to provide fixed income–like returns on equity, despite the fact that the business risks taken by the providers of capital are much higher than fixed income–type risk in practice. Although fixed income returns with equity risks may be acceptable to the first round of equity holders—as they also receive psychic income in the form of the personal satisfaction of doing the "right" thing and serving their clients the way they think they should be served—it can create insurmountable challenges for the next generation of owners, except when they, too, have bought into the philosophy and accept as sufficient compensation the satisfaction of being special.

CONTRARY EXAMPLES IN THE LEGAL AND MEDICAL FIELDS

I certainly hope that I will not be offending medical doctors and lawyers with the statements I am about to make, but I do make them with a great deal of admiration for their insightfulness and with no implicit or explicit criticism for the business model they adopted.

---

[1]Cain, Daylian M., George Loewenstein, and Don A. Moore, "The Dirt on Coming Clean: Perverse Effects of Disclosing Conflicts of Interest." *The Journal of Legal Studies,* 34(1), January 2005, pp. 1–25.

Let me start with the medical field. In virtually all instances of my personal dealing with medical practitioners in the United States—because I could not say the same thing in many other countries, France clearly among those—I have found that physicians are substantially leveraged. Most dental care practices employ a number of more or less specialized para-dental practitioners, who allow the actual dentists to experience and enjoy leverage. Similarly, most ophthalmologists employ personnel who can focus on all the less sophisticated tasks—ranging from basic optometry to complex computer-assisted diagnostic tools. Whether with my own dentist or ophthalmologist, it is not unusual that I do not see the top individual for more than five to ten minutes in an hour-long appointment.

Changing gears and looking at law firms, it is equally clear that legal assistants of various qualifications play a major role. Sure enough, one will meet the actual senior lawyer at the time the problem is described and the issues initially debated. Yet, as actual work is done, legal assistants and junior lawyers or associates take over and do most of the drafting, often using word processing tools to create the most mundane and least customized part of a document. In contrast with the medical example, where one does not see the medical specialist as much as his or her associates, one does principally interact with the most senior lawyer, although the work is still carried out in large measure by associates.

Both examples illustrate three very important points. First, a highly customized work product does not require all elements to be absolutely unique. Each piece of work involves a variety of tasks, a few or even many of which can somehow be standardized. In the Introduction, we used the example of customized suits that do not all have to come from a Saville Row tailor. There is plenty of room between the poorly made, cheap, and totally off-the-rack suit and one that only the very wealthy can afford.

Second, very few people can claim the status of undisputed leaders of their professions. Wealthy enough individuals who have major legal or health problems—real or imagined—typically want to work only with the very top practitioner in the field, who will often charge considerably more than his or her less distinguished peers. People at the top of their respective specialties can most often dictate their fees, because their services are in high demand, as there are more potential clients than their own time constraints would allow and differentiation from their competition is straightforward and readily accepted. Unfortunately for the many who are not yet at the very top of their professions, competitive differentiation is harder and they are therefore "fee takers" rather than "fee makers." They must charge what the competition charges, even if, objectively, the service they provide is better or—and this is the important element—more expensive to deliver.

Third, the essence of business profitability is in being as productive as possible given client constraints. Productivity in the medical or legal field rests in part on being able to differentiate between tasks that only the most qualified individual can perform and those that less expensive associates can provide—certain people will even argue that the specialization of many of these more "junior" individuals allows them to be as good as if not even better at these simpler tasks than more senior practitioners who do not have as much practice performing them.[2] Understanding which duties can—and should—be delegated versus those which should not, can be the differentiating factor between practitioners who are successful and profitable and those who are not.

A SIMPLE ILLUSTRATION

Consider the typical challenge posed by the typical individual or wealthy family and divide the process into three stages to reflect three important kinds of services: initial consultations geared to help the client formulate his or her investment policy, ongoing management and reporting processes, and continuous advisory processes to verify that goals are being met and that the client is satisfied. Each of these phases requires different talents and skills operating in different ways and in the appropriate sequence. I am sure that readers will agree with the postulate that the current, "normal" firm will place the same individual in front of the client for each of these phases. Yet, is this truly both necessary and even advisable? The fact that I asked the question suggests that the answer I prefer is that it's not.

The initial consultations are typically focused on starting the advisory process. Upstream from that moment, the prospect probably met with salespeople and was introduced both to senior management and to the person who would likely be his or her advisor. Many of the most sophisticated firms select that advisor based on the perceived preferences of the client, the professional skills he or she is most likely to need, and some assessment of personal chemistry. Note that the simple requirement that the advisor be just that, a good advisor, is nowhere in this list. This easily explains why so many firms suffer from unmet client needs or dissatisfied clients. Advising a client, particularly when it comes to complex wealth management, extends

---

[2]I remember a very sophisticated ophthalmic surgeon joking that certain pieces of equipment have become so sophisticated that he would rather have an associate handle them. In many ways, he is no different from the older generation—mine—at times musing at how easy certain apparently difficult computer manipulations seem to a five-year-old grandchild!

beyond a single discipline, as we saw in Chapter 1 and will dig deeper into in Chapter 14. Even if it were true that the initial diagnosis by the sales team as to the new client's main issue was spot on, how can a self-respecting firm take it for granted that the diagnosis is accurate and complete? How can one proceed with delivering a wealth management service without having totally satisfied oneself that all the various structural issues that should be covered were indeed covered? Certain firms actually are smart enough to do this, but often this is done in the context of a massive request for documentary information, rather than in a give-and-take session where the individual's or the family's goals are inventoried, the various actions discussed, and a wealth management policy developed. I personally remember a situation where a very wealthy family was ready to give a mandate to a well-known multi-family family office only to change its mind when it was asked to provide so much information that it felt is was being subpoenaed in some legal proceeding... How sad!

Turning to what I called ongoing management and reporting, it is often the case that firms bring the same team plus one or two "product" or "discipline" specialists. I say "product" or "discipline," because I do not want to focus solely on those instances where the main mandate is related to asset management. Trust management, bill paying, tax preparation or management, family education or governance, philanthropic management, and many other activities would still require our lead "advisor" to be present, together with other specialists. Experience suggests that the lead advisor who always seems to attend is often neither the most qualified to handle most questions, nor the best in terms of bedside manner, but quite frequently the most senior individual in the room. This is true except when some member of senior management is brought in to opine on some specialty or broad firm issue. This raises at least two important questions. The first relates to meeting the client needs: Rather than having some senior individual who is not the most qualified to discuss matters, would it not be better for the client to have access to a specialist who might offer deeper insights? The second deals with the firm's operational efficiency: Is it really essential to have so many people in the meeting at the same time? Even if it is not, only a well-qualified advisor will ensure that the meeting is well-enough organized so that different actors can come in and out without disrupting the flow or leaving an important question unanswered. Thus, people often stay in the room just in case the client should ask a question that they are best suited to answer.

The continuous advisory process geared to ensuring both that the client's needs are met and that the current understanding of these needs is accurate is frequently not a formal affair. In the many circumstances I have had the opportunity to observe, I must admit that I have not seen too great a focus on this activity. At best, certain firms conduct periodic senior management client audits, at which point one or another member of senior management meets with the client to discuss how things are going. Although a few excellent firms make sure that this is done at a specially scheduled meeting, many others, unfortunately, use client events for such meetings, allowing minimal time for real, sincere, and comprehensive client interaction with senior management. I cannot resist the temptation to believe that certain "lead advisors," in fact, deliberately avoid scheduling such meetings, as they want to remain the sole contact with the client, in a not-so-disguised form of employment insurance! Taking this one step further, I find the annual industry ratings of "the best advisors" somewhat misleading at best when a few of the laureates actually work for or lead larger firms. I do not deny that a few of these people are excellent. Rather, I am concerned by the idea that clients view them in isolation, rather than as members of a team within the firm that serves them. To me, the crucial element must be that the advisor is the focal point of the delivery of a firm-wide service, rather than an independent entity.

SUMMARY AND CONCLUSIONS

In short, the current structure—with its many variations—is more a product of evolution than of serious strategic consideration. Although it is most—if not all—of the time designed with the best intentions, it tends to fail on three important counts, which we will look into in Chapter 14:

1. Firms often lack the depth they should have in many disciplines, relying on a small number of stars, rather than on a solid and well-thought-out team of current and future stars.
2. Firms often lack the focus on the importance of the client advisory activity. Although many understand that clients are seeking a service and fewer, but still quite a few, believe in the concept of integrated wealth management, they continue to suffer from a discipline focus, rather than on a holistic approach to helping a client meet all his or her needs.
3. Firms often lack sufficient leverage to allow the most important tasks to be carried out by the appropriate staff and yet provide for more specialized—although not necessarily less sophisticated—activities to be delegated to people who can work to be the best in a narrower field. It has, for instance, remained a total mystery to me why a senior client advisor would feel he or she has to be specialized in manager selection. Sure, clients may want to talk about individual managers, but what is wrong with bringing the specialist in to answer the question? By the way, doing that would also allow the manager selection specialist to develop client relation skills over time, which might open the road to becoming an advisor to him or her if he or she eventually feels that this is the preferred career route to travel.

CHAPTER 14

Teams Versus Individuals

As we just saw in Chapter 13, the genesis of many multi-family family offices and independent fee-only financial advisors has led them to be a collection of a few highly successful and qualified individuals. In this chapter, we discuss the need to think in an alternative manner: develop firms that are based on the notion that clients are better served by teams, not by an individual.

TOO MANY DISCIPLINES FOR ANYONE TO MASTER ALL OF THEM FULLY

If we go back far enough in history, prior to the advent of wealth management advisors, wealthy individuals and families hired specialists. Their choice, as we have already seen, was most often driven by the one need they saw as the most crucial. This is what led to an initial advisory industry structure that comprised private banks, lawyers who specialized in fiduciary and estate transfer issues, or tax advisors. I vividly remember attending meetings of family boards or serving on them and noticing that the most crucial advisor was an individual who, although incredibly competent in his or her discipline, was literally "punting" when it came to the others. As an asset manager by professional background, I most often noticed it when the lead advisor was an estate or a tax lawyer who made it appear that he or she knew everything there was to know about investment management, but was rarely much more than a gifted amateur, at best. I even remember when the chair of a family board was an estate lawyer who really did not know much, if anything, about alternative assets or strategies and yet pontificated at length—and at times carried the day!—basing his "experience" on the fact that he had served on the board of directors of a mutual fund!

The first thing that advisors need to learn is that they do not know everything, and, most importantly as said to me once by the CIO of the family that we have been serving for the longest time, "We do not know what we do not know!" A corollary to this is to observe that each and every discipline has become so complex that it is virtually impossible for anyone to master it unless he or she dedicates all efforts to it.

I often remind myself that the historical personage I admire most is a Frenchman who lived in the middle of the 17th century, Blaise Pascal. I admire him because he could, simultaneously, be more than proficient at many disparate disciplines. First, after inventing the first mechanical calculator, he proved to be a solid mathematician—he gave us Pascal's triangle. Eventually and in collaboration with Pierre de Fermat, Pascal gave birth to the mathematical theory of probabilities. He was also a well-respected philosopher who drew on his probability theory experience to develop Pascal's wager, a proposition that it is safer to believe in God than not to—irrespective of whether God exists or not—based on what we would today observe is the nature of the outcomes under each of the two assumptions. His philosophical work actually extended into theology when, after a night of religious ecstasy, he worked on a book we know as "Les Pensées" (or "Thoughts"), which he wanted to entitle "Apology for the Christian Religion." He also became a top flight physicist, working particularly in the field of hydraulics and developing the idea that a vacuum existed. Although readers probably are tired of this historical trivia, they surely appreciate how unusual an individual Pascal was. I suspect that there may well be a few other people who could be said to share Pascal's breadth, but I am pretty sure that there are not many of them ...

The foregoing also illustrates that it would be next to impossible to replicate Pascal's prowess today. Indeed, while most sciences were at somewhat embryonic stages back then, massive theoretical developments have brought us to a point now at which no single man or woman could simply understand all arcane details across such a wide spectrum.

Obviously, wealth management is considerably simpler than any of the complexities of physics, sophisticated mathematics, or medicine, to name three disciplines that experienced mindboggling developments in the last couple of centuries. Yet, it is still true that the intricacies of the tax code, the complexities of securities markets and of the instruments and strategies available, or the advances in psychology and education are such that knowing all of them in depth is simply too much for a single person. A long while back, being a "jack of all trades and a master of none" might have been sufficient, if only because competition could not offer anything much better. Today, being satisfied with such a status is a virtual guarantee of business failure and, even if the business does not fail, of some form of intellectual and ethical frustration, as one would have to know that one could do better for clients.

SPECIALISTS, WHEN LEFT ALONE, LEAD TO SILOS

Note that our prior discussion highlights the need for specialists rather than well-meaning but skills-limited generalists. One could argue that wealth advisory firms should simply develop their own specialists in the various disciplines and be done with it.

This idea, unfortunately, falls flat because, as we observed earlier, clients are asking us what time it is, not how to make a watch! The service a client requires is not simply an accumulation or aggregation of specialized elements. Clients require a package. A car is comprised of many different pieces that are often engineered by different specialists with detailed knowledge of chassis, engine, suspension, brakes, aerodynamics, ergonomics, styling, and many others fields; yet, it remains a whole that can be used and enjoyed without caring about individual parts. Similarly, a wealth management service is an aggregate. It is essential that the various parts be brought together. We will come back to this point in a minute.

Before going there, however, it is also important to realize that specialists, when they are left to their own devices, tend to want to go deeper and deeper into their disciplines. This an entirely laudable attitude in that it fits with the desire to improve one's skill level and contribute to the development of one's discipline over time. But this tends to lead to a silo mentality, where one ignores—or is simply not even aware of—the various interactions that one's discipline has with other aspects of the "client solution." I vividly remember how so many of my colleagues at J.P. Morgan in the early days of my tenure at the Private Bank simply ignored the issue of our clients having to pay taxes. It was a case of "allowing the tax tail to wag the investment dog," I was told. Yet, once one went past that initial criticism, as we saw in Chapter 2, one began to understand that a new sub-discipline was being created: tax-sensitive investing, I also remember how I had wanted to develop a "trust-aware" investment discipline to deal with the somewhat rigid split interest trust policies of the day and, to my chagrin, fell flat. I could not gain traction and I have been regretting that for a long time. With the benefit of hindsight, this probably was the first time I found myself confronted with conflicting goals: the trustee and the investment manager had to arbitrate between the needs and rights of beneficiaries and remaindermen. Imagining what could have been, I can see that had goals-based wealth management been established then there would have been a great opportunity for investment managers and trust lawyers to cooperate and draft a new form of split interest trust document that allowed a finer and more balanced treatment of both beneficiaries and remaindermen.

The challenge was not and still is not limited to investment folks. Trust officers and tax lawyers also became deeply involved in their own discipline and I could just as easily mention times when investment horrors were proposed for the sake of some measure of tax-efficiency. Philanthropists also tend to care more for the details of their granting processes and successes and rely on funding that they view as simple; yet, for a long time, they ignored the opportunity that tax-aware charitable giving, such as a gift of appreciated securities, provides to enhance the tax-efficiency of a taxable securities portfolio.

In short, there is nothing wrong with having the sharpest, most skilled, and most knowledgeable specialists on one's team. However, it is essential that these people appreciate that they do not operate in a vacuum, but rather should combine their efforts to serve a higher purpose. Having the best performing engine is nothing if chassis and suspension designs are such that the car cannot seem to remain on the road . . . . The same is true here: having the best investment strategy or the most sophisticated and original wealth transfer structures are only one of the many dimensions of the challenge that our clients face. I suspect that this silo mentality is one of the major reasons why the goals-based wealth management process described in Part 3 of this book did not catch on for quite some time. Thinking that way forced specialists away from their original comfort zones, requiring them to consider issues differently from the way they had originally learned. In my opinion, it is not a coincidence that the Das, Markowitz, Scheid, and Statman papers quoted in Chapter 5 required the collaboration of top-flight authors and thinkers is various fields of finance. This is not to say that any one of them, individually, could not have thought of—or did not think of—the solution they eventually offered; but I believe that collaboration across disciplines—or sub-disciplines in this case—holds a much higher chance of providing the best solution.

THE CRUCIAL ROLE OF THE TEAM COACH

Team sports provide a frequent and vivid illustration that there is more to a team than the strengths of each team member. It is not a coincidence that doubles tennis champions rarely comprise the top-rated players of the time, or that the Ryder Cup in golf was won a number of times by the European team, despite the fact that, objectively, the members of the U.S. team were higher in the golf rankings individually. This simple observation, taken from sports that comprise both individual and team performances, offers an important first insight: teams must be made to become teams, and a collection of individuals will not do the trick. I cannot resist saying something only an asset manager would offer: there is more to creating an equity portfolio than simply assembling a list of stocks; the various stocks one eventually uses must be carefully selected to create a whole that has a good chance of earning higher returns, but also avoids taking risks for which one should not rationally expect to be compensated. The various stocks have to be brought together in some sensible manner.

Someone is needed to bring and keep the team together. The analogy I prefer comes from the world of music. I like to think of the crucial role of the conductor in any orchestra. I prefer this analogy because conductors can limit their roles to conducting the orchestra, but can also extend it and conduct the orchestra while playing an instrument, such as the piano. Many argue that the crucial role of the conductor is during rehearsals when he or she puts a stamp of approval on the way the piece is played and the sound that the orchestra produces. It is a well-known piece of classical music trivia that Herbert Von Karajan innovated by doubling the size of the string section of the Berlin Philharmonic Orchestra, allowing him to create a particularly powerful sound. The point is clear: each of the musicians in the orchestra produced his or her own best, but those individual bests needed to be brought together by someone who ensured that one plus one can at times be equal to three, or four, or five!

Bringing and keeping the team together is not the simplest thing, particularly when one is dealing with industry leaders, a few of whom have been accurately accused of being "prima donnas." Thus, it may be appropriate to pick specialists not only on the basis of their professional prowess, but also based on their willingness and ability to work together and for some higher goal: the good of the client. In a team, there will necessarily be times when one or the other player has a bigger role to play, must operate under more pressure, or is experiencing some short-term counter performance. Keeping the team together involves managing it through these challenging episodes. I remember one of my first bosses at J.P. Morgan, Karl R. Van Horn, telling me, as I was about to "graduate" to a world where I would have to manage a few people, of what he called the *investment paradox*—which I have come to believe extends beyond the world of investment. The message was simple: "Your team comprises good people; once in a while a good person will be a bit off and it is your job to go and encourage him or her to persevere, with the message that [they] are there because [they] are good and that [they] should not worry if things are not working as well as [they] would like. Once in a while, too, someone will be on a serious hot streak and it is your job to go and remind him or her that he or she does not walk on water; [they] are good, but not that good." The message may have initially been a bit counterintuitive, but it was absolutely right on: short-term disappointment must not be allowed to deter someone from keeping the faith, nor should short-term success allow someone to start getting too big for their britches.

The coach—or conductor—also has another very important role. He or she must be the interpreter![1] This function has two dimensions, inbound and outbound. The interpreter must be able to assemble the team that will best meet the specific needs of each client; although he or she may not be a real specialist in any of the key disciplines, he or she must be familiar enough with the issues in each discipline to retain credibility with specialists and understand all the various interactions between the various disciplines to ensure that the law of unintended consequences does not strike. In other words, the individual must be enough of a generalist to be able to see the full picture, but sufficiently good at understanding specialty points that specialists can fully trust his or her judgment. The analogy of the conductor of the orchestra comes back here in that the challenge is to design the composition of the orchestra for a particular musical piece and bring the best out of it by working with the various instruments. The conductor may not be able to play the oboe as well as the orchestra's oboe principal, but he or she must be able to impress the oboe player by not making stupid statements or having stupid expectations and be sure that the challenges associated with the instrument are understood. Note that some measure of appropriate humility and even deference to the specialist are also subsumed into that example.

The outbound communication or translation role is equally important and brings the package together. Although a client may ask quite a number of specialized questions, one cannot assume that each client wants to go deeply into each discipline. I call this "the reverse funnel" principle, thinking that one should communicate in increasing levels of complexity as a client keeps probing. At the outset, the communication is simple, possibly even simplistic: one focuses on a pithy message that is designed to answer the basic question we feel is most crucial at that point; most often it relates to discussing how goals have or have not been met, with little specificity. Then, helped along by the client's probing, one can go deeper and deeper into details, always allowing the client to be the driver and decide the depth at which he or she wants to look into the issue.

This idea highlights further the need for a team approach, as the different depths at which each issue will be discussed drives the need for a specialist.

---

[1]Note that I purposely use the word "interpreter" rather than a synonym such as "translator." To me, the fundamental difference between the two is that a translator might simply translate from one language to another, while an interpreter must convey the meaning intended in one language into some other. Although this can—and often is—pretty much a distinction without difference, it can matter a great deal at times. An example would be when the interpreter appreciates that his or her client could not understand a word or a phrase as literally translated and must make the effort to convey the meaning, even if it means adding to what the text was in the first language.

Just as a conductor will call on one instrument to come forth at one time or another during a concert, the team coach should be able to call on all members of the team when needed and yet remain in control so that the needs of the client are met, but the client is not overwhelmed with detail that he or she really does not care to know or with the impression that he or she has everybody and their dog in the conference room at the same time.

ONLY ONE INDIVIDUAL CAN PLAY THAT ROLE

Although it is true that no formal professional background best qualifies or prepares an individual to be the team leader, I strongly believe that the role should not be played by someone who also has other, specialized responsibilities, except possibly for selected members of top management. Music trivia—to remain in the same analogical sphere as in the prior section—often claims that string or piano players make the best conductors. Certain conductors do conduct from the piano or substitute themselves for the first violin. Yet, the overwhelming majority of all conductors view and play their roles as a specialized function and without "competing" with their specialists. In a few instances, particularly for clients at the very high end of a firm's typical client size range, it would not be unusual for senior management, even the chief investment officer, the chief fiduciary officer, or even the chief executive officer, to assume the role of lead advisor. This is more to illustrate to that client the importance he or she carried vis-à-vis the firm than because any such individual will do a better job. In fact, when this is the case, the senior manager often has a junior associate next to him or her to make sure that nothing falls through the cracks.

This coach or conductor is the person I like to call the lead advisor in the wealth management sphere. This function remains, in my eyes, the single most important role when it comes to clients, who are the life blood of the firm. I mentioned earlier the notion communicated to me by senior management in my J.P. Morgan days: "Clients pay your compensation, not the firm!" Thus, it is important to remember that the lead advisor must be the key player when it comes to client communication. He or she must be viewed as one of the firm's key success factors. That notion should not be allowed to go too far: lead advisors ought to be viewed as the people most knowledgeable when it comes to client needs and preferences, but they should never be allowed to overrule specialists when it comes to the fundamentals of any specialty. An advisor must remain descriptive and should never become prescriptive. He or she can make points as to how certain strategies or approaches may be viewed by clients; they are the representatives of all clients within the firm. But he or she cannot dictate what can and should be done within any specialty. Only a lead advisor who has a strong measure of self-confidence can walk that at times difficult line.

Senior management has a crucial arbitration role to ensure that the intelligence that comes from working deep in the weeds is never allowed to be lost simply because the initial reaction of a few clients might be negative. Similarly, senior management must also ensure that appropriate education is provided to clients before something new and possibly disturbing (or even threatening) is introduced. I have not encountered too many successful models of this interaction thus far, but I believe that a greater focus on client goals—the essence of goals-based wealth management—inevitably will lead to a sharper understanding of the new advisory role that is being created and of the need for the firm to be structured around the client. Figure 1.3 made the point rather well: the client is at the center, and the lead advisor sits right next to him or her. In fact, in Figure 1.3, he or she sits in the same circle as the client. The various disciplines surround them and are available to the client, and the advisor is responsible for identifying which will be needed and which will not.

SUMMARY AND CONCLUSIONS

The move from a firm comprising a few stars to one that may or may not comprise stars but is centered on the client and his or her needs is a crucial element before embarking on the process of adopting goals-based wealth management. Success is not possible if individual specialists are not willing to view themselves as team members with a specific role to play behind the lead advisor who delivers the firm and its services to each client. Similarly, success will likely elude firms that allow lead advisors to view themselves as better than the firm's specialists and thus overrule them or belittle their roles to clients.

Although this represents an upending of traditional hierarchies and structures, it is a sine qua non of the vision that the role of the firm is to bring together the resources that are needed to serve each client. With any change in hierarchy, particularly when one function is elevated that was previously overlooked, the transition must be managed carefully and the goals clearly stated to avoid the inevitable creation of a monster. No orchestra conductor will ever be successful if he or she so annoys the musicians that they refuse to play! Senior management has a crucial role to play, and if experience is any guide, one of the keys to success is for senior management to model and promote the notion of humility and collective success. One of the elements that might help in this process is the development of clearly defined individual performance measures that include both function-specific factors and some tool to assess cross-functional effectiveness. J.P. Morgan had a system of peer review that included peers, subordinates, and bosses, and I confess that I have yet to see something that works a lot better!

CHAPTER 15

An Alternative Structure

Philippe Néricault Destouches, a French dramatist of the early 18th century once said, "Criticism is easy, and art is difficult." It would be fair to apply this same saying to the first two chapters of Part 4 of this book. I can hear someone say, "If the current structure doesn't work, what might work instead?" This is the point of our final chapter, which combines two thoughts: first, the lead advisor plays a central role and, second, some leverage must be built into the process to allow some satisfactory profitability for the wealth management firm, without having to fall into the trap of "selling" products.

THE PRIMORDIAL ROLE OF THE ADVISOR

No one should be surprised by the contents of this first section, which will be short. The notion that there is a need for an interpreter is the most important insight. As already discussed in Chapters 3, 10, and 14, clients need someone to help translate whatever occurs in "financialese" into their native tongues. We concluded that translation goes in two directions: clients rely on the firm to make sure that their needs are truly met, and because of this, there is a crucial role for someone to translate their goals and needs into actionable strategies. Clients also must be prepared to learn what can be done and what cannot be done. It is unfortunate that many individuals think they know markets when, in fact, they have only limited experience, colored by the many behavioral biases aptly described by Daniel Kahneman and Mark Riepe,[1] who pointed to the disutility of losses versus the utility of gains, limited framing, hindsight biases, overconfidence, illusion of control, and regrets as the most important. That people should suffer from these biases is simply

---

[1]Kahneman, Daniel, and Mark W. Riepe. "Aspects of Investor Psychology." *Journal of Portfolio Management*, Summer 1998, pp. 52–65.

a reflection of our nature and the way our brains are wired. Unfortunately, our biases color the way we remember whatever experience we may have had in markets, whether recent or distant. Wealthy individuals as well as families must be helped to put their experiences into the appropriate perspective. This may well be the most difficult element of the interpreter's role, as he or she is often dealing with a client who does not know that the need for translation exists.

It is a very delicate role that requires a very unusual and sophisticated mind.[2] At some obvious level, no advisor can be really successful without some solid grounding in several disciplines so that he or she can possess the perspective needed both to interact with the firm's various specialists and to appreciate and to uncover interactions between disciplines that specialists might not perceive or even understand. Although such qualities might be viewed as sine qua non, there is much more to the role. The advisor has to be able to interact with clients and to fulfill the mission diplomatically, making his or hers the definition offered by Caskie Stinnett,[3] who said: "A diplomat is a person who can tell you to go to hell in such a way that you actually look forward to the trip." Similarly, in the case of an advisor, although sharing roles of both wealth management professional and educator, one must be able to help a client, who has every right to see himself or herself as someone quite special, "get it right," without seeming overpowering, abrasive, pretentious, obsequious, or pandering. Honesty forces me to admit that most of the really good advisors I have met tended to have at least some measure of "white hair." That should not surprise: some serious industry experience naturally conveys the message that one has had a chance to learn the ropes and, thus, can reasonably be expected to provide perspective. Being able to point to a measure of achievement in a prior life is the proverbial cherry on top of the cake.

As discussed in Chapter 14, the role must be as divorced as possible from any individual specialty within the multitude of disciplines that comprise wealth management. This provides the needed credibility for helping to determine trade-offs between the benefits and the costs associated with diverse multi-disciplinary solutions.

---

[2]It might be worth adding a comment. Daniel Kahneman, in his most recent book, *Thinking Fast and Slow* (Farrar, Straus and Giroux, 2011) makes the point that we have two distinct decision systems within our minds: one is fast, but liable to jump to the wrong conclusion, and the other is slower and a heavier energy consumer, but more reliable. Being able to know how to help clients use the right "system" at the right time is one of the keys to being a great advisor.

[3]Caskie Stinnett was a travel writer, humorist, and a former editor of *Travel + Leisure* magazine who lived in the 20th century and died in 1998 at the age of 87, according to his obituary published in the *Chicago Tribune*.

THE MISSIONS THE ADVISOR SHOULD NOT ACCEPT

One can easily see why and how a superb advisor could become the client's advocate within the firm and be viewed by the client as his or her own consigliore, the individual who can be, in the words of Robert Hargrove,[4] like a "friend and companion, a Delphic seer, a thinking partner, and master psychologist." Many great leaders have had consigliores through time and credited them with helping them get things done in a successful and appropriate manner. But it is one thing to sit—or stand—right next to clients and help them achieve their goals; it is quite another to accept the role of "doing it" for them. This role an advisor should eschew, for both self-preservation and ethical reasons, can take several dimensions, all of which can be lethal.

A client can become convinced that his or her advisor is a genius and want him or her to make all decisions. This phenomenon can be interpreted using Kahneman's and Riepe's definition of "illusion of control." I remember a client at J.P. Morgan who was convinced that I—as a member of senior management and not as an individual—had to "know" where currency and other markets were going, given "the bank's reach and history of success!" Clients, particularly after a period during which the advisor happens to have had a run of successful suggestions or calls, can become mesmerized and want to delegate all decisions to the advisor. This is an extremely dangerous challenge, because, as I used to remind the members of my team: "God does not work for [fill in the blank with the name of the appropriate firm]." It is virtually a guarantee that a series of unfortunate suggestions will follow a string of good ones, just as one can defy the odds and get ten "tails" in a row in a coin flip exercise, without having in any way changed the basic 50/50 probability of obtaining a head or a tail!

An extension of this problem, potentially an even more challenging one, is when a client not only adopts the advisor as "a serving genius" but expects the advisor to offer his or her own, rather than the firm's view. I remember several clients of a multi-family family office who had allowed a few of the firm's advisors to see themselves as better than any of the firm's specialists. They were prepared to offer investment advice that ran in a different direction than the firm's investment group, legal advice that trust and estate specialists within the firm might not condone, or even governance and education advice without feeling it was necessary to seek the opinion of the firm's family governance and education team. The potential legal and regulatory costs associated with such a distortion of the role of and expectations for a lead advisor can be huge. No one is better than the firm for which one works, and the role of the advisor is simply to deliver the firm's insights to the client,

---

[4]Robert Hargrove is the founder of Masterful Coaching and has served as director of the Harvard Leadership Project.

while helping the firm understand what the client needs and helping the client to appreciate what is possible and what is not. Yet, clients too frequently tend to view the successful advisor as capable of walking on water and seek more from him or her than should be reasonably sought.

Changing gears, there is another equally noxious challenge for any advisor, which involves accepting a mandate that he or she feels is not realistic. At J.P. Morgan, we had a well-established and long tradition of formally "accepting" a mandate before it became effective. I cannot remember how many times I had to tell this or that advisor, "It may well be his—or her—money, but it is our mandate" (as first mentioned in Chapter 9). My point was not to pretend that I knew better than the client, or the advisor for that matter, what the client really needed; I did not. However, I knew—or at least believed I knew—what markets could deliver and strongly argued that we should not condone unrealistic expectations. Further, just thinking that the client would learn, through time, that his or her expectations were not realistic and change is just as dangerous as marrying someone with the belief that he or she can be changed: perfection does not exist in this world. We should accept our lot and deal with it. Yet, it is worth adding that one may need some measure of flexibility—and avoid ideological rigidity or dogmatism. Thus, it is not a bad idea to be prepared to accept a mandate that might be a bit rough around the edges, provided we are talking of roughness and not of fitting a square peg into a round hole: elementary principles do exist, and any mandate that violates them is an accident waiting to happen.

I mentioned earlier that there are self-preservation and ethical reasons not to fall into any of these traps—and a few others. Self-preservation has two dimensions here. First, is the obvious: a client who loses confidence in the advisor for failing to achieve some goal that had been accepted as feasible when it was not—or not understanding the importance of allowing sufficient time for the goal to be reached—will typically not only leave the firm, but may also say unflattering things about the firm to others. This has got to be bad news.[5] A second, potentially more lethal dimension is legal or regulatory damages. Loose speak—which here is less extreme than accepting a goal that is not reasonable—can have dramatic consequences. Years ago, I knew an incredibly smart and well-respected advisor who had come to call hedge funds "industrial-strength fixed income." That many of the strategies that were covered under that label had an expected volatility that fell within the range commonly accepted to apply to fixed income strategies may have been correct. That it made life easier and avoided complexity that certain clients might not have understood is also true. Yet, the fact is

---

[5] I remember a saying that a satisfied client talks to a couple of people, while a dissatisfied client talks to at least five times that number.

that so-called non-directional hedge funds usually comprise minimal inter-est rate—or duration—risk; that they do not trade or follow credit cycles; that they comprise investing in instruments that have special features; and that they often have return distributions that are not similar to a classic bond portfolio return, being frequently not normal (the mean and median rarely overlap), involving measures of illiquidity, pricing and model risk, and requiring leverage that can come back and bite one in the tail. Numer-ous multi-family family offices have, in the more recent past, faced client lawsuits—and, in some instances, regulatory reprimands—for having failed to be specific enough.

The ethical dimension of the issue is equally important, in my view, and it becomes orders of magnitude more so when one accepts a goals-based wealth management framework. Recalling the points made in Chapters 8, 9, and 10, a crucial activity in the process is to determine how much money is required to "fund" each goal the client has, over the required time horizon and with the required probability of success. To me, there is an important ethical dimension in advising the clients at that stage; making believe that some goal is achievable when one actually believes it may not be or letting the client believe that he or she has sufficient assets to meet all of his or her goals when this is not true, is ethically flawed. A lawyer might eventu-ally label this a "gross negligence" or "dereliction of duty" in a complaint, but, to me, this is much simpler. It is plainly wrong—and an obvious mis-take in the interpreting process—not to tell the client that this or that belief or conviction is inaccurate. After all, even if it is not fun to have to work with a client whose goals are not collectively achievable, one never knows how he or she will trade one goal against another one until the possibility has been contemplated. I feel that, as an advisor, I owe each client my best guess and should work with him or her to live with whatever consequences there might be. I honestly admit that I lost a few mandates here or there because of this, but I still prefer to be able to look at myself in the mirror each morning.

In short, advisors should understand both the central role that they play and the clear limits to that role. They should remember, as discussed in Chapter 14, that they are members of a team and that they must not operate outside of that team. They should also remember that they owe their clients their best, unvarnished, and honest views.

THE DIFFERENCE BETWEEN MUST AND DOES NOT NEED TO BE TAILORED

This last sentence provides a great—and somewhat unintended segue—to the next issue. We discussed in the Introduction, in Chapter 7, and in Chapter 13 the notion that not everyone needs—or can afford—a Saville

Row suit. Mass customization is an important dimension of the need to deliver tailored services to clients and to do it in a way that assures that the firm remains profitable. From my days in Hong Kong and Singapore, I remember a Chinese saying that you should always leave some fat on the table for the next customer. I also remember an admonition by my boss at the time, who told me we needed to get the best trade execution for our clients, but that the need had to be balanced against being equally mindful of allowing enough profitability for our broker intermediaries because we could not trade without them and we needed for them to stay in business. I have since used that principle many times, including in situations that have nothing to do with wealth management. We need service providers to earn enough to stay in business, yet not so much that we are fleeced. In other words, one is quite frequently faced with situations that require balancing what might superficially seem like competing, practically incompatible goals. In fact, they might, at first blush and in a first degree sense, be competing and opposite; a more thorough analysis demonstrates that they are linked and that one cannot be suppressed for an extended period of time without the other becoming unachievable.

Thus, one can superficially conclude that each client needs a fully customized solution—and mentally apply the word "customized" to every element comprising that solution. Yet, this would be—is and has been—a big mistake, as there are elements of each client situation that are like those of other clients. For instance, does it really matter what individual client circumstances are when it comes to observing how capital markets behave on a day-to-day basis? "No!" In the end, it does not really matter how much money one has—within the obvious test of reasonableness—most, if not all, investors are "price-takers," rather than "price-makers" when it comes to security markets. I used to joke with clients that the only way they could be "price-makers" was when they had a very large position in a security and elected to dump the whole thing on the market at one time, requiring an instant fill of the trade. A few of us can overwhelm the market, but doing so is nothing short of silly.

Examples abound of what I'm talking about here. Let me go back to the example I used in the Introduction of a super high-tech racing bicycle. Do I really need all the various elements of the frame to have been made to measure, starting with my own piece of carbon fiber, molded into my own tubes of the appropriate sections, and then cut to my own measurements? Do I need my own set of mechanical gears, specially machined for me? Obviously, the answer is a resounding "no!" What I do need is for the frame to be made of the best carbon fiber tubes possible and to be cut to my own measurements; whether these tubes were made especially for me or for a broader array of potential customers does not really matter, as long as they are cut to my own measurements. The same applies to all the other mechanical pieces.

A similar story could be told about many so-called fully customized and made-to-measure goods. In fact, back to our Saville Row suit; even there, the fabric is rarely if ever made especially for any specific client. The message is that the final product must be absolutely first class and uniquely fitted to each client, but this does not require each step along the way to be unique. In fact, one could take this a bit further and argue that there are certain steps where excessive customization can reduce quality. Why should manager selection be client-specific, for instance? Should each client have his or her own reporting system made from scratch, or should the same reporting system be designed to produce the reports needed by each client and in the format required by him or her? Economies of scale do exist that allow the use of specialists who might otherwise be too expensive.

In short, one of the most misunderstood elements of the private wealth management space relates to customization. It stands to reason that individuals expect their portfolios to be totally customized to their needs. Nothing makes a client more upset than the perception that an advisor is trying to pigeonhole him or her into some "model portfolio." Unfortunately, many advisors think this means that everything that remotely touches the portfolio must be unique to each client. Nothing could be further from the truth, in my opinion. Consider this question: Is the amount of money invested for you in fixed income assets a reason why the outlook for interest rates should be different for you than for any other client of the firm that advises you? The answer is obvious. It has to be a clear "no!" Note that this does not mean that you will not have a certain number of constraints or preferences—for instance, in the municipal bond market, with respect to the U.S. states in which you are prepared to invest or, more globally, on whether you are interested in lower credit obligations or in non-local bonds hedged in your home currency. Yet, assuming that the firm must make a series of assumptions on these preferences as they apply to their "average client," whether you have 25 percent or 75 percent of your financial assets invested in fixed income, there is no reason why your fixed income portfolio should not be broadly similar to that of the average client, adjusting for tax and other considerations. Similar assertions can be made with respect to other asset classes or strategies.[6]

---

[6]In fact, I once served a family with assets totaling more than a half a billion U.S. dollars who invested in fixed income mutual funds rather than individual bonds. The insight was that there was considerably more "instant" liquidity in a mutual fund, or an ETF now, than in a portfolio where a decision to cut the exposure would require a proportional liquidation of each holding! I should add that the ability to use institutional share classes made that decision also quite sensible from the point of view of management fees.

This is an important element because it should help any firm create a dichotomy in its own investment process:

1. Certain parts of the process can be generic to the firm. Except for firms that deal with exceptionally wealthy individuals, it is not unreasonable to expect a firm to create a list of the generic types of goals they will accept to try to meet and, thus, of the portfolio modules that will be used to meet each of these goals. A firm may accept that it will modify its portfolio modules for an exceptionally large client, but the costs associated with such an exception would have to be justified in terms of both the fee the firm earns and the real—as opposed to perceived—uniqueness of the client circumstances.

2. Other parts of the process must be totally unique to each client. The determination of the amount of assets required to meet each goal cannot be anything but unique. Thus, even if each client shares in the same underlying goal portfolio modules, the overall weighted allocations to the various strategies comprised in each module will differ across the full client universe. In fact, as seen in Chapters 6 and 10, basic arithmetic principles tell us that there are 1,001 possible overall allocations if one takes the share of assets allocated to each goal simply to the first decimal—as in 35.1 percent allocated to goal A, 22.7 percent to goal B, and so on.

IMAGINING A DIFFERENT FIRM AND PROCESS ARCHITECTURE

The next four figures outline a process that rests totally on the dichotomy we just discussed. They involve recognizing that there are elements of the process that must be the same for all clients, while there are others that are absolutely and totally client-specific. Just as it should inform advisory firms, this discussion could help the wealthy identify the kind of advisor they might seek and the areas in which customization is non-negotiable and those in which it is unnecessary.

Figure 15.1 presents the first step and, in fact, comprises the various tasks that were discussed in Chapter 8. The fundamental purpose of this first step is for the firm to develop a series of goals-based modules, or sub-portfolios, designed to meet a category of goals defined by their time horizon and their required probability of success. These two characteristics set out the risk that can be taken to achieve the given goal, and the interaction of that risk profile and capital market realities provides us with a single optimal sub-portfolio. Conceptually, this process is similar—even

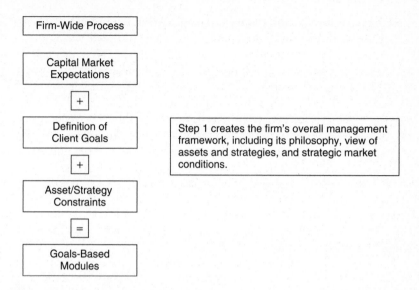

FIGURE 15.1 First Step of a Three-Step Process

analogous—to the one described in Figure 4.2 for the institutional world: a constrained efficient frontier is drawn and the given risk profile—which can be viewed as a utility function—is tangent to the frontier at one point, and that point represents the optimal portfolio. Things are a bit more complex in reality, and the analogy breaks down to the extent that, as discussed in Chapter 8, we do not apply the same constraints to the construction of each module. Yet, for the purposes of linking goals-based investment with the traditional finance case, the analogy is still broadly valid.

Note that the case arguing that this step requires specific client tailoring is quite weak, but not non-existent. Indeed, one could easily suggest that each client may have a different set of constraints and that forcing the generic constraints on all clients goes too far. Although real, this logic breaks down in most cases when one incorporates the notions of cost and capital market realities. Although one could indeed readily have individual client constraints—that could, in fact, simply be client preferences—the real test of the validity of the objection comes at the point when one checks whether these preferences really make any difference in the end and how much they cost. Ostensibly, certain preferences will make a difference, for instance, for clients who want to exclude certain geographical areas from their investment universe. There might be good reasons for these exclusions, for example, when the client is excluding home country securities from a global portfolio. Yet, there and in similar circumstances, one can make two arguments that can reduce the critical importance of such tailoring. First, one could—I would argue that one should—look at all assets when devising an investment policy. Home country assets would be just another "account" in the nomenclature we used earlier. That this would still lead to the need for different modules is not in question, and the process might allow for some measure of flexibility to deal with that requirement. There are, however, clear incremental costs involved, and both firm and client should know and account for them. The second argument rests on the idea of education: certain preferences reflect history or biases that, although real, may not be relevant or the client would benefit from being educated away from them. Again, the process might incorporate a measure of flexibility to allow that education to be provided over time—we are not talking centuries, but it could take a few quarters or even years for it to sink in.

In short, while a common set of modules will typically meet the needs of most clients, there are valid reasons to believe that some flexibility might be needed. Each firm must decide how much flexibility should be provided, given the nature of its client base. For instance, a firm that typically deals with a small number of ultra-affluent clients may need to build more flexibility into its process than one that has a large number of relatively less wealthy clients. Competitive realities will dictate the "right" level of customization, although it is probably clear that the first activity, which deals with capital market expectations, will rarely—if ever—tolerate any measure of real customization.

The second step of the process, as discussed in Chapters 9 and 10, is the polar opposite of the first and illustrated in the second column in Figure 15.2. While the first step was meant to be common to all clients, the second is totally tailored to each client. It is focused on matching goals with modules suitable to achieve them and, thus, with the assets required to meet them. It goes beyond mere investment management issues, as it has to include such dimensions as asset location (who owns which assets and how) and the specific features of each of these locations (which asset is available to whom and in what circumstances, and the relevant tax statuses). At this point, the needs of each client and his or her specific circumstances are nothing short of primordial, and the role of the firm is to help each client understand what is and what is not achievable. More likely than not, this is where a firm—and each advisor—will encounter a perceived need and some pressure to modify the modules the firm uses to make it easier for the client to square the proverbial circle when needed. Although dogmatism is to be eschewed at

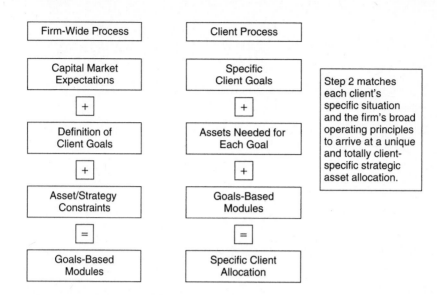

FIGURE 15.2 Second Step of a Three-Step Process

all costs, this is also when some internal fortitude will be needed to make sure that one does not fall into any of the three main traps discussed in the previous section of this chapter. Arguing that the expected return and return volatility of any strategy must be raised because the client feels he or she knows managers who have achieved higher returns in the past will have to be resisted: either the capital market framework is sufficiently robust and well-thought-through or some global rethinking is necessary. But modifying capital market expectations to make goals and assets fit when they should not is a very slippery slope.

Figure 15.3 depicts the last step in the process, in its extreme right column: the actual ongoing tactical tilting of client portfolios to reflect perceived capital market opportunities. Although it labels the process as "firm-wide," it is important to appreciate that this can be a bit of a misnomer. The process starts being firm-wide; there should be but one firm view. But it can involve some measure of client interaction, as we saw in Chapter 11. Indeed, there can be instances when the client has significant assets and, thus, has the wherewithal to maintain his or her own internal unique investment committee, on which the advisory firm would be represented. At that point, the tilt scoring activity within the process can—and often should—leave room for the client having a word—or more than a word—to say. In fact, there can be cases in which the balance of the decision weights allocated to each

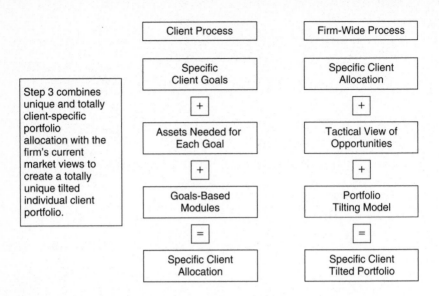

FIGURE 15.3 Third Step of a Three-Step Process

member of the investment committee will leave the client with control, if not full authority. This can be seen as the gradual shifting of relative positions along the discretionary/advisory axis. Yet, one must be clear in the role that the wealth management firm purports to play: one cannot be a minority partner in the voting and the sole entity responsible for poor performance.

Ostensibly, there will be circumstances when the client will be seeking a mere advisory relationship under the terms of which the advisor is only expected to offer certain recommendations with, or without, the requirement that he or she helps execute any trade. There is nothing wrong with such an arrangement, although it does place a fairly heavy burden on the client and requires the advisor to make sure he or she understands the limits of what he or she is expected to do and say. In fact, I have found a whole range of advisory behaviors in these types of situations. At one end of the spectrum, the advisor is happy to provide his or her firm's views and insights, but really sticks to that; at the other end, the advisor can become an almost independent agent, participating in decisions alongside the client, whether he or she (the advisor) truly has had the time or the skill to do the work. To me, this latter end is incredibly treacherous. I do not see what the advisor has to gain, while it is clear that he or she has everything to lose in taking market views that differ from those of the firm or condoning the use of a manager the firm either does not recommend or does not know.

Figure 15.4 brings the prior three figures together and illustrates how a process can be designed to ensure that all the activities that require total

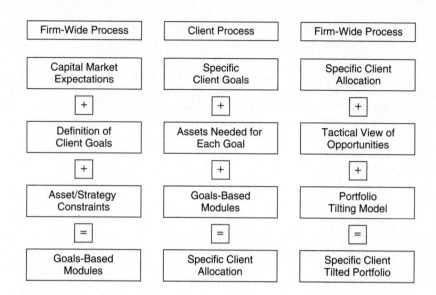

FIGURE 15.4 Goals-Based Wealth Management Process

client involvement can be preserved, while those that allow firm-wide leverage can be executed without loss of true client customization.

THE KIND OF LEVERAGE THAT CAN BE BUILT

This design allows the firm to start to create meaningful leverage along at least three dimensions. First, it *focuses the firm on the client* through the advisor, who is the most crucial interface as he or she controls—in a humble manner—the various activities and skills that must be brought to bear in order to serve the client best. Note that I did add that it must be done in a "humble manner:" the firm employs numerous professionals who are specialists in certain disciplines and who, in these specialized areas, can and often do run circles around the advisor. Thus, the advisor must see himself or herself as a "client specialist," rather than as the be-all and end-all in the firm. He or she must remain respectful of the skills of the various other specialists and avoid circumstances where the fact that a client currently desires something makes that something the absolutely best solution. Typically, however, this problem only arises when senior management has not been careful in its hiring and training processes: a first-class advisor must be a good listener—to the client—and these skills naturally extend to listening to his or her corporate peers.

Second, it provides *room for leverage being built within each of the functions*, as seniority is not necessarily a requirement to be placed in front of a client. Thus, using manager selection as an example, a relatively junior analyst can participate in client meetings, as long as he or she is "chaperoned" by the advisor, who is typically a senior person within the firm. Besides allowing the firm to plan for succession in those "specialized" dimensions, it allows it to decide what will be built within the firm and what can be purchased from outside vendors if that is more economical, more sophisticated, or both. That it allows firms to manage their costs more effectively is icing on the cake.

Finally, it also provides *room for leverage within the advisory function*. Although it stands to reason that the lead advisor should be present in most client meetings, it is not a foregone conclusion that all advisory activities must be done by him or her. In fact, there is plenty of room for associates—more or less junior, depending on the circumstances—to be in charge of a majority of the activities, subject to the management and approval of the lead advisor. Thus, an advisor can handle a considerably larger client load to the extent that it is distributed among the associates on his or her team, each of whom handles a much smaller load, in order to make sure that there is ample "extra" time to be responsive to the needs of a client who might call unexpectedly. This takes us straight back to the law firm example and the difference between the rain-making partners and the worker bee associates.

It is clear that such a process, with its well-defined and differentiated activities, brings the wealth management firm closer to the models we discussed earlier, such as law firms or medical practices. This can materially increase margins, as it allows for a much better and finer matching of costs with the various individual activities.

DEALING WITH OBJECTIONS

Conceptually, there are probably two sets of possible objections, split between objections arising from clients and objections arising from managers or advisors.

Clients typically must be educated in the benefits associated with the process. Although I have personally found that clients, in fact, are more comfortable with this approach, which they see as centered on themselves, I can imagine that its inherent greater internal complexity can raise questions. I can think of three sets of objections.

The first relates to clients who are still in a wealth-building mode—economists might characterize them as clients whose human capital is still greater than their financial capital. They may find the need to define specific goals somewhat artificial. Imagine an individual who is in his or her forties and inherits some money. Imagine further that the inheritance is material but not substantial in relation to what he or she expects to be able to save through work-related compensation for the next however many years. The advisor will have to be very careful to focus on the potential changes wrought by the inheritance. There will be a need to discuss the individual's full goal list, but it will be extremely important to help the client determine whether the inheritance allows additional goals or speeds up the achievement of currently existing goals. The key focus is identifying what the inheritance enables the individual to do or dream differently—and what may or should not change.

Second, clients who are moving to one firm from another advisor might find the changes in the way their portfolios are strategically allocated over-whelming. Although there is a favorable bias toward the newly appointed advisor, the sales process might be where the complexity and the objections arise. The focus of the advisory—or sales—activity must be on how well the client or prospect currently feels his or her goals are met. One should be very careful not to default too quickly to how the portfolio might be struc-tured; rather one must remain sharply dedicated to discussing goals, time horizons, and required probabilities of success. This will help the advisor conduct an "audit" of the current portfolio and to point to features—if there are any—that should be expected to prevent the achievement of one's goals. I remember a family whose portfolio was way overinvested in equities given their lifestyle expenditures and who initially found it very difficult to detach themselves from the potential for higher returns. The solution involved care-fully and sensitively bringing them back to the last market downturn—in that case the 2000–2001 bubble bursting in the United States—and keep asking them how they felt then. That was the trick needed to help them recognize that the current high equity exposure and the loss of wealth that resulted from the bear market were exposing them to serious risks that they might need to cut back on their lifestyle if another bear market came to pass. With the benefit of hindsight, the transition that they made was incredibly lucky—at least in its timing—as they sold in the bull market that preceded 2008! One shudders at the thought of where they would be today if they had gone into that sell-off with their prior equity position.

Finally, the third objection relates to clients who have substantially different views with respect to capital market expectations. I have found most—but not all—of these challenges arise with respect to clients who made their "fortunes" in the financial services industry. Although most of them either did not operate in the asset management world—they might have been investment bankers—or managed money in a narrow segment of the market—hedge fund managers or proprietary desk traders—many felt they knew what they needed to do and how markets behaved. The solution I successfully used focused on massive amounts of data. After all, most of these people when I met them had surely been more successful than I, and confronting them directly with a professorial style would have been both arrogant and probably quite misplaced. By contrast, showing them the wide range of the various scenarios that played out across a multiplicity of time periods and geographical locations typically led them to appreciate that their experiences might have been narrow or exceptional. Helping them differentiate between their "internal assets"—as defined in Chapter 8, those for which they keep the management responsibility—and those they delegate, and discussing why they might not keep the management responsibility for all their assets is a good trick to help them focus on risk and their own limitations.

In short, client objections can be addressed by being confident as to why the goals-based process is superior and by humbly, but without fear, explaining these benefits to each client or prospect. The astute reader will have noted that I did not discuss objections that come from individuals who disagree with the advisor in terms of strategy, tactics, or manager selection. I did not include such clients as I believe that they should have remained prospects. It is a basic fact of life that nobody can be all things to all people. Just as I saw institutions in Asia follow strategies that made me cringe because I saw these strategies as totally unsuited to their needs and decided they would be the wrong clients for J.P. Morgan, there are people today who are unsuited to goals-based wealth management. Typically, they are people who do not understand the benefit of addressing individual goals separately and have not yet appreciated the existence of a conflict between these goals. I admit that it is a lot easier for a small practice, like ours currently is, to take that view than when one works for a large organization. Yet, there is a great deal of wisdom in making sure that we develop a clear understanding of those clients we can serve versus those we cannot.

The other set of objections comes from the changes that are required within the wealth management firm that transitions to this new approach. Ten or twenty years from now, one might anticipate that many of the objections that naturally arise currently will have disappeared. In the short term, however, this approach and process architecture involve material change, and the people who will naturally fill many of the roles will have been trained in a different environment. Thus, one can predict that they will bemoan the loss of certain prerogatives and the added responsibilities placed on them. I can think of four main sets of objections as well.

The first is linked to the greater clarity with which duties are defined and the fact that one moves from an individual to a team approach; this will upset many advisors and professionals who used to operate like a solo practitioner within a larger firm. The management challenge is to show how much better served clients are with a team approach. Although certain advisors will put themselves above clients, most advisors are strongly focused on their clients and on how well they are served. Therefore, their objections come from misguided beliefs that they alone are able to help their clients. Call it "control-freakness" or an inability to delegate.

Also, the ability to tell a client that certain requirements that he or she is seeking are counterproductive and costly will upset advisors who have historically been loath to refuse to do anything a client suggests. Many advisors have not always been crystal clear in terms of what they should and should not do. The challenge is to build a sufficiently strong philosophical basis within the advisory group that they come to believe that the solutions offered by the firm are truly superior and in the best interests of clients. After all, few patients will approach their internist and tell him or her that they need an appendectomy; if they did, they would likely be told that the surgeon sees the problem as a stomachache. Analogously, this means that clients should be helped to be descriptive about their issues, rather than prescriptive. However, unless an advisor has such a strong and well-understood belief in the benefit of any solution being offered, he or she often folds, rather than confront—however diplomatically—the client. In short, a solid and continuous cycle of advisor education is needed, particularly because advisors, in this framework, truly are generalists and cannot be expected to remain up-to-speed on all new insights on their own.

Third, the greater leverage brought about by the more systematic nature of the process and by the presence of more junior team members will upset those who wanted to be responsible for all actions: again, the control freaks! Although they might have countenanced the idea of having associates helping them, these advisors were not used—or even ready—to have them outside of their direct line of control. In the modern firm, these associates may have to report into other centers of excellence, both to provide them with the proper career and development paths and to ensure their professional integrity. Further, regulatory constraints may be such that these associates actually must comply with broader firm procedures that advisors are ill-equipped to manage. The real challenge is to help advisors to see that it is in their—and their clients'—interests to take advantage of leverage; we've already seen how to deal with objections that relate to fears that clients will not be served well. The next dimension must be to show advisors how leverage will actually help them. Although a small part of this—realistically speaking—can come from helping advisors remain at the industry's leading edge, the truth is that this leverage must in some way translate into higher compensation.

Finally, the greater firm focus on profitability combines with activities that are much more carefully and clearly defined to allow for a more pervasive individual performance measurement. For those for whom detailed performance measurement is a part of life today, the change will not be so great. Others who have been laboring in an environment in which performance measurement is much more qualitative than quantitative will find it harder to adapt. This is the toughest challenge to overcome, as few people like being told that they are not doing as well as they should be. I experienced it when I tried to introduce the notion of assessing the input of individual investment committee members to an old client of ours. The solution I have found is to start in a coaching mode, effectively "divorcing" performance and compensation for some intermediate period of time. This is a sensible tack as performance measurement and assessment can only become meaningful after some period of time, after which skill and luck can be reasonably distinguished from each other. In this intermediate period of time when performance does not directly affect compensation, one can use the insights provided to coach each individual with respect to what the data say they are doing well or less well.

Helping identify biases, a false sense of conviction, or any other performance shortfall can help an individual look forward to performance assessment. While this is clearly true and relatively easy to implement for disciplines that lend themselves to quantifiable measurement of results, it is also true when dealing with disciplines for which success is more qualitative. A well-designed process focused on the appropriate measures and with a solid basis of objectivity can prove invaluable; in fact, my own experience suggests that this is where the most good can be done. Quantitative disciplines naturally lead their practitioners to self-assess, whether formally or informally. Thus, helping practitioners in "softer" disciplines develop that same measure of sensitivity to what works and what does not can be a major management opportunity.

In short, one should accept that any change will generate objections. Humans are often described as creatures of habit, and anything that disturbs their equilibrium will be viewed as threatening. The client and management challenge cannot be ignored, but it should not be feared, but managed.

A DIFFICULT DECISION

Certain client types might appear only marginally to benefit from the approach described above, and a few firms will find it difficult to move from their current models to goals-based wealth management.

Innovation is always a challenge, but one should still recognize that standing against the march of history might be a better solution, but only until history marches all over those who have resisted its progress. It would

be somewhat arrogant on my part to describe goals-based wealth management as the inevitable historical trend. That I believe it is should not surprise,
as I was one of a few who stood at the birth of the new approach, and I
came to it because I saw the alternative approaches fail clients and prospects.
However, in a world where uncertainty is high and where it can take decades
to be able to tell whether one has succeeded, some measure of humility is
needed. I can only state that I have found it so much more practical to help
clients using this systematic approach that I have decided that it is better than
others, all the while recognizing that the jury is still out and that it is totally
possible that someone will think of something even better and that someone
may actually even be working on it as this is written.

So, although I believe that the decision should be made to adopt the
goals-based approach, I am willing to accept that there may be circumstances
under which the change could be more disruptive than beneficial. I can think
of three cases where making the move may not be wise unless one is prepared
to take a truly long-term view.

The first such case touches advisors whose clients are still in a significant wealth accumulation mode, as we discussed above, who will find the
approach less beneficial. I have long argued that a possible definition of afflu-
ence involves a state where one could meet all of one's lifestyle needs without
having to take nominal investment risk. Clearly, this definition is extreme,
but it helps focus the mind: the decision to take risk is objectively more
sensible when there is no alternative option. Consider the young executive
whose sole important savings, other than possibly a home, are in defined
contribution plans. That he or she must take investment risk is not optional:
without investments in equities, for instance, the likelihood of being able
to retire at some point is really more a dream than a reality. Traditional
finance justifies this by pointing to the fact that future contributions mean
that the individual is long in both equities—in the portfolio—and cash—in
those future contributions. Yet, the role of a financial advisor here is more to
help the individual plan his or her budget, design savings plans, and invest
those savings wisely. At that point, it is not unreasonable to argue that there
is but one goal: build enough financial savings to be able to retire. There
are a couple of dualities here. The first is when the client also has children
whose education will need to be financed. Here, one does have two goals
and two different time frames; and it may make sense to begin to consider
the benefits of goals-based wealth management, but the case remains less
strong in the face of potential disruptions—unless one is perceptive enough
to realize the long-term benefits and feels that these actually may provide an
additional selling point. The other is when the individual is unsure that he
or she will be able to stick with the program in the event of a major market
disruption. Even there, solid education is probably a better weapon than the

artificial creation of multiple goals—one with a shorter-term horizon and a higher required probability of success—when there is still probably only one, successful retirement.

Second, well-established, large multi-family family office practices will often find the change cumbersome. By definition, the firms I have in mind here already have substantial infrastructure, human resources trained in a different process, and client bases that may have become used to "the way it has been." There, although the client benefits may actually be immediate, management must be philosophically convinced before embarking on a change. At some level, my own experience suggests that biting the bullet may be at least as much a defensive as an aggressive move. Newer firms pop up on an almost daily basis, and those can be seen as "industry disrupters." Just as many well-established companies that used to have a virtual monopoly on certain products and services—think of Polaroid, Kodak, or even IBM—eventually had to change or die, many traditional multi-family family offices are faced with potential death if they stick to old-fashioned approaches. In fact, I have seen arguments that the multi-family family office of the future will view investment management as a commodity, while non-investment services will be the differentiators,[7] and find myself in agreement, although more with the conclusion than with its argumentation. *I believe that asset management for the sole purpose of investment performance that somehow disconnects with the complex and multiple needs of families is more than futile: it is dangerous!* Yet, when it is planned and executed through a well-structured goals-based wealth management process and integrated with other wealth management disciplines, I feel it remains a crucial ingredient. Assuming that it can become secondary only makes sense, in my view, if one also assumes that it is divorced from all relevant interactions with other wealth management disciplines. If that is the case, it deserves to be secondary; if it is not it can remain an essential element.

Finally, institutions that retain a product manufacturing dimension will also find the naturally open-ended process difficult to square with their competing business needs. Yet, perhaps paradoxically, they seem to have been at the forefront of the adoption of the terminology. Squaring that circle requires recognizing that there may be a marketing benefit to "talking the talk" without "walking the walk." Experience demonstrates that many clients almost instinctively take to the goals-based wealth management approach, if only because "the talk" is incredibly enticing: "Whoa, they are interested in me

---

[7]Hauser, Barbara R., and Kirby Rosplock "The Family Office Landscape: Today's Trends & Five Predictions for the Family Office of Tomorrow." *The Journal of Wealth Management*, Winter 2014, pp. 9–19.

and in my needs; what a change!" I do not want to bite here the hand that fed me quite well for so many years, but it is a fact that product manufacturers are more in the business of making and selling products than in the business of meeting individual client needs. Client needs are important when products are designed but, once that is done, the point is to sell what is made. At that time, crafting the correct sales message is what matters; and fashion can take over.

Aside from these exceptions, I believe that, however difficult the decision and its implementation are, goals-based wealth management will eventually take over, at least in the upper reaches of the wealth range. The greater focus on the client, the potential for virtually ultimate customization, and the ability to integrate all dimensions of the wealth management challenge are just too great not to become overwhelming relative to approaches that are materially less customized and responsive.

SUMMARY AND CONCLUSIONS

Except with respect to the greater procedural complexity and of the changes that it requires among the practitioners who adopt it, goals-based wealth management seems to be the right answer to the question posed by many clients. It does require advisory firms that adopt the framework to execute a number of important process changes, but that disadvantage is more than offset by the potential it offers to raise the profit margins of many practitioners. It therefore makes sense for clients to insist on it. The challenge posed to many financial advisors indeed rests on the competing requirements to meet the needs of clients—needs that can be extremely varied—and to meet the expectations of stakeholders—employees and stockholders have the right to expect competitive compensation. Offering a more clearly defined series of process steps and thus providing the opportunity to leverage those activities that lend themselves to it are two of the most compelling arguments for firms to bite the bullet and make the move to the newer thought process; that it also allows a more tailored solution to be created for each client is, however, the ultimate rationale, as virtually all advisors think of their clients first.

The wealthy themselves can play a particularly important role in the transformation of the industry. They can be the motivating force that will provide the impetus for advisors to change if they want to keep serving this market successfully.

Conclusion

Dealing with the needs of wealthy individuals has been the focus on this book, and our principal area of attention has been in the area of asset management, because this is the area within which the proposed change—the adoption of a goals-based wealth management approach—is the most needed and arguably imminent. We certainly recognize and discussed the extent to which asset management is but one of many facets of the challenge. In conclusion, it is necessary to broaden the discussion to suggest that many of the principles we developed here apply to most other disciplines.

The most important such principle relates to leverage and thus to the need for wealth management advisors to adopt much more systematic processes. I hope one of the many insights discussed will have been that the asset management needs of wealthy individuals and families are varied and differ considerably from one individual to the next. This should serve to dispel the notion that systematization is possible in the world of asset management, but does not work when it comes to other disciplines, be they related to taxes, estate transfers, philanthropy, or family governance and education. Each and every discipline has its own axes around which client services must be structured, its own goals that can be specified, and its own processes that should be designed and executed.

The first critical element, which is common to all disciplines, relates to information. Client data must be acquired and managed.[1] How many times has an advisor been asked to authorize or opine on a routine transaction, simply because the specifics of the transaction, what it entails, who may or may not authorize it, and how it should be executed are not codified into a database that would allow a much more junior individual within a firm to take responsibility for it? From a pure investment standpoint, I have seen many instances where on- and offshore vehicles coexist and where there is no comprehensive set of guidelines outlining what vehicle is allowable in one or the other set of structures: does it really make sense to have a international

---

[1]Robert E. Mallernee, W. Jackson Parham, and Teresa Eriksson, the principals of Eton Advisors L.P., shared that insight with me and appear to have done more thinking about the issue than anybody else in this industry.

tax lawyer or tax accountant opine on the suitability of each investment decision? Similarly, how many times has it been necessary to verify that a transaction can be carried out in a trust simply because what can and cannot be done is not clearly specified, the decision being left, each and every time, to a fiduciary administrator who should be too senior an individual to be involved in it, most of the time? Even when it comes to dealing with family members across several generations, most families are not invited to codify what activity is required and permissible. Thus, a time-consuming and costly effort is needed each time an activity is contemplated to make sure that one does not step on anyone's toes or make a mistake.

It should be a simple matter of routine for client data to be aggregated in a single file, with someone in charge of verifying the accuracy and timely nature of it, to make any needed amendment and to keep it current. Years ago, I remember that, in the institutional asset management world, all quarterly client meetings started with a review of the investment policy and of all the client information it contained, extending to constraints and preferences that the manager had to accept and with which one had to comply. Ostensibly, such information is orders of magnitude simpler than all the various elements that describe the inner workings of a wealthy family, with multiple generations, multiple structures and asset locations, multiple goals and time horizons, and a wide variety of assets and asset types. Yet, conceptually, the problem is no different; it is simply more complex and requires more attention to be kept up-to-date.[2] Somehow, however, the wealth management and fee-only financial advisory industry has managed to convince itself that it is not necessary—or it is too complex—to maintain the appropriate database to help a family—in all its dimensions—manage its wealth. Investment policies, which would be a good although not the only place to start, are often written in a way to protect the advisor rather than summarize client goals and constraints. To me, this is a shame and it needs to change; it would be much preferable for the industry to originate the change than to have it imposed through regulations that can at times be counterproductive or even worse.

The second element is a bit more difficult, but considerably less cumbersome: it involves specifying the key activities that each discipline requires. Again, our industry has allowed itself to remain in a "loosey-goosey" world

---

[2]Considering how much more computer memory is available today and how much cheaper it is, it is not a huge intellectual leap to argue that the codification that is required in this activity is not really that much more complex—if at all—than what had to be done at a time when computers were still made of vacuum tubes and word processing, spreadsheet, and database management software mere sparkles in someone's eyes.

where nothing can be set, because "doing so infringes on the need to customize everything to all clients." Yet, interestingly, as per the example we used in Chapter 13, law firms—who should be, and most often are, the epitome of customization to each client—do maintain databases of paragraphs, or even whole documents, from which they can source detailed language that is eventually incorporated into each client's own, customized document. There is no need for a partner to draft all the wording each and every time; a partner is needed to review the draft before it is sent to the client to make sure that it holds together and fits with the specific circumstances; but more junior—and cheaper—staff can do the bulk of the heavy lifting before the partner's time has to be spent. Educating a member of some "next generation" should not be a case of "re-inventing warm water" each time; rather, there should be—as many educational institutions do and as exemplified by the Chartered Financial Analyst Institute for its CFA exam—a clear set of "learning outcomes" that can then be compared with the current knowledge of the individual to be educated and a specialized program designed to plug any hole. Each learning outcome can easily be associated with a list of underlying concepts and of the appropriate elements of literature that can be drawn upon to teach the required concepts. The list could go on, but the point is hopefully made. It is not easy, but it is not rocket science either to codify the critical elements of any process that should be used to achieve certain outcomes, whether related to asset management, family education, or trust and estate planning.

Importantly, such a transformation of the firm from a rough practice based on the knowledge, experience, and dedication of a few senior individuals to an institution, which can effectively represent that it possesses all the required knowledge and experience, is helpful to both the firm and its clients—and, I should add, to the employees of the firm. That it should help clients is a given, to the extent that instead of flying blind each advisor knows what the best practices of the day are. Note that these best practices are not set in stone. In an industry that is still very much in flux, new ideas will come up as new challenges arise or new tools are developed. Yet, having a solid sense of what these best practices are must help each client gain the benefit of all that a firm has to offer, rather than the best than an individual in a firm has to offer. After all, there is no need to re-invent the wheel at each turn, and regulatory requirements mandate that each client receive the same treatment and benefit from the same insights. More importantly, having a list of current best practices provides the basis on which one can build.

A firm staffed with highly creative partners and associates is bound to come up with instances where prior practitioners had missed one or another dimension of the challenge or had failed to realize that certain solutions lead to potentially nasty situations quite a bit down the road. Imagine how powerful it could be to have the opportunity to audit one's own activities over time and to see how the law of unintended consequences is at work: a great iconoclastic idea that survived all the firm's best efforts to make sure that one does not make stupid mistakes can still lead to a problem at some future point in time. Yet, this does not make the idea irremediably wrong: What if it was simply a small comma in the process that should have been changed? Without a clear codification of how things are done, one may never be able to identify where the error occurred. How sad it must be not being able to learn from one's mistakes!

The third element is where art meets science. Only a fool would believe that everything can fit neatly in a box. The classic proverb states that the ultimate form of insanity is to keep repeating the same actions and expect different results. The corollary of this is to keep reminding oneself that the same actions applied to different circumstances are more likely than not to generate different results. Despite the fact that the universe of potential clients for wealth managers is relatively small and represents an even smaller fraction of the whole population, it is fair to assume that circumstances will vary, in an almost infinite manner. The science of the effort postulates that there are many specific activities that will likely have to be a part of a client solution. The art recognizes that tweaking will probably be necessary here or there. The point where the twains meet is where one can effectively see the difference between a requirement that has proven to be misguided in similar—although not necessarily the same—situations in the past and one that reflects a truly different need.

I would argue that this third element actually is the province of senior professionals and management. To me, cynically, experience is the name that we give to our past mistakes. Thus, having some white hair—physically or metaphorically—means that one has made a number of mistakes already. I usually add that I am convinced that I am creative enough to be sure that there are many more mistakes for me to make! Yet, having made mistakes and hopefully learned from them combines—or should combine—with raw brain power to allow someone to resolve the earlier dichotomy between a misguided change and one that seems to make sense. Thus, allowing senior professionals, individually or as a group, to suggest and vet exceptions may be both the most successful and the least risky way for a firm to grow with its clients.

Interestingly, this may be a part of the non-financial compensation that accrues to seniority: being able to remain in a problem-solving mode and contribute innovation both to one's clientele and to the industry. As the editor of the *Journal of Wealth Management,* I can testify that a number of the articles that are submitted and eventually make it through the peer review process to publication are the result of the brainwave of one or several individuals; they encountered a situation in which they thought that standard approaches did not or would not work and came up with a better solution that they are now willing to share with the rest of the industry.

It is now the time to craft the final paragraph. The concept of goals-based wealth management came to me—and I am sure others experienced a comparable although likely different epiphany—when I found myself disappointed with traditional finance as it applied to wealthy individuals and families. A labor of love ensued that took me from where I was in 2002 to today, where I feel that several contributions by other practitioners have combined with my own modest insights and allowed me to describe a systematic process that possesses the right balance between client customization and standardization. In my own practice, it has been immensely useful and has certainly helped me provide better advice to quite a few clients. It taught me the need to apply the same kind of intellectual discipline, rigor, and honesty to all the facets of our industry, whereas a clear-cut case cannot be made that subjectivity and responsiveness to specific circumstances are the only elements of a viable approach. I must confess that I have yet to see a situation in which some form of systematic approach does not work, but I am prepared to accept that my universe and knowledge are still too small or narrow to allow me to believe in the universality of the need for some sort of systematic approach to the many interrelated and integrated challenges that comprise wealth management. Yet, until I do, I will keep trying to stay faithful to the principles expounded upon in this book and to work to improve the value of the help I endeavor to offer to our clients. I hope you, dear reader, will now join me in this journey.

About the Companion Website

This book has a companion website, which can be found at www.wiley.com/go/wealthmanagement. Enter the password: brunel123.

The companion website offers an opportunity to browse articles that are relevant to this topic. Also available is a simplified Excel model that allows readers who can input certain capital market and model portfolio assumptions to perform a simple hypothetical goals-bases strategic asset allocation exercise.

About the Author

Jean L.P. Brunel, CFA, is managing principal, Brunel Associates LLC, a firm founded in 2001 to serve ultra-high-net-worth individuals and their advisors. Prior to founding Brunel Associates, Jean spent the bulk of his career with J.P. Morgan, becoming the chief investment officer of J.P. Morgan's global private bank and a director and member of the Executive Committee of J.P. Morgan Investment Management, Inc., in 1990.

He has been the editor of the *Journal of Wealth Management* since its founding in 1998, and the author of the book *Integrated Wealth Management: The New Direction for Portfolio Managers,* as well as many peer-reviewed articles. During his more than thirty-five-year career, Jean has been based in the United States, Japan, Hong Kong, Singapore, and Australia and has served clients around the world. His three most notable areas of focus have been tax-aware investing, goals-based wealth management, and the role of alternative assets in balanced portfolios.

In 2011, Jean received the prestigious C. Stewart Sheppard Award from the CFA Institute; this award is presented annually to an individual CFA charter holder in recognition of outstanding contributions in fostering the education of professional investors and the development of programs and publications to encourage continuing education in the investment profession. In June 2012, Jean was named the 2012 Multi-Family Office Chief Investment Officer of the Year by Family Office Review. He is a graduate of Ecole des Hautes Etudes Commerciales in France (HEC) and holds an MBA from the Kellogg School of Business at Northwestern University, Evanston, Illinois.

Assets:
  alternative, 106
  "authentic," 13
  of institutional investors, 50
  internal vs. external, 96
  location of, 112–113, 169, 214
  in multiple modules, 173–175
  real, 135
  sizing of, to meet goals, 69,
      122–123
  types of, 13
Asset allocation:
  based on scoring results, 157,
      159
  example of tilted, 163, 165
  and long-term risk, 2
  strategic, *see* Strategic asset
      allocation
Asset classes, 38, 39
  broad definition of, 28
  consistent with risk profiles, 69
  interacting with client goals,
      73–74
  mapped to goals, 85–87
  market expectations of, 94–95
  mega, 134–135
Asset liability analysis, 55
Asset management, complexities
      of, *see* Complexities of wealth
      management
Asset size, 51–53, 69, 122–123
Assumptions:
  client disagreement about, 89
  of models, 87, 144
  in portfolio optimization,
      104–105
Australia, 40
"Authentic" assets, 13

Barbell portfolio, 29–31
Behavioral biases, 205–206
Behavioral finance, 59, 62

Behavioral portfolio, 60–61
Behavioral portfolio theory, 71
Berlin Philharmonic Orchestra,
      201
Bernatzi, Schlomo, 117n.3
Berra, Yogi, xix
Beyer, Charlotte, xviii, 13, 15
Biases, behavioral, 205–206
Bite sizes (derivatives), 32
Black-Litterman framework, 104
Bonds:
  as asset class, 38
  convertible, 38n.2
Bond immunization, 55n.2
Bottom-up approach, 67
Business models, 191–193

Capital:
  forms of, xvii
  multiple sources of, 11–13
Capital gains:
  realized, 24
  and taking of losses, 26
  unrealized, 24
Capital losses:
  analysis of, 25–26
  realized, 24
  unrealized, 24, 25
Capital markets:
  cyclicality of, 61
  forecasting, 39–42
  long-term returns from, 25
  short-term fluctuations in, 25
Capital market expectations,
      93–95
  of clients, 219–220
  for creating goal modules, 107
  goals and assets fitting, 215
  in portfolio optimization,
      104–105
Capital preservation, 97
Carnegie, Andrew, 11n.1

DATE DUE

2-25-16	
4-19-16	
1-3-18	
6-29-18	
7-17-18	
3-23-2020	
	PRINTED IN U.S.A.